Lecture Notes in Computer Science 731

Edited by G. Goos and J. Hartmanis

Advisory Board: W. Brauer   D. Gries   J. Stoer

Alexander Schill (Ed.)

DCE –
The OSF Distributed
Computing Environment

Client/Server Model and Beyond

International DCE Workshop
Karlsruhe, Germany, October 7-8, 1993
Proceedings

Springer-Verlag

Berlin Heidelberg New York
London Paris Tokyo
Hong Kong Barcelona
Budapest

Series Editors

Gerhard Goos
Universität Karlsruhe
Postfach 69 80
Vincenz-Priessnitz-Straße 1
D-76131 Karlsruhe, Germany

Juris Hartmanis
Cornell University
Department of Computer Science
4130 Upson Hall
Ithaca, NY 14853, USA

Volume Editor

Alexander Schill
Institut für Telematik, Universität Karlsruhe
Postfach 69 80, D-76128 Karlsruhe, Germany

CR Subject Classification (1991): C.2.1, D.1.3, D.2.6, D.4.2-3

ISBN 3-540-57306-2 Springer-Verlag Berlin Heidelberg New York
ISBN 0-387-57306-2 Springer-Verlag New York Berlin Heidelberg

Typesetting: Camera-ready by author
Printing and binding: Druckhaus Beltz, Hemsbach/Bergstr.
45/3140-543210 - Printed on acid-free paper

Table of Contents

Introduction

DCE Analysis and Comparison

Application Support

Methods and Tools

RPC Extensions

Object-based Systems

Invited Talk

Appendix

Preface

Client/server applications are of increasing importance in industry; they are a significant first step towards a global distributed processing model. A very recent response to this trend is the Distributed Computing Environment (DCE) of the Open Software Foundation (OSF), the emerging new industry standard for distributed processing. The papers in this volume discuss the client/server approach based on DCE, illustrating and analyzing the functionality of important DCE components and applications. Moreover, a number of contributions also focus on new models beyond traditional client/server processing and beyond DCE.

The material summarized in this volume was presented at the International Workshop on the OSF Distributed Computing Environment on October 7 and 8, 1993 in Karlsruhe, Germany. This workshop was organized by the German Association of Computer Science (*Gesellschaft für Informatik*, GI/ITG), together with the University of Karlsruhe and the Nuclear Research Center in Karlsruhe.

Major subject areas of the workshop were analysis and overview of DCE, methods and tools for DCE applications, extensions of the DCE remote procedure call, and distributed object-based systems on top of DCE, including the Object Request Broker (ORB) of the Object Management Group (OMG). Most papers are of practical orientation but typically have a strong technical and conceptual background. A more detailed overview of the papers is given at the end of the first contribution which gives a survey of distributed systems, DCE, and approaches beyond DCE.

We would like to thank all people who contributed to the success of this workshop. The members of the program committee did a very good job in reviewing about 10 papers per committee member. The Institute of Telematics of the University of Karlsruhe, especially Prof. Dr. Gerhard Krüger, made the workshop possible by providing a lot of organizational support. The university supported the workshop by making the required lecturing halls available. The background organization of the workshop was made possible by the *Gesellschaft für Informatik*, especially by its working groups on operating systems and on distributed systems (FA 3.1 and 3.3). We would also like to thank the speakers and authors and the colleagues who did the industry demonstrations on DCE; their technical contributions were a major prerequisite for this workshop. Moreover, the work force who helped with the local organization, especially the colleagues and students from the Institute of Telematics did an excellent job.

Finally, we would of course like to thank all companies that supported the workshop in various ways, including Daimler-Benz AG, Digital Equipment Corporation, Hewlett-Packard, IBM, the Open Software Foundation, Siemens-Nixdorf, and SUN Microsystems. The local organization was particularly supported by Dr. Lutz Heuser of Digital Equipment's Campus-based Engineering Center (CEC) in Karlsruhe and by the Volksbank Karlsruhe. Moreover, we would like to thank all other colleagues who supported this workshop in one way or the other during the last few months.

Karlsruhe, August 1993   Alexander Schill

Workshop Organization

General organization:

German Association of Computer Science (GI/ITG),
particularly the working groups "Operating Systems"
and "Communication and Distributed Systems"

University of Karlsruhe, Institute of Telematics

Nuclear Research Center Karlsruhe

KfK

Workshop chair:

Alexander Schill
University of Karlsruhe, Institute of Telematics,
Postfach 6980, 76128 Karlsruhe, Germany
e-mail: schill@telematik.informatik.uni-karlsruhe.de

Program committee:

Martin Bever (IBM European Networking Center ENC, Heidelberg)
Kurt Geihs (University of Frankfurt)
Lutz Heuser (DEC Campus-based Engineering Center CEC, Karlsruhe)
Elmar Holler (Nuclear Research Center, Karlsruhe)
Winfried Kalfa (Technical University of Chemnitz)
Klaus-Peter Löhr (Free University (FU) of Berlin)
Klaus Müller (R&O Software Technology, Chemnitz)
Max Mühlhäuser (University of Karlsruhe)
Alexander Schill (University of Karlsruhe)
Peter Schlichtiger (Siemens-Nixdorf, Munich)
Gerd Schürmann (GMD Research Center (FOKUS), Berlin)

Local organization:

Lutz Heuser (DEC Campus-based Engineering Center CEC, Karlsruhe)
Monika Joram (University of Karlsruhe)
Ludwig Keller (University of Karlsruhe)
Dietmar Kottmann (University of Karlsruhe)
Gerhard Krüger (University of Karlsruhe)
Markus Mock (University of Karlsruhe)
Max Mühlhäuser (University of Karlsruhe)
Alexander Schill (University of Karlsruhe)
Jörg Sievert (University of Karlsruhe)

Distributed Systems, OSF DCE, and Beyond

M. Bever[1], K. Geihs[2], L. Heuser[3], M. Mühlhäuser[4], A. Schill[5]

1) IBM European Networking Center, Vangerowstr. 18,
69115 Heidelberg, Germany; e-mail: bever@dhdibm1.bitnet

2) University of Frankfurt, Dept. of Informatics, P.O. Box 111932,
60054 Frankfurt, Germany; e-mail: geihs@informatik.uni-frankfurt.de

3) Digital Equipment GmbH, CEC Karlsruhe, Vincenz-Prießnitz-Str. 1,
76131 Karlsruhe, Germany; e-mail: heuser@kampus.enet.dec.com

4) University of Karlsruhe, Institute of Telematics, Postfach 6980,
76128 Karlsruhe, Germany; e-mail: max@tk.telematik.informatik.uni-karlsruhe.de

5) University of Karlsruhe, Institute of Telematics, Postfach 6980,
76128 Karlsruhe, Germany; e-mail: schill@telematik.informatik.uni-karlsruhe.de

Abstract. This introduction paper presents basic foundations of distributed systems and applications and then shows how OSF DCE addresses the requirements imposed by distributed environments. The DCE architecture is illustrated, the basic functionality of the DCE components is explained, and the DCE RPC as the major base for client/server applications is presented in closer detail.

The paper also discusses requirements and new models beyond DCE in order to enable even more advanced distributed applications. In particular, distributed object-oriented DCE extensions are outlined and directions towards distributed multimedia applications are pointed out. Moreover, other requirements and trends such as advanced tool support or distributed transaction facilities are also discussed. Finally, an overview of the papers within these proceedings is given.

1 Introduction and Overview

The potential benefits of distributed processing systems have been widely recognized [1,2]. They are due to improved economics, functionality, performance, reliability and scalability. In order to explore the advantages of distributed processing, appropriate support is needed that enables the development and execution of distributed applications. A distributed application consists of separate parts that execute on different nodes of the network and cooperate in order to achieve a common goal. A supporting infrastructure should make the inherent complexity of distributed processing transparent as much as possible. The infrastructure is required to integrate a wide range of computer system types and should be independent of the underlying communication technology.

The Open Software Foundation (OSF) has presented such an infrastructure called Distributed Computing Environment (DCE). It is a collection of integrated software components that are added to a computer's operating system. DCE provides means to build and run distributed applications in heterogeneous environments.

Let us illustrate the role of DCE by an example: Figure 1 shows a distributed office / manufacturing procedure that implements a product management scenario. Several distributed activities are performed by a collection of processes. We assume that each process is allocated to a different network node, and that nodes are connected by a physical network. The processes cooperate as shown by the arrows by forwarding forms or control data between each other. Some of the activities can be executed in parallel (such as the manufacturing and marketing activities) while others are sequential, or alternative (such as regular quality control, simplified quality control or by-passing according to the product type). Each activity can be subdivided hierarchically.

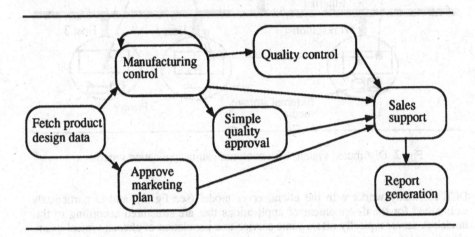

Fig. 1 Example of a distributed office procedure application

An example of an underlying distributed system is shown in figure 2. Two hosts and three workstations are interconnected via an Ethernet and a Token Ring. The two networks are coupled via a gateway. Each computer system offers local resources (at least CPU and main memory, but possibly also printers and secondary storage). These resources can also be accessed remotely and can be shared among different computers. Resource control is performed in a decentralized and mainly autonomous way. On each computer system, a set of application processes are operating - as found in our distributed application. These processes can communicate over the interconnected networks via basic interaction mechanisms such as remote procedure call. At this level, the underlying physical network topology is already considered to be relatively transparent.

Role of DCE and client/server-model: The OSF Distributed Computing Environment (DCE) can now be classified as being a distributed system, while also offering a set of services that support the development of distributed applications. Basically, DCE closes the gap between the physical components of a distributed system and the application components.

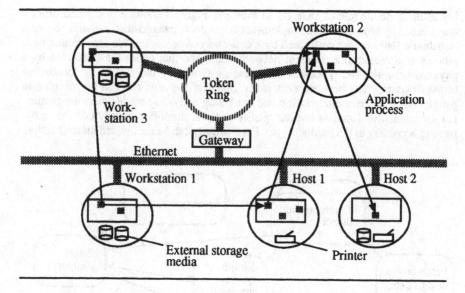

Fig. 2 Distributed system with communicating application processes

DCE internally works with the client/server model (see fig. 3), and is particularly well-suited for the development of applications that are structured according to this model: A server typically offers some service to a population of clients; typical examples are print services, computational services or name translation services. A client can make use of a service by sending a service request message to a suitable server. The request can contain input parameters (e.g. data to be printed). The server performs the requested service and finally sends a service response back to the client. The response can contain output parameters (e.g. a status indication).

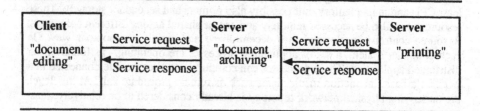

Fig. 3 Client/server model

As shown in the figure, a server can also act as a client of another service, i.e. delegate parts of a service request to a peer server. For example, a document archiving server could request a print service in order to offer a more complete document management functionality to its clients.

2 DCE: Strategy and Architecture

Based on the introduced foundations, this section presents the general strategy of the Open Software Foundation towards products for open systems and then illustrates DCE as one of these products in more detail.

2.1 Goals and Strategy of the Open Software Foundation

The Open Software Foundation (OSF) is a not-for-profit research and development organization. Its members comprise computer hardware and software vendors, end users, universities and other research institutions. One of the major goals of the OSF is to enable global interoperability among heterogeneous systems by providing a practical open computing environment [3].

To achieve this, the OSF solicits proposals for open systems software technology, then evaluates the submissions, and finally licenses the selected solutions for incorporation into the OSF open computing environment. That environment is a collection of technologies that provide for interoperability of diverse systems as well as application portability.

Its main parts are currently

- the OSF/1 Unix operating system,
- the OSF/Motif graphical user interface,
- the OSF Distributed Computing Environment (DCE) and
- the OSF Distributed Management Environment (DME).

From a distributed systems point of view, DCE and DME are of primary importance. While DCE is the base for building distributed applications and also offers a set of distributed services directly to the end user, DME addresses the issues of network and system management; it should suffice to mention that it offers an object-oriented infrastructure for distributed management applications, together with support for the management protocols SNMP and CMIP. It also provides a management user interface and several supplemental management services [4]. Moreover, DME uses certain DCE components. The DME development has not yet reached the same mature stage as DCE.

In the meantime, DCE tends to become an industry standard for distributed processing; most of the major computer vendors are members of the OSF and offer (or have announced) DCE compliant products for their computing platforms. As opposed to other standards, the implementation of the components existed first, and standardization was performed by the OSF thereafter. This seems to have major advantages concerning the resulting functionality, system performance and timeframe of delivery.

2.2 DCE Architecture and Services

Fig. 4 shows the overall DCE architecture [5-6]. All DCE components are based on local operating system services (e.g. Unix) and transport services (e.g. TCP/IP). Distributed applications make explicit use of *fundamental DCE services* (in *italics* in the figure) via C programming interfaces. The other DCE services are used implicitly via the fundamental services or via modified operating system services.

Fundamental DCE services: The *Thread Service* provides a portable implementation of lightweight processes (*threads*) according to the *POSIX Standard 1003.4a*. Threads enable concurrent processing within a shared address space, and are especially used by RPC for implementing asynchronous, non-blocking remote invocations and multi-threaded servers.

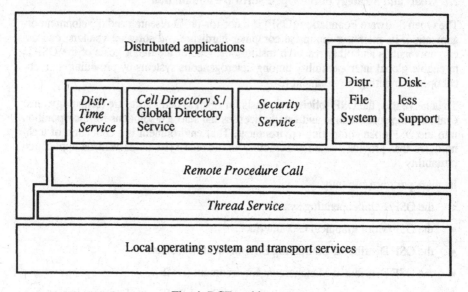

Fig. 4 DCE architecture

The *DCE RPC* is the major base for heterogeneous systems communication. Based on RPC, a client request for a remote procedure (i.e. a service request) is transferred to the server, mapped to a procedure implementation, executed, and finally acknowledged by sending back results to the client. All input data and results are encoded as RPC parameters similar to local calls. All parameter conversion and transmission tasks are handled by call marshalling facilities that are part of so-called RPC stub components at both sites. This way, the remoteness of a call be be masked to a large degree at the application level. The stubs are generated automatically from an interface description which specifies the signatures of the invoked procedures. DCE offers a C-based *Interface Definition Language (IDL)*, various kinds of call semantics, nested parameter structures, secure RPC with authentication and authorization based on the DCE Security Service, global (up to worldwide) naming of servers based on the X.500 directory service standard, backward calls from servers to clients, and bulk data transfer based on typed pipes (logical channels).

The *Cell Directory Service (CDS)* supports distributed name management within dedicated management domains. Name management basically comprises mapping of (attributed) names to addresses, and update of name information. Most important, it is the base for mapping RPC server addresses to client requests. Its functionality is integrated into the DCE RPC programming interface via *NSI (Name Service Interface)*.

CDS exploits replication and caching to achieve fault tolerance and efficiency. An advanced CDS programming interface is offered by the standardized *X/Open Directory Service Interface*.

The *Security Service* implements authentication, authorization, and encryption. These mechanisms are tighly integrated with DCE RPC; for example, RPC clients and servers can be mutually authenticated, servers can dynamically check access control lists for proper client authorization, and all RPC messages can be encrypted on demand.

Finally, the *Distributed Time Service (DTS)* implements distributed clock synchronization, a common problem in distributed environments. It guarantees that local clocks of participating nodes are synchronized within a given interval. Moreover, synchronization with exact external time sources (e.g. with radio clocks) is supported. This functionality is important for implementing timestamp-based distributed algorithms. It is also directly exploited by other DCE components.

Other DCE services: The *Global Directory Service (GDS)* extends CDS by global naming facilities across administrative domains. It is based on the X.500 directory service standard. Therfore, it enables interoperability not only with other DCE directory servers but also with other X.500 servers worldwide. As an alternative, the *Internet Domain Name Service* can also be used for global naming.

The *Distributed File System (DFS)* implements cell-wide transparent distributed file management. Files can be stored at different servers and can also be replicated. Clients, i.e. application programs, can access files by location-transparent names similar to a local Unix file system. File access is quite efficient based on whole-file caching at the client site. This technique also supports scalability by offloading work from file servers to clients during file access [7]. Interoperability with the widely used *Network File System* is enabled via an *NFS/DFS interface*. DFS is augmented with a *Diskless Support* component; it provides boot, swap, and file services for diskless workstations.

In summary, DCE provides a rich and integrated functionality for distributed applications. Moreover, DCE supports heterogeneous systems interoperability and is offered in product quality.

2.3 DCE System Configurations and Application Example

DCE supports structuring of distributed computing systems into so-called cells in order to keep the size of administrative domains manageable. A cell can consist of all nodes attached to a local area network but is usually defined according to organizational considerations rather than physical network structures. Therefore, it is basically a set of nodes that are managed together by one authority.

Cell characteristics: Most DCE services are especially optimized for intra-cell interactions. While cross-cell communication is possible, interactions within a cell are usually much more frequent, and can therefore benefit from such optimization significantly. Moreover, cell boundaries represent security firewalls; access to servers in a foreign cell requires special authentication and authorization procedures that are different from secure intra-cell interactions. Finally, the distributed file system within a cell provides complete location transparence; as opposed to that, explicit cell names must be specified for file access across cells.

Example: Fig. 5 shows an example of an application framework based on DCE to implement an office / manufacturing scenario as discussed above. It consists of three cells A-C for product data management, manufacturing and marketing / sales. Within each cell, various nodes with dedicated application services exist (such as manufacturing control, machine management, and quality control processes on three different nodes in cell B). Moreover, each cell has a set of DCE system servers, including security, directory, time, and file servers. Typically, two or more servers of each kind are configured within a cell in order to improve availability of DCE services and performance of service access. One or several global directory servers are available in the example to enable cross-cell naming, e.g. to identify and access an application server in a remote cell. Finally, a diskless workstation pool is part of cell A and is linked to DFS and other DCE services via the diskless support component of DCE.

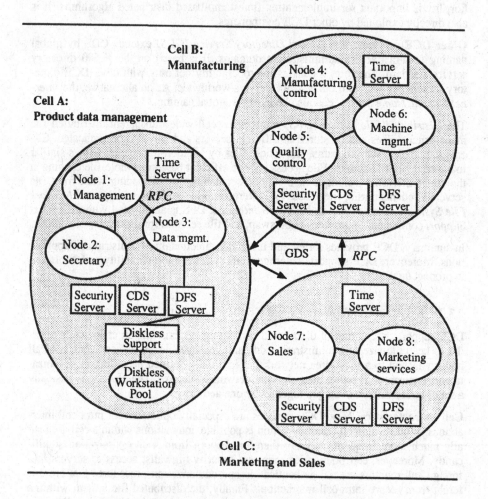

Fig. 5 DCE application example and cell structure

All nodes, respectively the application processes, and also the DCE components interact via DCE RPC. For example, this is indicated within cell A and between cell B and C in the figure. RPC servers are located via CDS based on logical names, and via GDS across cells. RPC communication can be made secure by the protocols offered by the security servers. Each process can comprise a number of threads to serve multiple RPCs concurrently (server site) or to issue multiple RPC requests in parallel (client site).

Data management can be based on the distributed file system. This way, different processes such as the management, secretary, and data management components of cell A can share file data in a location-transparent way. On the other hand, these files can also be accessed from remote cells upon request, provided that the accessing client is properly authorized and authenticated in both cases.

3 DCE Remote Procedure Call

As the RPC tends to be the most important mechanism within DCE, it shall be described in more detail, augmented with practical examples.

3.1 Properties of DCE RPC

Language integration and data representation: The implementation of DCE RPC is based on the C programming language; all interface specifications are given in a specific *Interface Definition Language (IDL)* that is a superset of the declarative part of C, corresponding to C header file code portions. Moreover, the RPC programming interface is offered as a C library - similar to the interfaces of other DCE components.

IDL allows the specification of arbitrary parameter data types with virtually the same facilities as found in C. The RPC runtime system, namely the stubs generated from IDL, are able to handle nested data structures by flattening them recursively, transmitting them to the server, and rebuilding them there. All differences concerning data representations at the client and server sites are masked by DCE by converting data formats accordingly. This principle is called "receiver makes right" and means that data are transmitted in the sender's representation and are adapted to the receiver's format at the destination site. The DCE implementation of a particular vendor must therefore know all other possible data formats of peer nodes - however, in practice, only a few different formats actually exist.

Call semantics: The application programmer can choose between different kinds of call semantics. For example, the default, at-most-once, makes sure that a call is executed once even if communication messages are temporarily lost. This is achieved by message retransmission combined with the detection of duplicate messages. Although node failures cannot be tolerated, message loss can be masked this way. Other selectable semantics provide weaker guarantees in the case of failure but achieve an improved efficiency.

Thread support: Based on threads, it is possible to implement multithreaded servers; this just requires an appropriate parameter setting during server initialization. Then a (static) pool of concurrent server threads is allocated initially. The application programmer, however, must take care of correct thread synchronization in case of shared data modifications. On the client site, threads must be started explicitly to do concurrent, asynchronous calls to multiple servers. Within its body, each thread then performs a synchronous call while different threads are mutually asynchronous.

Security: As mentioned above, secure RPC communication is possible based on the security service. First, the application client and server run a distributed authentication protocol in cooperation with a security server. In this phase, they mutually validate their identity based on a private key encryption approach. In a second phase, the actual call is executed; before the server starts acting upon it, it checks the proper authorization of the client based on a local access control list. Finally, the call data can optionally be encrypted in order to enable complete privacy during communication.

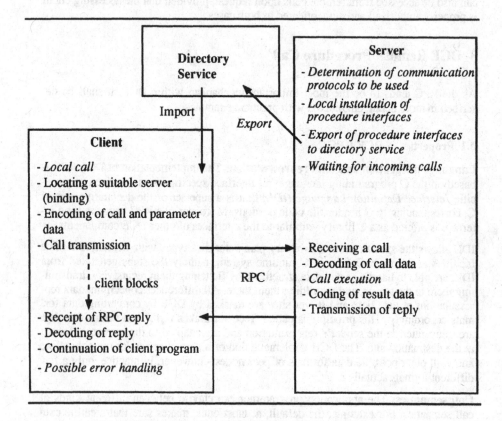

Fig. 6 Typical DCE RPC runtime scenario

3.2 Building Applications with DCE RPC

Building distributed applications with DCE RPC requires the following steps:

- *Interface definition:* An IDL interface must be specified with all procedures that shall be offered by a server.

- *Server implementation:* The server procedures must be implemented as ordinary C code. Moreover, DCE-specific server initialization steps must be performed by the implementation.

- *Client implementation:* In the simplest case, the client site is implemented as a standard C program. Advanced DCE features such as explicit selection among a group of servers or execution of secure RPC require additional code, however.

RPC runtime aspects: A typical DCE RPC runtime scenario is illustrated in fig. 6. All functionality that has to be implemented explicitly by the application developer is shown in italics, everything else is or can be performed automatically by DCE RPC.

The first step is the server initialization. The servers determine which communication protocols to use (such as TCP/IP or UDP/IP), installs its offered procedure interfaces with the RPC runtime system, exports the procedure interface information to the directory service (i.e. CDS), and finally waits for incoming calls.

To invoke an RPC, a client calls the corresponding procedure locally. However, based on the stubs that are generated from IDL, an internal handler routine is executed instead of a local application procedure implementation. It contacts the directory service for locating a suitable server. The input is a logical name for the server and the required procedure interface, the output is a server address, a so-called binding handle. This whole process is called RPC binding. Then the remote call and its input parameters are encoded and transmitted to the server. While the server executes the call, the client blocks. The remaining steps of call decoding, execution and result transfer have already been explained earlier. Finally, the client should include some error handling due to possible transmission problems etc.

Example: A program example shall illustrate the required code; it implements a remote client query against a server that manages product data. The interface definition consists of a header with a unique interface number (generated automatically) and with versioning information. The interface body comprises the required C type definitions and procedure interfaces with fully typed parameter specifications. Some attributes beyond C are required to distinguish between input and output parameters, for example.

```
[
uuid(765c3b10-100a-135d-1568-040034e67831),
version(1.0)
]
interface ProductData {                          // Interface for product data
    import "globaldef.idl";                      // Import of general definitions
    const long maxProd = 10;                     // Maximum number of products
    typedef [string] char *String;               // String type
    typedef struct {
        String productName;                      // Product name
        String productAnnotation;                // Textual annotation
        Plan manufacturingPlan;                  // ...Type defined in globaldef.idl
    } ProductDescription;                        // Product description data type

    long productQuery (                          // Remote query procedure
        [in] String productName[maxProd],        // -> Product names
        [out] ProductDescription *pd[maxProd],   // <- Product descriptions
        [out] long *status );                    // <- Call status
}
```

Server: The server initialization implements the steps discussed above by calling a number of DCE RPC system functions. A simplified example program looks as follows:

```
#include "productdata.h"                    // Generated by the IDL compiler
#define entryName "/.:/ProductServer"        // Name of server's directory entry
#define maxConcCalls 5                       // Max. number of concurrent invoc.

main ()   {
    unsigned status;                         // Return status
    rpc_binding_vector_t *bVec;              // Vector of binding handles

    // *** Perform some local initializations (not detailed here)
    // *** Get the actual vector of binding handles: ***
    rpc_server_inq_bindings (&bVec, &status);

    // *** Register the interface with a machine-local RPC manager process: ***
    rpc_ep_register (ProductData_v1_0_s_ifspec, bVec, NULL, NULL, &status);

    // *** Export the interface to the directory service under the given name: ***
    rpc_ns_binding_export (rpc_c_ns_syntax_default, entryName,
            ProductData_v1_0_s_ifspec, bVec, NULL, &status);

    // *** Now be ready to accept incoming invocations concurrently: ***
    rpc_server_listen (maxConcCalls, &status);
    }
```

The implementation of the server's application procedures, i.e. of *productQuery* in this case, is identical with a local implementation and is therefore not detailed here.

Client: The client site is also independent from DCE or distributed systems aspects (if no advanced RPC functionality is desired):

```
#include "productdata.h"                    // Interface definition header file

main ()    {
    String product[maxProd];        // Product names
    ProductDescription *pd[maxProd];        // Requested product descriptions
    long rc, status;                        // Status values

    inputProductNames (product);            // Input function (appl. specific)
    rc = productQuery (product, pd, &status);  // RPC
    // ... check status value and handle errors
    }
```

In summary, building DCE applications based on the client/server model is a relatively straightforward task for C programmers. However, the use of advanced features is more difficult. In the following, such features are summarized briefly; for deatails, see [6].

3.3 Advanced DCE RPC Features

Binding: During binding, the client can control the selection of a specific server explicitly; this mode is called *explicit binding* as opposed to the *automatic binding* applied above. The implementation of explicit binding is based on directory service interaction procedures to be called by the client via system RPCs. Moreover, DCE offers facilities to register groups of servers with the directory service and to specify client-specific search paths through the directory entries. This way, the server selection process can be controlled in detail.

Callback: With DCE RPC, it is possible for a server to issue a callback to a client during remote procedure execution; the client must offer an appropriate call interface for that. This way, a server can deliver intermediate results or can request further input data.

Pipes: For bulk data transfer, logical pipes can be established between client and server by passing pipe references as RPC parameters. A server can then request large chunks of data via the pipe dynamically from the client, and can also send bulk data back to the client this way.

Context: For multiple client/server interactions in a row, it is sometimes useful to establish some context information between both sites. An example is information about an open file of a file server that is read by a client by several RPCs. DCE RPC offers explicit mechanisms to handle such context information.

Other features such as asynchronous RPCs and secure RPCs have already been discussed. Altogether, a quite rich RPC functionality is provided by DCE.

4 Challenges and Models Beyond DCE

While DCE is a major step towards open distributed computing, the approach is still limited to relatively conventional client/server applications. This presents a number of ongoing research and development challenges to provide advanced support and new models beyond DCE. Examples are advanced development and management tools, distributed object-oriented systems, distributed transaction support, and multimedia extensions.

4.1 Advanced Method and Tool Support

Only few commercially available dedicated tools exist for client/server type applications. As a consequence, programmers use design methods, debugging tools and other software development aids that were developed for the sequential programming languages used as RPC host languages. The situation is similar for management components such as source code control tools. The distribution and parallelism exhibited in client/server applications, however, requires dedicated development aids. This requirement becomes even more important as we move to programming paradigms beyond client/server, such as the ones described later.

We will, for the remainder, focus on a number of important aspects of tool support which can be divided into three categories: development tools (here we will discuss formal specification and design), runtime-level tools (debugging and cooperation), and management tools (runtime management and distributed system management). For some of these topics, we will separately discuss support for DCE-like client/server applications and for advanced distributed applications.

Formal specification techniques have gained a lot of attention in the context of communication protocols. This is due to the fact that such protocols are complex (i.e. hard to describe unambiguously with informal techniques) and that implementations of different vendors have to interoperate in open distributed systems. The formal techniques used for communication protocols can be applied to distributed applications as well [8]; the application of Lotos, Z, and SDL to distributed systems is described in [9]. However, the corresponding formal specification techniques usually do *not* focus on any of the most interesting aspects of distributed applications, such as dynamic reconfiguration of the network of processes (active entities and communication links beeing added and removed at runtime), hierarchical decomposition, and asynchronous communication. Moreover, the feasibility of formal techniques for large software projects, and the close coupling of formal techniques to DCE (in the sense of automatic code transformation) have not been achieved to a satisfactory degree yet. Moreover, in the client/server context, formal techniques for reasoning about the correctness of RPCs as such ought to be included.

Design: Specific design tools for distributed applications are hardly in use, either. The software engineer would want them to support visual programming, early animation of coarse designs, and automatic code generation. An example for a prototype tool with these features, VDAB, is described in this volume. It also supports the design of the dynamic behaviour of distributed applications "by example", based on dedicated *call scenarios*. The tool translates into a distributed version of C++, which is in turn implemented on top of DCE.

Debugging: Distributed debugging is widely recognized as one of the most important issues to be resolved on the way to cost-effective development of distributed applications. This owes to the fact that sequential debuggers do not help resolve some of the most predominant problems with testing distributed programs: the interference of the debugger with the code (which can make it impossible to detect the effects of race conditions), the presence of indeterminisms (which hinder the reproducability of subsequent debugging sessions), the vast amount of parallel events to be perceived by the user, and the lack of support for notions like "distributed breakpoint" and "distributed single-step". While uncountable contributions to these issues can be found in the literature, hardly any commercially available distributed debugging tool exists in the wider DCE context.

Runtime management: For sequential program development, the management of different versions and branches of source code and executable code in the development environment has been considered an important problem; to resolve this issue, code management tools were developed. In contrast, the *installation* of the final software version in a target environment (i.e. at the customer site) was usually deferred to a one-shot installation procedure. The installation of a distributed application however, i.e. the management of executable code in a distributed environment, is often an iterative and cumbersome task. Executables have to be copied to all sites, parameters and input files have to be considered at these sites, nameserver, network, and operating system setups have to be adjusted, etc. During execution, performance monitoring is desired, e.g., as a base for reconfiguration decisions. Such tasks are mostly carried out by hand today. But with the increasing deployment of distributed applications and the continuing sophistication of these applications, the need for user-friendly (e.g., graphics-based) and highly automated runtime management tools will increase drastically.

Distributed system management: As DCE shows, distributed system management is a rather complex task. For example, CDS or Security servers must be installed, managed, and replicated. Security information such as passwords or access control lists must be maintained. DFS management comprises an even wider variety of different tasks. Therefore, graphical management tools are required to provide simplified management user interfaces. Beyond this, further higher-level programs are desirable which automate other routine management tasks in a distributed system such as backups or software upgrades.

To summarize, tool support for distributed programming has, for the most part, not yet left the academic stage. With DCE, however, the development of distributed applications *has* left this stage and more and more commercial sites get involved in distributed programming. The expected aggravating effects on the software crisis will probably lead to rapid changes in the scene of support tools in the years to come.

4.2 Distributed Object-Oriented Systems

A step beyond RPC are distributed object-based systems as extensions of programming languages like C++, Smalltalk, Trellis, Modula-2 or Eiffel. An object can be defined as a data structure associated with a set of operations. The data structure could refer to other objects by which an object graph can be built representing a so called complex object. Thus, as opposed to RPC servers, the granularity of objects is scalable and ranges, in general, from a couple of bytes up to thousands of bytes.

The fine granularity of objects and their capability to form complex objects lead to a unit of mobility, i.e. the object, which is easy to handle. Objects interact with each other through "message passing", i.e. an object sends a remote message to a peer object to initiate the execution of one of the provided operations. At the communication level, message passing is performed by RPC-style location independent object invocations whereby interacting objects can reside at different nodes.

However, as opposed to RPC with call-by-value parameter semantics, object references (i.e. pointers to objects) can also be passed remotely, leading to call-by-object-reference semantics. In addition, single objects or even complete object graphs could be passed as parameters to the callee [10].

The resulting approach is more flexible than RPC and, in particular, enables a more natural modeling of distributed applications. Due to the mobility of objects, they can be relocated dynamically. This way, communicating objects can be co-located in order to reduce communication costs or to increase availability during execution of a joint action of a set of objects.

Example: The discussed office / manufacturing system can directly be mapped to a distributed environment this way (see fig. 7). Distributed office procedures can be represented as task objects transferred between server objects. Typical operations of task objects are start, stop, suspend, or status inquiry while servers provide actual service invocations, status inquiries, or accounting functions. Data/document objects attached to an office procedure can also be modeled as objects. Moreover, since each document has a certain structure like chapters, paragraphs and so on, it is likely that such document objects are object graphs as mentioned earlier.

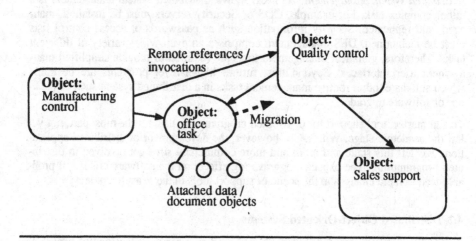

Fig. 7 Distributed object-oriented office procedure modeling

Class structure: The mechanisms to create remote objects, to locate and invoke them, and to relocate them dynamically can be implemented by superclasses from which all relevant application classes inherit. As an example, a C++ superclass is given below [11]; it also offers methods to fix objects at a certain location in order to prevent migration, and to unfix them later:

```
class DistributedObject {
// ... Instance variables like location, size etc.
public:
DistributedObject (Location*); // Constructor to create at a given location
~DistributedObject ();          // Destructor
Location *locate ();            // Locate the object
boolean move (Location*);       // Move to a given location
boolean fix ();                 // Fix at current location (prevent from moving)
boolean unfix ();               // Release for migrations
void Invoke (//...);            // Perform generic
invocation
};
```

Such functionality can be implemented on top of DCE RPC as illustrated by other papers in the proceedings. This requires sophisticated additional mechanisms for locating mobile objects (e.g. via forwarding addresses), for synchronizing migrations and computations, for controlling object migrations according to a given goal, and for monitoring and controlling the overall system behaviour.

OMG/CORBA: The industry consortium Object Management Group (OMG) has defined the Object Management Architecture (OMA) for managing objects in distributed systems. This approach aims at providing support for distributed object interaction in a heterogeneous environment. In OMA, objects usally tend to be much larger than they are at programming language level, i.e. a whole application could be an object. This approach differs from object graphs in the sense that these "coarse-grained objects" are treated as monoliths.

A key component of OMA it is the Object Services Architecture [12-13] that offers the required services with a very broad spectrum of functionality. In general, these services provide a higher level of abstraction than DCE does and cover a broader technological area. Examples are database- and transaction-oriented services, version control of software objects, concurrency control, and distributed object replication. Location independent object interactions are supported by the Common Object Request Broker Architecture (CORBA); it supports mechanisms for identifying, locating, and accessing objects in a distributed environment. However, the Object Management Architecture has not yet reached the same level of maturity that DCE has. Moreover, some functionality of distributed object-oriented systems mentioned above, namely mobility, is not yet supported by CORBA. Several vendors implement - at least partially - CORBA on top of DCE.

Open Distributed Processing (ODP): Distributed system technology has become a major focus in international standardisation and harmonisation activities, too. As an important example, work in ISO and related standardisation committees is in progress to define a reference model for Open Distributed Processing (ODP). The reference model will include a descriptive as well as a prescriptive part. The descriptive part defines terminology and modeling gear that can be used to model arbitrary distributed systems. The prescriptive part specifies when a distributed system may be called an ODP system. It prescribes architectural properties that an ODP system must have. After the ODP reference model has been finished, individual ODP standards conforming to the reference model will be defined. Most likely, one will first work on standards for infrastructure components similar to those that we find in OSF DCE today. ODP and OSF DCE are two projects that are completely unrelated from an organisational point of view. However, the ODP work on an abstract reference model benefits significantly from the design of an infrastructure such as OSF DCE. The latter shows what functionality is needed in distributed processing systems and how components can be integrated into a common framework. Furthermore, when individual ODP standards will be sought for, the OSF DCE technology will certainly be a suitable and promising starting point. OSF and OMG (see above) have expressed their interest in advancing the ODP standardisation.

4.3 Distributed Transactions and Workflows

Transactions are a well-known approach found in database systems. It guarantees so-called ACID semantics (atomicity, consistency, isolation, and durability). Atomicity means that an operation is only performed as a unit; it is either fully completed (commit) or its effects do not become visible (abort). Consistency means that a transaction transforms data from one consistent state into another consistent state. Isolation means that concurrent transactions execute like in a sequential system without interference. In particular, a transaction T1 will never see any intermediate state of data caused by another transaction T2 before T2 is completed. Finally, durability means that the effects of a transaction (data manipulations etc.) remain persistent after transaction completion; for example, they do not get lost after a system crash.

Distributed transactions: The transaction properties have proven very useful for implementing processing functionality with strict consistency requirements (like credit/debit transactions). Therefore, extensions of the basic concept towards distributed systems have been developed [14]. Some of them are based on RPC or distributed object interactions, others on pure message passing. The implementation typically relies on the two-phase commit protocol. In the first phase, all transaction participants are polled by a coordinator whether they are able to successfully commit. In the second phase, the uniform decision is propagated to them in order to commit or abort jointly.

This concept has also been extended towards nested transactions with hierarchical subtransactions. This allows for running subtransactions in parallel, and for selective rollback and restart of subtransactions. Standards and implementations on top of DCE: Meanwhile, there are several emerging product-level implementations of distributed transactions that conform to new standards. Most notably, the *X/Open* consortium has defined the *X/Open Distributed Transaction Processing (DTP)* application programming interface named XA [15]. This approach is designed to work with standardized ISO/OSI transaction protocols, namely CCR and TP.

Conforming to the XA standard, there are several implementations available. The origins of XA have evolved according to the *Tuxedo* system [16] of Unix System Laboratories that is available on numerous hardware platforms and operating systems. The *Encina* transaction processing system [17] of Transarc is an open, XA standards-based family of components that provide online transaction processing based on DCE. Transactional integrity is added to DCE programs through Transactional-C, Transactional RPC (TRPC), two-phase commit and the management of recoverable data. Transactional-C consists of C language extensions to indicate transaction demarcation, concurrency control and exception handling. TRPC adds exactly-once semantics to DCE RPC. When a remote procedure is called from within a transaction, it is executed exactly once, if the transaction commits and not at all if the transaction aborts. Besides this basic support for transactional integrity, Encina offers a Structured File System (SFS) and a Monitor as an administrative, runtime and development environment for transactional applications. Functionality of the Monitor comprises, for example, monitoring active clients, performing load balancing and connecting front-end tools (like OSF/Motif). SFS is an record-oriented file system (in contrast to DCE DFS) that meets the requirements of transactional systems for record-style and recoverable resource managers.

Workflows are a rapidly emerging technology area that deals with long-lived, well-defined activities like office procedures. A workflow system controls the execution of the global control flow and in some cases provides certain reliability support by using transaction mechanisms. Workflows are distributed by nature and thus are one of the key application domain for distributed processing. On the other hand, workflows introduce a new style of programming since execution order and principles should be extracted from the single application part and be moved to a separate workflow program.

Workflow systems could benefit from all DCE services. Especially RPC for communication between the workflow and the application parts, authorization and authentication of users performing the individual steps, and directory services for locating workflow servers are important.

4.4 Distributed Multimedia Systems

A multimedia system is characterised by the computer controlled generation, manipulation, presentation, storage, and communication of independent discrete media such as text and graphics and continuous media such as audio and video [18,19]. Application domains for multimedia systems are, e.g., multimedia e-mail, multimedia-supported teaching, virtual reality simulation systems, and workstation conferencing systems. Many of these domains are inherently distributed. A workstation conferencing system, for example, allows sharing of window based applications among participants at different locations supported by multimedia services for audio communication as well as video conferencing.

Distributed multimedia systems impose new challenges for the communication of continuous data. Whereas discrete media have time independent values, the values of continuous media change over time and these changes contribute to the media semantics: Each single value in an audio or video stream represents stream information for some fraction of time. Changes in the times at which values are played or recorded result in the modification of the original data semantics and must not happen unintentionally. The timing demands of continuous media require operating and transport system support for connections with guaranteed quality-of-service (QoS) for the transmission of continuous data [20]. This is achieved by allocating some fraction of the end-system and network resource capacity and scheduling these resources appropriately. Another meaningful requirement is the support of multicast since a continuous stream often must be transmitted from one source to multiple sinks.
For the development of distributed multimedia applications it is reasonable to model sources (e.g. a microphone) and sinks (e.g. a loudspeaker) of continuous streams as objects. A source object, for example, offers operations to connect itself to a sink object and to start, stop or suspend the production of a stream. This kind of control operations is performed by conventional DCE RPC communication. When control operations must be submitted to multiple sinks, a multicall extension to the RPC is convenient. Directory and security infrastructure is crucial to identify appropriate sources and sinks. The establishment work for the respective connections, however, that comprises the negotiation of the required QoS, and the transmission of the data itself can be left to the "multimedia" transport system. As a result, sources and sinks must be able to cope with the coexistence of dedicated runtime systems for conventional RPC communication as well as processing of continuous data.

Special support for producing, processing and consuming continuous data is needed, when the data get manipulated within the application. Manipulations are, for example, encrypting or compressing audio or video information, or mixing and synchronising different but related streams. A useful construction in this context is to conceive the connection between a source and its sink as an object in its own right. Such an object exhibits two categories of operations: a lower level category acting on the established transport connection and a higher level for controlling it.

5 Overview of the Technical Contributions

The technical contributions in this volume are concerned with DCE implementation issues, with applications and tools, but also with models and approaches beyond DCE. In particular, the following areas are covered:

DCE analysis and comparison: DCE is compared with the ANSAware environment developed in the UK. Moreover, DCE RPC is compared with SUN RPC and with other RPC approaches. Two performance analysis studies evaluate DCE RPC and CDS in detail. This also leads to concrete recommendations, for example concerning the configuration of a CDS name space. This way, the conceptual overview given above is augmented with practical DCE analyses and experiences.

Application support: This part focuses on DCE application support tools and on actual DCE applications. Two different tools for enabling Fortran access to DCE services are presented. The first tool supports the conversion of existing non-distributed Fortran applications to distributed DCE applications. The other approach enables direct program-level access from Fortran to C-based DCE functions. One paper presents a practical DCE application for stock broker support. This contribution emphasizes how DCE is used for real-world applications and reports experiences with DCE application development. Another application implements print services and a heterogeneous interface to various mail systems based on DCE RPC, using a generic services architecture.

Methods and tools: Several other DCE support tools are presented. A formal method and tool approach focuses on the problem of converting monolithic, non-distributed programs to distributed applications on top of DCE. A similar transition approach is presented for DCE Security, helping to incorporate conventional Unix security environments into a DCE framework. Finally, advanced tools for resource monitoring in DCE cells are presented. Altogether, tool examples from all three categories of development, system management and runtime-level are discussed.

RPC extensions: This part covers direct extensions of DCE RPC. The first example is multimedia support based on new media types and quality of service attributes in IDL, and on runtime mechanisms for time-constrained RPC and realtime thread scheduling. Another paper introduces an integration of RPC and message passing, leading to a more flexible set of communication facilities. Moreover, optimized RPC server selection is also addressed in order to relieve the application developer from the selection process discussed above. Finally, an ambitious distributed object model is implemented by an object-oriented RPC extension. It provides the facilities discussed above, but also supports dynamic typing of objects. This allows a more natural integration of common generic services in a DCE environment.

Object-based systems: Several other papers focus on object-based DCE extensions, too. An operating implementation of CORBA on top of DCE is presented, showing that there's a strong practical relationship between CORBA and DCE. The design and implementation of a distributed object-oriented framework with mobile objects beyond CORBA, but on top of DCE, is illustrated by another contribution. A related paper shows how the more conventional DCE functionality can at least be offered via higher-level, object-oriented class interfaces. This way, an improved abstraction is provided to the application developer. Finally, an object-based tool for graphical support of DCE applications is presented. This also extends the tool discussion towards the early phases of application design.

In summary, the papers in this volume illustrate that DCE is a practical environment for building distributed programs. However, they also make the need for higher-level tools, models and abstractions obvious. It is hoped that directions for further research and development in the context of DCE are pointed out this way, and that such work will help to make DCE a success for open distributed environments.

References

1. Mullender, S. (Ed.): Distributed Systems; *Addison-Wesley, Reading, Massachusetts, 1989*
2. Tanenbaum, A.S.: Computer Networks; *Prentice Hall, 1991*
3. Open Software Foundation: Interoperability: A Key Criterion for Open Systems; *OMG, 1992*
4. Open Software Foundation: OSF Distributed Management Environment (DME) Architecture; *OMG, 1992*
5. Open Software Foundation: Introduction to OSF DCE; *Open Software Foundation, Cambridge, USA, 1992*
6. Open Software Foundation: DCE Application Development Guide; *Open Software Foundation, Cambridge, USA, 1992*
7. Howard, J.H., Kazar, M.L., Menees, S.G., Nichols, D.A., Satyanarayanan, M., Sidebotham, R.N., West, M.J.: Scale and Performance in a Distributed File System; *ACM Trans. on Computer Systems, Vol. 6, No. 1, Feb. 1988, pp. 51-81*
8. Misra, J., Chandy, K.M.: Proofs of networks of processes; *IEEE Trans. on Software Engineering, Vol. SE-7, 1981, pp. 417-426*
9. Special Issue on the Practical use of Formal Definition Techniques in Communications and Distributed Systems; *Computer Communications, Vol. 15, No. 2, March 1992*
10. Achauer, B. The DOWL Distributed Object-Oriented Language; *Communications of the ACM, Vol. 36, No. 9, 1993*
11. Schill, A., Zitterbart, M.; A System Framework for Open Distributed Processing; *Journal of Network and Systems Management, Vol. 1, No. 1, 1993, pp. 71-93*
12. Object Management Group: The Common Object Request Broker: Architecture and Specification; *OMG, 1991*
13. Object Management Group: Object Services Architecture; *OMG, 1992*
14. Gray, J., Reuter, A.: Transaction Processing - Concepts and Techniques; *Morgan Kaufman Publishers, San Mateo, CA, 1993*
15. X/Open Distributed Transaction Processing; *X/Open Ltd., Reading, Berkshire, England, 1992*
16. Tuxedo System Transaction Manager; *Unix System Laboratories, 1992*
17. Encina Transaction Processing System; *Transarc Corp., Pittsburgh, PA, 1992*
18. Herrtwich, R., Steinmetz, R.: Towards Integrated Multimedia Systems: Why and How; *in 21th. Jahrestagung GI, Darmstadt October 1991, Informatik-Fachbericht 293, Springer-Verlag, 1991*
19. Davies, N.A., Nicol, J.R.: Technological Perspective on Multimedia Computing; *Computer Communications, Vol. 14, No. 5, June 1991, pp. 260-272*
20. Vogt, C., Herrtwich, R., Nagarajan, R.: HeiRat-The Heidelberg Resource and Administration Technique Design Philosphy and Goals; *in N. Gerner, H.-G. Hegering, J. Swoboda, Kommunikation in Verteilten Systemen ITG/GI-Fachtagung, Munich, March 1993*

Comparing two Distributed Environments: DCE and ANSAware

Ashley Beitz [1], Paul King [2] and Kerry Raymond [3]

[1] ashley@dstc.edu.au
CRC for Distributed Systems Technology,
University of Queensland,
Brisbane 4072 Australia

[2] king@dstc.edu.au
CRC for Distributed Systems Technology,
Digital Equipment Corporation, Networks and Communications R&D Centre,
Burnett Place, Bond University Research Park, Robina 4226 Australia

[3] kerry@dstc.edu.au
CRC for Distributed Systems Technology,
Centre for Information Technology Research, University of Queensland,
Brisbane 4072 Australia

Abstract. A distributed environment is used for the development and operation of distributed applications. This paper compares two distributed environments: the Distributed Computing Environment (DCE) from the Open Software Foundation (OSF) and ANSAware from Architecture Projects Management (APM) Limited. The results indicate that DCE and ANSAware have many differences. These differences reflect the fact that ANSAware was built up from an innovative architectural model for distributed systems with a focus on providing a vehicle for technology transfer, while DCE was built by integrating existing technology with a focus on providing the functionality necessary for commercial viability.

1 Introduction

Distributed environments are the collection of utilities, languages and libraries which support the development and operation of distributed applications. A distributed environment has a similar purpose to a distributed operating system, but sits on top of an existing operating system as opposed to replacing it entirely. Therefore, the distributed environment is easier to port and its installation causes minimal impact to the system (i.e. the operating system is not replaced). Unfortunately, a distributed environment is not usually as efficient as a distributed operating system and it is difficult to implement migration and load balancing in a distributed environment. In this paper, the term distributed environment is synonymous with the terms: distributed computing environment, distributed processing environment and distributed systems environment.

This paper compares two prominent distributed environments: DCE 1.0.2 [1] [2] [3] and ANSAware 4.0 [4]. Distributed Computing Environment (DCE) is produced by the Open Software Foundation (OSF) through its Request For Technology process. Its technology originates from a number of vendors and research institutions, including Digital Equipment Corporation, Hewlett-Packard, Siemens-Nixdorf, Transarc and

MIT. ANSAware is the realisation of the Advanced Networked Systems Architecture (ANSA), an architecture for networked computer systems to support distributed applications. ANSAware was developed by the research organisation Architecture Projects Management (APM) Limited to serve as a technology transfer vehicle.

This paper compares DCE and ANSAware from a number of perspectives. Section 2 describes the software components within each distributed environment. Section 3 examines application development, which covers the computational aspects. Section 4 explores infrastructure issues, including the engineering and technological aspects. Section 5 addresses system administration and the effort of installing and maintaining a distributed environment. Our conclusions are presented in Section 6.

2 Software Components

ANSAware and DCE both comprise of a number of software components, shown in Figure 1 and Figure 2 respectively.

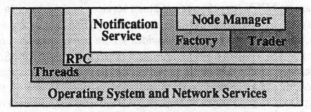

Figure 1: ANSAware components

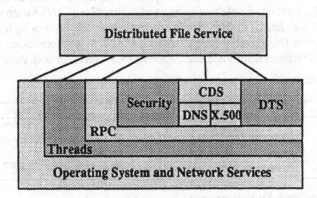

Figure 2: DCE Components

ANSAware and DCE have common components, such as *threads* and *Remote Procedure Call (RPC)*. The threads component allows the creation, management and synchronisation of multiple threads of control within a single process. The RPC component allows procedure calls to be invoked remotely.

Both distributed environments have a name service. The name service maps names that a user understands into names that a distributed environment (computer) understands. In DCE, the *Directory Service* component allows information about resources within the system to be stored and accessed. The directory service functionality is further divided into inter-cell and intra-cell parts. A *Cell* is a fundamental grouping of nodes into some administrative domain (see Section 5). A hierarchical naming scheme is provided by the *Cell Directory Service (CDS)* for intra-cell use. Inter-cell naming is handled by the *Global Directory Service (GDS)* which uses either the X.500 or the Domain Name Service (DNS) naming scheme. In ANSAware, the trader provides the name service functionality. The trader allows a client to find the service that it requires via a lookup based on attributes. ANSAware's and DCE's name services are very different; DCE provides a white pages service (straightforward name to entry lookup), while ANSAware provides a yellow pages service (lookup based on attributes). DCE provides groups and profiles for the logical grouping of directory entries; such groupings can be based on attributes and thus can support a yellow pages style of search.

Both ANSAware and DCE provide a few distinct services of their own. In DCE, these are the *Security* service, the *Distributed Time Service* (DTS) and the *Distributed File Service* (DFS). The Security component provides secure communications and controlled access to resources within a distributed system. The Distributed Time Service component provides synchronised time to nodes within the system. The Distributed File Service component allows users to access and share files anywhere on the network without having to know their physical location. ANSAware's distinct services are the *Notification Service*, the *Factory* and the *Node Manager*. The notification service advises interested parties of the termination of an object. The factory provides the dynamic instantiation and termination of objects. The node manager provides an architectural interface for the creation, simple monitoring and destruction of ANSAware services on a node. ANSAware has no distributed file service; it relies on systems such as the Network File System (NFS). As a general comment, ANSAware focuses on distributed processing and neglects distributed data, whereas DCE caters for both these aspects.

2.1 Summary

	DCE	ANSAware
Software Components	RPC, Threads, Name Service, Security Service, DTS and DFS	RPC, Threads, Name Service, Notification Service, Factory and Node Manager
Name Service	Directory Service (white pages)	Trader (yellow pages)

3 Applications Development

3.1 Paradigm

The architecture for both DCE and ANSAware is based on the object model [5]. An object is a discrete component which makes available a particular resource, or service, through a restricted set of operations. Objects play an important role in distributed applications, as they provide a natural partitioning for these applications. In both DCE and ANSAware, an object's operations are usually partitioned into smaller sets known as interfaces, where the operations in each interface usually serve some related purpose.

Both DCE and ANSAware support the client-server paradigm; the objects which provide the service are the servers and the objects which use the service are the clients. A client accesses a service by invoking an operation on the server's interface via an RPC.

3.2   Interface Definition Language

In both DCE and ANSAware, an interface definition language (IDL) is used to specify the data types and operations applicable to each interface in a platform-independent manner. Semantically, DCE's IDL and ANSAware's IDL are very similar; syntactically, they are very different. DCE's IDL builds on the C language syntax for function and data type definitions, augmented by *attributes* which define properties not representable in the C language. Figure 3 illustrates how a simple interface providing Unix-like file operations is defined using DCE IDL; the attributes appear in brackets.

```
[
        /* An interface type id comprises of a unique universal id (uuid) and a version number.      */
        /* It is required if interfaces of this type are to be registered with name servers.      */
        uuid(907F0E10-D3C2-11CB-BCCE-08002B2D0880),
        version(1.0)
] interface UnixCall
{
        typedef struct {
            long                        length;
            [length_is(length)] char        data[BUFSIZE];
            /* length_is() indicates the variable which stores the array length */
        } Buffer;

        /* for the functions below, any error status is returned as the (unnamed) function result */

        long Open ( [in, string] char path[], [in] long flags, [in] long mode, [out] long *fd );

        long Read ( [in] long fd, [in] long nbytes, [out] Buffer *buf, [out] long *nread );
}
```

Figure 3: Example of Unix system calls using DCE IDL

ANSAware's IDL is based on the Courier IDL from Xerox [6] and syntactically resembles Modula-2. Figure 4 illustrates the simple file interface using ANSAware IDL.

```
UnixCall: INTERFACE =
BEGIN
        Buffer: TYPE = SEQUENCE OF CHAR;

        Open: OPERATION [path: STRING; flags, mode: INTEGER]
                RETURNS [fd: INTEGER; err: INTEGER];

        Read: OPERATION [fd: INTEGER; nbytes: INTEGER]
                RETURNS [buf: Buffer; nread: INTEGER; err: INTEGER];
END.
```

Figure 4: Example of Unix system calls using ANSAware IDL

Data Types

The primitive data types supported in both ANSAware and DCE are very similar. Both support the common data types: boolean, cardinal, integer, character, real, byte and string. Variants of the common data types are also supported, e.g. short integer and long real. The major difference is that DCE alone supports pointers allowing DCE to exchange complex pointer-linked structures during an RPC. ANSAware also provides ANSAware-specific data types; such as object id, interface id and interface reference.

New data types can be constructed using data type constructors. The data types constructors supported in both ANSAware and DCE are very similar. Both provide enumeration, arrays, records, variant records and aliases. The only difference is that ANSAware provides sequences (or variable-sized arrays) directly, while DCE supports variable-sized arrays by having an explicit length variable indicated by the length_is attribute on the array declaration (see the definition of Buffer in Figure 3).

Operation Signatures

In DCE, there are three methods to exchange information during an RPC: named input parameters (indicated by the in attribute), named output parameters (indicated by the out attribute) and the unnamed function value (e.g. the error codes are returned as function values in Figure 3). There can be any number of input and output parameters (or none), but there is at most one unnamed function value. A parameter can be used for both input and output (i.e. declared as [in, out]). ANSAware only has two methods: named input parameters and optionally named output parameters (which can also be regarded as function values). ANSAware can have zero or more of the input and output parameters, but no parameter can be both for input and output.

ANSAware supports two types of operations: interrogations and announcements. Interrogations (the default form) are operations that return results; the client waits until those results are returned. Announcements do not return results and the client does not await any response. By not awaiting a response, the client cannot be informed of the failure of the announcement operation; this is a risk that the client must accept. The normal RPC in DCE is identical to ANSAware's interrogation operation. ANSAware's announcement operation is equivalent to DCE's maybe operation (an operation annotated with a maybe attribute does not return results and is not guaranteed to execute).

Interfaces

Both ANSAware IDL and DCE IDL have a method of inheriting *data type definitions* from another IDL file. In ANSAware, it is the NEEDS statement; in DCE, it is the import statement. Additionally, ANSAware has a means to inherit *operation definitions* from another IDL file. The IS COMPATIBLE WITH statement in an ANSAware IDL file inherits operation definitions while the IMPLEMENTATION IS COMPATIBLE WITH statement also allows code re-use.

In ANSAware, an interface type is identified by a simple name (e.g. UnixCall in Figure 4). Although a DCE interface type can be given a simple name (e.g. UnixCall in Figure 3), a DCE interface type is actually identified by its uuid and version attributes. The uuid attribute defines a unique name for the interface while the version attribute indicates the compatibility between different versions of that interface type. The DCE utility uuidgen generates uuid values making it easy for the application developer to ensure world-wide uniqueness.

3.3 Distributed Programming Language

Distributed programming languages are used to implement distributed applications. DCE does not provide a new programming language. DCE applications are written and compiled using conventional programming languages and compilers, typically C. The benefits of this approach are that application programmers do not have to learn a new language and existing applications can be more readily ported to DCE.

In contrast, ANSAware provides a new language, a combination of the C language and ANSAware's PREPC language, which provides additional syntax for distributed systems functions. ANSAware applications must first be preprocessed to yield a conventional C program before compilation using a regular C compiler. The advantage of ANSAware's distributed programming language is that it gives syntactic support to the concepts of interfaces, not directly representable in the C language and, hence, in DCE applications.

Offering an Interface

In order to provide an interface to clients, a server must first create and export its interface. The following code fragments in Figure 5 show how this is done using ANSAware. Note that lines commencing with a '!' are PREPC code.

```
! DECLARE { if_ref } : UnixCall SERVER    /* PREPC declaration for the interface reference (if_ref)    */
                                          /* interface type (UnixCall) and role (SERVER) are specified */

  ansa_InterfaceRef  if_ref;              /* C declaration for the interface reference                 */

!{ if_ref } :: UnixCall$Create( ... )     /* create an interface of type UnixCall                      */
                                          /* this operation returns an interface reference             */
!{ } <- traderRef$Export("UnixCall", ... , if_ref)  /* export an interface offer to the trader         */
                                          /* traderRef is the trader's interface reference             */

! if_ref$Discard                          /* withdraw the interface offer from the trader              */
                                          /* and destroy the interface                                 */
```

Figure 5: Offering an interface in ANSAware

In comparison with ANSAware, establishing a server's interface in DCE requires a series of calls to register the interface at a number of levels (viz. RPC runtime, name service and endpoint mapper). An outline of the DCE code to establish an interface and the main loop which provides service at the interface is shown in Figure 6.

```
rpc_server_register_if( ... );                    /* register interface with RPC runtime      */
rpc_server_use_all_protseqs( ... );               /* establish protocol sequences             */
rpc_server_inq_bindings( ... );                   /* get binding handles for this server       */
rpc_ns_binding_export( ... );                     /* export entry to name service             */
rpc_ep_register( ... );                           /* add endpoints to local endpoint map      */
TRY
        rpc_server_listen( ... );                 /* listen for client calls                  */
FINALLY
        rpc_ep_unregister( ... );                 /* remove endpoints from endpoint map       */
        rpc_binding_vector_free( ... );           /* relinquish binding handles               */
ENDTRY
```

Figure 6: Offering an interface in DCE

An important difference between ANSAware and DCE is that ANSAware treats interfaces as "first class" entities. By "first class" entities, we mean that the interfaces are not contained within an object, instead they are distinct entities which may be offered by an object. Through ANSAware's support of interfaces as "first class" entities (viz. the interface reference data type and interface-specific state) ANSAware object's can offer multiple instances of the same interface type. A DCE object cannot readily offer multiple interfaces of the same interface type (as an interface can only be identified via its interface id and its object id); it can, however, be split up into sub-objects and, thus, offer multiple interfaces through multiple sub-objects.

Implementing the Server's Operations

Servers must provide code for each of the operations defined in the interface type. The code fragment in Figure 7 shows the ANSAware server code for the Read operation defined in Figure 4. Notice that the interface type has been prepended to the operation name and that the first parameter _attr (which is used to access interface-specific state) is added to the parameters defined in the IDL file.

```
int UnixCall_Read (_attr, fd, nbytes, buf, nread, err)
        ansa_InterfaceAttr *_attr;        /* this parameter may be used to access the interface's state */
        ansa_Integer fd;
        ansa_Integer nbytes;
        Buffer *buf;
        ansa_Integer *nread;
        ansa_Integer *err;
{
        buf->data = buffer;               /* buffer is a static variable */
        *nread = buf->length = read (fd, buf->data, nbytes);
        *err = errno;
        return SuccessfulInvocation;
}
```

Figure 7: Implementing a Server Operation in ANSAware

Although establishing a DCE interface is rather complex, the code to implement the operations offered by the interface is relatively straightforward as shown in Figure 8. Like ANSAware, the first parameter IDL_handle is additional to those parameters defined in the IDL file. The IDL_handle parameter can be used to obtain details of the binding.

```
long Read (IDL_handle, fd, nbytes, buf, nread)
        handle_t IDL_handle;
        int fd;
        int nbytes;
        Buffer *buf;
        int *nread;
{
        *nread = buf->length = read (fd, buf->data, nbytes);
        return (errno);
}
```

Figure 8: Implementing a Server Operation in DCE

Binding Clients and Servers

Before a client can invoke the operations of a server, the client must first be bound to the server's interface. DCE provides three different forms of binding:

- automatic, where the client program simply calls the procedures specified in the interface. The client stub binds to any server offering that interface. Successive calls might be made to different servers.

- implicit, where the client program initially binds to a single server. Any call to the procedures defined in that interface will automatically be made to the bound server.

- explicit, where the client program binds to one or more servers. Each call made to the procedures defined in the interface must specify which bound server is to be used (the binding handle for that server is passed as the first parameter to the procedure).

Automatic binding is the simplest for the applications programmer, but there is a loss of control. Explicit binding is the most complex for the applications programmer, but provides maximum control. Implicit binding lies between the other two. The choice of binding is expressed as an attribute in an optional Attribute Configuration File (ACF), which customises the IDL file. In our experience, explicit binding is required for all but the more trivial applications.

DCE and ANSAware have a different approach to binding. In DCE, the directory service provides the node that offers the interface, the node (and the object id) identifies the endpoint to be used, and then binding can occur. In ANSAware, the trader combines the ability to select an interface based on quite complex criteria (if desired) with the node and endpoint information required to establish a binding. Although there is an explicit binding action in ANSAware, our experiences suggest that the trader's Import operation (which combines the selection and binding) is normally used.

DCE's two-stage method of locating an interface (node, then endpoint) appears to be based on the assumption that an interface is unlikely to be offered more than once by a single node. If multiple instances are offered on a single node, then both entries in the directory service point to the same node. The interface's object ids are required to enable the end-point mapper to distinguish between the instances. As ANSAware's trader maps interfaces directly to endpoints, multiple interfaces of the same type offered by the same node cannot be confused.

The ANSAware code fragment in Figure 9 demonstrates the client code for selecting and binding to a server interface.

```
! DECLARE { if_ref } : UnixCall CLIENT      /* PREPC declaration for the interface reference (if_ref)   */
                                            /* interface type (UnixCall) and role (CLIENT) are specified */

  ansa_InterfaceRef   if_ref;               /* C declaration for the interface reference               */

! {if_ref} <- traderRef$Import("UnixCall", ... )   /* select an interface offer from the trader        */
```

Figure 9: ANSAware code for selecting and binding to a server interface

The explicit binding process performed by the DCE client is in Figure 10. Again, considerable detail of this complex mechanism has been omitted. Note that this code is not required if automatic binding is used.

```
rpc_ns_binding_import_begin( ... );                              /* begin scanning binding handles   */
while (1) {
        rpc_ns_binding_import_next( ... );                       /* import a binding handle          */
        rpc_binding_to_string_binding( ... );                    /* translate to string              */
        rpc_string_binding_parse( ... );                         /* parse the binding                */
        rpc_string_free( ... );                                  /* free all rpc-allocated strings   */
        /* exit loop when suitable binding handle is found */
}
rpc_ns_binding_import_done( ... );                               /* end of scanning binding handles  */
```

Figure 10: DCE code for selecting and binding to a server interface

Calling Remote Procedure Calls

As DCE uses conventional programming languages for applications development, invocation of RPCs is syntactically similar to the invocation of local procedure calls as shown in Figure 11. Once the DCE client has established the binding, calls to the operations of the remote interface can be made quite simply. Notice that the first parameter (not present in the IDL file) is the binding handle (this is using explicit binding).

```
errno = Read (binding_h, fd, BUFSIZE, &buf, &nread);
```

Figure 11: DCE RPC invocation

In contrast, invocation of RPCs in ANSAware is done using PREPC code as shown in Figure 12.

```
! {buf, nread, errno} <- if_ref$Read (fd, BUFSIZE)
```

Figure 12: ANSAware RPC invocation

An ANSAware invocation comprises of five parts. The first part is the result list (contained in { }), the second part is the interface reference for the interface being invoked (if_ref), the third part is the operation name (Read), the fourth part is the argument list (contained in ( )) and the fifth part is used for exception handling (this part is not used in the above example).

As mentioned in Section 3.3, DCE does not give any syntactic support to interfaces. Therefore, name clashes occur if the client uses another interface which has a Read operation. The simplest solution is to rename the operation in one of the interfaces, but this affects all existing clients and servers of that interface (and assumes that the programmer has the privileges to modify the IDL file). By adopting the convention of prepending the interface name to each operation name in the IDL file, e.g. call the operation UnixCall_Read, these problems can be avoided.

Exception Handling

In ANSAware, exception handling is supported syntactically as part of remote invocation. As shown in Figure 13, each invocation can choose to continue, abort, or invoke an exception handler in response to any of 27 invocation outcomes, e.g. ok (when the operation returns SuccessfulInvocation), abnormalReturn (when the operation returns UnSuccessfulInvocation), transmitTimeout (when a communications time-out occurs).

! {b, n, e} <- file_ops$Read (f, B) Continue ok Signal transmitTimeout Abort *

Figure 13: ANSAware RPC invocation with exception handling

In DCE, invocation failures are separated into two groups: failures of communications (e.g. time-out) and failure at the server (e.g. unable to make the call). By using the ACF attributes comm_status and fault_status, the operations of the interface can be modified to return these error codes as either output parameters or function results. The programmer can then test these error codes and react appropriately. DCE provides syntactic support for exceptions through the use of macros, e.g. RAISE and TRY.

Advanced DPL Concepts

In addition to the DPL concepts discussed in the previous sections, DCE provides two additional concepts: context handles and pipes. Neither of these concepts are provided by ANSAware.

A DCE server can store the state (or context) associated with a client's session. This allows the communication overhead to be reduced, as there is no need for the state to be transferred (back and forth) for each of the client's invocations on the server. The context handle is the reference used by the client to associate itself with a particular state maintained by the server.

A pipe is a mechanism used to transfer data of a particular type between a client and a server. This transfer can be bidirectional, i.e. the client can use the pipe to transfer data to the server and the server can use the same pipe to transfer data to the client. This mechanism is normally used to transfer large amounts of data or when there might be a sporadic stream of data between the client and the server. One limitation of the pipe mechanism is that it cannot transfer pointers or data containing pointers.

3.4 Concurrency

In order to exploit the potential for parallel execution in a distributed system, the applications must be capable of concurrency. Although the RPC is an excellent paradigm for programmers, awaiting the return of the call does not exploit the parallelism of the distributed system. As RPCs are the basis for interworking in both DCE and ANSAware, it is important to understand how the concurrency of applications can be increased when required.

DCE supports concurrency via three mechanisms: threads, broadcast RPCs and maybe operations. A thread is a light-weight process and allows an application to have multiple execution paths. A broadcast RPC is an operation invoked on all servers of a particular type within the local network; the client awaits the first successful result while the others are ignored. Broadcast RPCs are only possible in restricted circumstances; in particular, the UDP transport protocol is required. Operations with the maybe attribute do not need to await results.

ANSAware supports three concurrency mechanisms: threads, announcements and vouchers. ANSAware threads and announcements are similar in concept to DCE's threads and maybe operations. Vouchers enable an ANSAware interrogation (RPC) to be invoked without awaiting the results, which are collected later as shown in the code fragment in Figure 14. Note the use of the := operator rather than the normal <- operator.

```
ansa_Voucher        v;        /* declare a voucher */

! {v} := if_ref$Read (fd, BUFSIZE)
/* processing continues without awaiting the results */
! {buf, nread, errno} <- if_ref$Redeem (v)
```

Figure 14: ANSAware vouchers example

3.5   Security

ANSAware has no security mechanisms while DCE provides authentication and authorisation mechanisms directly. DCE also supplies the foundations for the construction of access control, privacy and integrity mechanisms by the applications developer (see Section 4.5).

DCE provides a superset of the access control list (ACL) data structure defined in POSIX 1003.6 to enable the implementation of an ACL manager for a server. Based on a client's privileges, the ACL manager determines whether that client has permission to perform the requested server functionality.

In DCE, confidentiality (privacy) can be provided in applications by using the Data Encryption Standard (DES) to encrypt/decrypt the parameters of RPCs. DCE provides conversation keys, which can be used by DES. Note that some implementations of DCE do not include DES libraries due to export restrictions.

Integrity can be guaranteed if applications include a checksum as one of the parameters for each of their RPC operations which require integrity.

3.6   Summary

	DCE	ANSAware
Paradigms	Object-based, client-server, RPC	Object-based, client-server, RPC
IDL syntax	C like	Modula-2 like

	DCE	ANSAware
Supported IDL Data Types	the common data types, the common data type constructors and **pointers**	the common data types, the common data type constructors, **object id, interface id and interface reference**
Methods of exchanging information during an RPC	named input parameters, named output parameters and the **unnamed function value**	named input parameters and **optionally** named output parameters
RPC parameter direction	in, out, **in/out**	in, out
Types of RPCs	default and maybe	interrogation (same as DCE default) and announcement (same as DCE maybe)
Inheritance from IDL files	data type definitions	data type definitions and **operation definitions**
Interface type identifier	**uuid + version number**	**string**
DPL	C	**C with embedded ANSAware PREPC**
Offering an interface	must register with **RPC runtime**, name server and **endpoint mapper**	must register with name server
Support for multiple instances of the same interface type by an object	**only with multiple sub-objects**	yes
Forms of Binding	**automatic, implicit**, explicit	normal (same as explicit)
Advanced DPL Concepts	**pipes and context handles**	**none**
Concurrency	threads, maybe operations and **broadcast RPCs**	threads, announcement operations (same as DCE maybe operations) and **vouchers**
Security	**authentication and authorisation mechanisms, and the foundations to build access control, privacy and integrity mechanisms.**	**none**

4 Infrastructure

4.1 Technology Supported

DCE is available (at various levels of functionality) from a variety of vendors on a number of platforms, including MS Windows, OS/2, VMS and UNIX variants. ANSAware is available from APM on a number of platforms, including DOS, VMS and UNIX variants.

DCE provides interoperability between the platforms on which it is available; so does ANSAware. Neither DCE nor ANSAware can interoperate with other distributed environments.

DCE is currently implemented using various transport protocols, including TCP, UDP, DECnet and Domain. ANSAware is implemented using sockets over TCP and UDP.

4.2 Distribution Transparency

Distribution transparency is the ability to mask some aspect of distribution from the user. The Basic Reference Model for Open Distributed Processing [6] identifies the following distribution transparencies:

- access transparency - hiding the different access mechanisms used for local and remote information and services

- location transparency - hiding the physical location and migration of information and services

- replication transparency - hiding the presence of and maintaining the consistency of multiple copies of information and services.

Location transparency can be regarded as a combination of location independence transparency (interaction can occur without awareness of physical locations) and relocation transparency (bindings are preserved despite changes in physical location).

For process interaction, ANSAware provides access and location transparency. ANSAware provides access transparency through stubs, which allow remote invocations to appear local through a combination of message passing and local invocations. Location independence is provided by mappings from location-independent service references to specific locations. If a client calls on a server which has relocated, a binding error will occur. The binding error triggers an exception handing routine which uses a service called the relocator (this service is provided by the trader in ANSAware 4.0) to determine the server's new location, allowing a new binding to be established. Together, the exception handling routines and the relocator provide relocation transparency.

For process interaction, DCE provides access and location independence transparency; for data, it provides location transparency and replication transparency. Like ANSAware, DCE provides its access transparency through stubs and its location independence through mappings. Unlike ANSAware, DCE does not provide relocation transparency for process interaction. DCE's distributed file service provides location independence for files (data) and masks the replication and migration of filesets.

4.3 Robustness

Robustness is comprised of three parts: availability, reliability and fault tolerance.

In the context of distributed systems, availability means the level of usage that an object might have of a particular service. Availability can be improved by minimising the number of critical components or through adding redundancy (replication). DCE employs both of these techniques to improve availability. DCE has two critical components: the CDS and the security service. DCE system services increase their availability through caching and replication. ANSAware has only one critical component, the trader (see Section 1). ANSAware system services do not employ redundancy to increase availability. Both ANSAware and DCE can provide the duplication of services (on separate nodes) increasing the availability of a type of service, but not the availability of a particular service instance.

Reliability is the level of trust that the user has in the system's behaviour, which can be influenced by both availability and fault tolerance. It can also be influenced by security (which is provided by DCE, but not by ANSAware) and atomicity, which is provided by neither DCE nor ANSAware as they do not directly provide any transaction processing capabilities.

Fault tolerance is the level of failure handling provided by the system. In both DCE and ANSAware, objects can be autonomous, so the failure of one object does not imply the failure of the entire system. Exception handling is provided to recover from errors in remote invocations. ANSAware also provides a notification service which can notify an object of the termination of other objects (see Section 1).

4.4 Scalability and Incremental Growth

Both DCE and ANSAware address the issues of scalability. DCE has the concept of a cell (an administrative domain) which can be used to partition the distributed system into manageable subdomains. If the performance of a cell is degraded by an overloaded system service, then the cell can be further partitioned into more cells. In ANSAware, the most likely bottle-neck is the trader service. ANSAware reduces the scalability problem by allowing duplication of the trader service and federation of these duplicates. Federation involves similar independent services working together to enhance the effectiveness of each service involved in the federation (e.g. by sharing resources).

The naming conventions used in interface definitions have a significant impact on scalability. The simple names used in ANSAware will not be an appropriate solution for a very large distributed system, whereas DCE's uuids are guaranteed to be unique.

Both DCE and ANSAware provide a dynamically reconfigurable object-oriented environment, which allows the introduction of new services and the removal of existing services. ANSAware's trader uses subtyping to determine which services can substitute for other services. In DCE, version control of the interface types is used for service substitution. A new service can substitute for an existing service if it has the same major version number and a larger or equal minor version number.

4.5 System Security

For security to be provided in a distributed environment, it is essential that the infrastructure provides either security mechanisms or the necessary foundations for an applications developer to build their own security mechanisms. ANSAware provides neither, unless the applications developer can modify the ANSAware source code to implement viable security mechanisms (due to the complexity of this task, it is highly infeasible). DCE provides authentication and authorisation mechanisms and also provides the foundations for constructing other security mechanisms (see Section 3.5). DCE's authentication service is based on MIT Project Athena's Kerberos Network Authentication Service Version 5 and provides facilities to authenticate both applications and users. DCE's authorisation service is based on Hewlett-Packard's privilege service and can control the extent of access to system resources.

4.6 Summary

	DCE	ANSAware
Platforms	MS Windows, OS/2, VMS and Unix variants	DOS, VMS and Unix variants
Interoperability between heterogeneous platforms	only platforms running DCE	only platforms running ANSAware
Transport Protocols	TCP, UDP, DECnet and **Domain**	TCP and UDP
Process interaction transparencies	access and **location independence**	access and **location**
Data transparencies	**location** and **replication**	Not applicable, as ANSAware has no support for distributed data
Support for Robustness	**two** critical components, **caching, replication, security**, autonomous objects and exception handling	**one** critical component, autonomous objects, exception handling and **notification service**
Support for scalability and incremental growth	dynamically reconfigurable object-oriented environment and **cells**	dynamically reconfigurable object-oriented environment and **federation**

5 System Administration

Administrative tasks include planning, installation, configuration, maintenance and evolution. Typically, such tasks are carried out at various levels of granularity; for example, some tasks must be performed once per organisation, others once per node. In this section, we consider administrative tasks from four levels of granularity (viz: global domain, local domain, node and object).

5.1 Global Domain

A global domain involves an entire (enterprise-wide or world-wide) distributed system. At this level of granularity, administration involves defining sub-system boundaries. These boundaries allow system resources (potentially users, services and files) to be partitioned into local domains for management simplicity, performance requirements or preservation of existing areas of local autonomy. Subsequently, mechanisms to deal with any resulting boundaries (e.g. naming and security boundaries) must be devised.

In DCE, system resources are partitioned into local domains called cells. Cells are an integral part of DCE usage. Both administrative and, to a lesser extent, performance issues are used to determine cell boundaries. DCE provides a global naming environment to identify cells within the global domain (using either the X.500 or DNS naming scheme). To participate in a world-wide environment, it is necessary to register each cell name with an appropriate standards body. In addition, inter-cell participation requires sharing of secrets across security boundaries.

In ANSAware, offered services are partitioned into local domains known as trading domains. Trading domain boundaries are determined by considering both performance and, to a lesser extent, administrative issues. Within each trading domain is a trader.

One particular trader will be designated as a master trader; the purpose of this trader is to share its trading domain (or federate) with all of the other traders (known as local traders). This allows local traders to learn the location of other local traders and thus federate with them.

While the trading domain is an important concept within ANSAware, not all parts of ANSAware use these domains. For example, the trading domains do not provide a basis for partitioning files or users. In addition, some infrastructure facilities such as the notification service and the master trader are required exactly once per global domain regardless of any trading domain requirements. Likewise, for development purposes, ANSAware's development environment must be installed on a global basis (at least one node per platform).

As each ANSAware global domain has only one master trader and one notification service, the merging of two such global domains involves the selection of a common master trader and notification service.

5.2 Local Domain

At the local domain level, tasks specific to a particular local administration domain must be performed. In DCE, this involves the installation of the DCE system services on nodes within the cell. The cell must contain a minimum set of core services (one security server, three DTS servers and at least one CDS server) and can make use of additional services (e.g. DFS server). All of these services involve ongoing administrative overheads. In ANSAware, local domain tasks include installing, maintaining and federating the local trader.

5.3 Node

A node usually denotes a single machine, but it can also refer to a set of machines running a closely-coupled distributed operating system, or to each of the operating systems running above a heavy-weight operating system on a single machine (e.g. MVS and AIX running on top of VM).

For each node, DCE involves the installation and maintenance of the appropriate DCE development and run-time environments (e.g. the endpoint database). In ANSAware, node administration involves the installation and maintenance of the factory and node manager. ANSAware and DCE are similar at this level.

5.4 Object

ANSAware allows sub-entities to exist within a process; these are known as objects. Each object has a management interface, which allows some of an object's functionality to be controlled by remote invocations. The only support that DCE provides for object management below the process level is a means to identify objects.

5.5 Summary

	DCE	ANSAware
Global Domain	define cell boundaries, devise secret sharing mechanisms and register global names	define trading domains, and administration of master trader and notification service

	DCE	ANSAware
Local Domain	administration of **core services**	administration of **local trader**
Node	administration of **DCE runtime**	administration of **factory and node manager**
Object	**identification**	**management interfaces**

6 Conclusion

In this paper, we have compared DCE and ANSAware from a number of perspectives (viz. software components, applications development, infrastructure and systems administration) and have summarised our findings in the form of tables, one for each of the perspectives.

DCE was built by integrating existing technology with a focus on providing the functionality necessary for commercial viability. The benefits of this are that DCE offers the important enterprise functions of security and global naming, and has the ability to readily merge existing global domains. The shortcoming of this is that DCE's architectural model was drawn from old technologies, and thus requires refinement if it hopes to compete with emerging distributed environments.

ANSAware was built up from the concepts of an architectural model for distributed systems in which the interface is a central concept. The benefits of this are that the overall design philosophy is elegant and offers an interface-oriented approach; this yields a number of practical benefits: mechanisms for inheritance and subtyping, simpler binding and the selection of interfaces based on interface properties. ANSAware is limited by the failure of its architectural model to cater for distributed data and enterprise functionality, such as security and global naming.

Acknowledgements

The work reported in this paper has been funded in part by the Cooperative Research Centres Program through the department of the Prime Minister and Cabinet of the Commonwealth Government of Australia. This research was also supported by Telecom (Australia) Research Laboratories through the Centre of Expertise in Distributed Information Systems (CEDIS).

We would like to thank David Arnold, Andrew Berry, Mark Fox, Barry Kitson and Ajeet Parhar for their invaluable comments on an earlier version of this document.

References

1.   W. Rosenberry, D. Kenney & G. Fisher: Understanding DCE, O'Reilly & Associates Inc, September 1992.

2.   J. Shirley: Guide to Writing DCE Applications, O'Reilly & Associates Inc, June 1992.

3.   OSF: OSF DCE Application Guide, Prentice Hall, 1992.

4.   Architecture Projects Management Ltd. (APM): ANSAware 4.0 Application Programmer's Manual, March 1992.

5.   A.K. Jones, The Object Model: A Conceptual Tool for Structuring Software, in R. Bayer, R.M. Graham and G. Seemuller (eds.) Operation Systems: An Advanced Course, Lecture Notes in Computer Science 60, Springer-Verlag, 1978.

6.   Xerox Corporation: Document Xerox Systems Integration Standard 038112, Stanford, Connecticut, December 1981.

7.   ISO/IEC CD 10746-3: Information Technology - Basic Reference Model of Open Distributed Processing - Part 3: Prescriptive Model, December 1992.

Comparison of DCE RPC, DFN-RPC, ONC and PVM

Rolf Rabenseifner[1] and Armin Schuch[2]

[1] Rechenzentrum der Universität Stuttgart, Allmandring 30, D-70550 Stuttgart, Germany, Tel. ++49 711 6855530, e-mail: rabenseifner@rus.uni-stuttgart.de
[2] Institut für Kernenergetik und Energiesysteme, Pfaffenwaldring 31, D-70550 Stuttgart, Germany, Tel.: ++49 711 6852122, e-mail: rpcas@ikeux1.energietechnik.uni-stuttgart.de

Abstract. Taking part in the Early Participation Program of OSF/DCE on IBM RS/6000 workstations, we have examined the RPC of DCE between workstation and compute server under aspects of performance, capability and functionality for scientific-technical applications programmed in Fortran, under user-account. A brief introduction shows the demands expected from a RPC tool taking a scientific-technical point of view.

1 Introduction

Taking a scientific-technical point of view, the demands, a RPC tool has to satisfy, are resulting from the profile of the user and from the application itself.

Users of scientific-technical applications are highly specialized, but they normally have only basic knowledge in computer science. Therefore, the user wants a short period of learning time to get his work done, this means the RPC tool must be easy to use. The lesser the difference between a distributed and a non-distributed application is, the better it is. The RPC tool should hide the distribution to the user as much as possible. The possibility of optimizations, which are only useful to users with good knowledge of the used tool, are not so important.

The features an application demands from a RPC tool can be shown looking at a typical, practical example. The program system ESTER has been developed for the shared-cost action for the reactor savety of the European Community [4, 12].

To harmonize the analyse of source terms beyond the countries of the EC, to strengthen the co-operation of single development groups and to develop a best-estimate code for source term analysis which can be used everywhere in Europe are goals of the ESTER development. This best-estimate code is based on modules which are developed at different research locations in countries which are members of the EC. The data exchange between these modules is made using a data base which is kept in the main memory because of efficiency reasons. These single modules are big program packages which were developed for specific computers. If you want to connect these modules, this can't be done anymore on a single computer. Therefore, communication between the modules and the data base with RPC tools is necessary.

The development of the modules has been done in projects over serveral years and the programming has been done exclusively in Fortran. At the moment, Fortran is a very important programming language for scientific-technical applications. So, a RPC tool must have a Fortran interface to satisfy these requirements. This interface must have the ability that remote procedures as Fortran subroutines and functions can be called from Fortran programs. Programming of C routines is undesirable.

The data exchange between the modules is made using a common data base which is kept in the main memory of any computer. When a calculation and afterwards a visualization is made where several modules take part, there are big data flows between the modules and the data base. Therefore, the ability of a RPC tool to use a high transmission speed is desirable.

In the summery, there are three demands a RPC tool has to satisfy: A RPC tool should be easy to use, should have a Fortran interface and should make it possible to use a high transmission speed.

2 Performance Comparison

To test the performance, we've compared the DCE RPC, IBM-Rel. 1.2.9310.0 (OSF-Release 1.0.1.) [8] with three other tools:

1. the DFN-RPC, Rel. 1.0, a RPC tool for the distribution of Fortran applications between workstation and compute server developed by us by order[3] of the DFN, the German Research Network Society [1, 9, 10, 11],
2. the PVM, Rel. 2.4.1 and 3.0, a message passing library to parallelize Fortran and C applications in a network of UNIX computers [2],
3. and the SUN RPC (ONC), a RPC tool for system programming [14].

For the first benchmark, shown in Table 1, two IBM RS/6000 workstations have been used, connected with Ethernet, FDDI, Cisco and NSC router. The RPC of DCE[4] and PVM are using UDP and an own protocol to do end-to-end flow control, while the DFN-RPC and the SUN RPC[5] are using TCP. The tests transmitted 1, 3 or 64 kbyte real numbers (each with 4 bytes length) as input or output arguments, the transmission speed was measured in kbyte/sec. The delay was measured by the round-trip-time of an empty call in ms/call.

The DFN-RPC was used with the default buffer size of 2400 bytes. The buffer size can be optimized between 600 bytes and 64 kbytes. Using PVM, the remote procedure call has been simulated by sending corresponding messages.

The results in per cent compare the speed of the DCE RPCs with the speed of DFN-RPCs, PVM and SUN RPCs. Looking at the empty calls, the per cent results are based on calls/ms. The more powerful CPU of the two CPUs taking

---

[3] registration number of the BMFT: TK 558 VA 005.3.

[4] In the next release, TCP will be available too.

[5] Also UDP is available, but only with may-be semantics, and therefore not evaluated in this test.

Table 1. Throughput and delay between two workstations

Calls with	Unit abs.	DCE RPC abs.	%	DFN-RPC abs.	%	PVM 3.0 abs.	%	SUN RPC abs.	%
64 kbyte In	kbyte/s	376	100	499	133	157	42	357	95
64 kbyte Out	kbyte/s	326	100	392	120	124	38	250	77
3 kbyte In	kbyte/s	141	100	196	139	82	58	134	95
3 kbyte Out	kbyte/s	140	100	124	86	78	56	117	84
1 kbyte In	kbyte/s	70	100	92	131	38	54	77	110
1 kbyte Out	kbyte/s	66	100	90	136	37	56	69	105
Average	kbyte/s	187	100	232	124	86	46	167	89
Empty Call	ms/Call	10.3	100	5.8	178	19.7	52	7.3	141

Table 2. Throughput and delay, if client and server process are on the same workstation

Calls with	Unit abs.	DCE RPC abs.	%	DFN-RPC abs.	%	DFN 64k abs.	%	PVM 3.0 abs.	%	SUN RPC abs.	%
64 kbyte In	kbyte/s	159	100	1081	680	1336	840	286	180	331	208
64 kbyte Out	kbyte/s	203	100	1099	541	1481	730	286	141	356	175
3 kbyte In	kbyte/s	433	100	593	137	750	173	185	43	268	62
3 kbyte Out	kbyte/s	433	100	577	133	778	180	185	43	268	62
1 kbyte In	kbyte/s	156	100	366	235	376	241	88	56	145	93
1 kbyte Out	kbyte/s	163	100	355	218	385	236	84	52	165	101
Average	kbyte/s	258	100	679	263	851	330	186	72	256	99
Empty Call	ms/Call	6.0	100	2.4	250	2.3	261	9.0	67	3.8	158

part (the side of the compute server) was loaded 100% with a daemon. All measurements were repeated three times, and all three results have differed only a little bit. Therefore, the average results shown in the table can be used to compare the products.

DCE RPC and SUN RPC have nearly the same transmission speed. The DFN-RPC is faster by 25%, while PVM is slower by 50%. Empty calls are rather slow with DCE. DCE RPC needs 10.3 ms for a an empty call, this means 1.8 times longer than DFN-RPC, although it uses UDP. On the other hand, this can be the reason for the slowness, because the end-to-end flow control has to be made in the application process. Looking at PVM empty calls, you can see clearly that another two PVM deamons are involved.

The asymmetry between In and Out measurements looking at the absolute numbers is probably caused by the different power of the computers. Another reason are the different routing paths through the network for both directions, while in both cases an Ethernet is the bottle-neck.

If client and server are on the same RS/6000 530, the differences are more visible, see Table 2. These measurements don't depend on a real network load and the computer has been used only for these measurements. Using DFN-RPC, two different buffer sizes have been used for the measurements, one with 2400 bytes (default) and one with 64 kbytes (64 kbytes is the recommendation for high speed networks >100 mbit/s). The buffer length can be changed by runtime, but can also be given in the interface definition file, used for the stub generation.

The DCE RPC shows a weakness if plenty of data has to be transferred. Other measurements on computers from Sun and Silicon Graphics [6] showed that SUN RPC has problems with a data quantity over 3.9 kbytes, which can cause in extreme cases a fixed round-trip-time of 200 ms and this means 19.5 kbytes/sec transmission speed for 3.9 kbytes of data, see also next section.

It's surprising that the performance of DCE, SUN RPC and PVM is so low in comparison with DFN-RPC, which uses internally only needed BSD socket system calls for a TCP connection, although the maximum network speed cannot be achieved with those sockets. To reach the maximum speed, more complex solutions are necessary, like the implementation in, e.g., the Peregrine High-performance RPC [3]. At least, the hope remains that a TCP based DCE RPC for applications under user account shows better performance and that, for kernel resident applications (like DFS), the UDP basis is not a disadvantage for the performance.

3 Possible Reasons for the Different Performance

The main topics of optimization of the DFN-RPC are:

- The DFN-RPC is making only an absolute minimal number of sytem calls. Only bsd socket write and read is done, using a TCP/IP connection, which is normally established the whole time during the execution of the program.
- The input and output arguments are copied only once within the user's space. They are copied between the argument list and an input or output buffer, which is used then for the write and read operations.
- The conversion – if necessary – is integrated into this copy and is done by loops with maximum length.
- These loops can be vectorized.
- The argument list on server side is allocated on a local stack and not by malloc.
- As transfer encoding of real and integer numbers one can choose between four formats: ieee big or little endian, cray or vax.

Because we have used the tools DCE RPC, SUN RPC and PVM only as a black box, it is difficult to say a lot about the reasons why these products don't reach the performance of the DFN-RPC. Nevertheless there are a few decisions in the design of those tools which must have a negative impact on the performance of these tools.

Table 3. In an empty Ethernet between two Silicon Graphics Indigo, IRIX 4.0.5F with E++, processor R 3000 and R 4000

Calls with	Unit abs.	DFN-RPC abs.	%	DFN 64k abs.	%	PVM 3.0 abs.	%	SUN RPC abs.	%
64 kbyte In	kbyte/s	800	100	663	83	286	36	487	61
64 kbyte Out	kbyte/s	699	100	753	108	312	45	499	71
3 kbyte In	kbyte/s	524	100	524	100	187	36	410	78
3 kbyte Out	kbyte/s	450	100	500	111	182	40	336	75
1 kbyte In	kbyte/s	294	100	300	102	92	31	238	81
1 kbyte Out	kbyte/s	294	100	307	104	87	30	195	66
Average	kbyte/s	510	100	508	100	191	37	361	71
Empty Call	ms/Call	2.1	100	1.9	111	8.6	24	2.3	91

Table 4. SUN RPC with 4 kbyte input or output data in an empty Ethernet between two Silicon Graphics Indigo, IRIX 4.0.5F with E++, processor R 3000 and R 4000

Calls with	Unit abs.	DFN-RPC abs.	%	DFN 64k abs.	%	PVM 3.0 abs.	%	SUN RPC abs.	%
4 kbyte In	kbyte/s	571	100	603	106	116	29	**20**	**3.5**
4 kbyte Out	kbyte/s	500	100	571	114	176	35	309	62

The DCE RPC in the tested release (the newest one that was delivered in the *Early Participation Program* of IBM in March 1993) is based only on UDP, which is also the default for system applications as the *distributed file system* (DFS). To obtain an at-most-once semantics and to guarantee the end-to-end-flow-contol, an additional protocol, executed by the RPC stubs, has to be implemented. This can lead to additional context switches between the application and the system kernel, which slows down the speed of data transfer and empty calls. I hope that this problem has no negative impact on RPC applications, like DFS, which are running in the kernel.

We have tested the SUN RPC also between two Silicon Graphics systems, see Tables 3–5. Looking at RPCs with 64 kbyte output data in Table 3 the DFN-RPC transfers 699 kbyte/s, i.e. it needs 5.6 μs for one real number. The SUN RPC transfers 499 kbyte/s, i.e. it needs 7.8 μs/number. Therefore, the loss of performance is 2.2 μs for each real number. The SUN RPC makes one conversion call for each real number (although this procedure makes only a copy). For the overhead of an additional procedure call on both systems we have measured 0.5 μs + 0.2 μs = 0.7 μs. This overhead is a significant part of the performance loss.

Table 4 shows a special problem of the SUN RPC. If one is using 4 kbyte of input arguments in a remote procedure call, then the call needs 200 ms with the consequence of a transfer rate of only 20 kbyte/s. This effect can be seen in a big

Table 5. Client and Server on the same Silicon Graphics with R 3000 processor

Calls with	Unit abs.	DFN-RPC abs.	%	DFN 64k abs.	%	PVM 2.4 abs.	%	PVM 3.0 abs.	%	SUN RPC abs.	%
64 kbyte In	kbyte/s	1012	100	1481	146	157	16	486	48	**320**	**32**
64 kbyte Out	kbyte/s	1040	100	1422	137	123	12	492	47	**320**	**31**
3 kbyte In	kbyte/s	705	100	868	123	105	15	331	47	450	64
3 kbyte Out	kbyte/s	727	100	938	129	91	13	326	45	450	62
1 kbyte In	kbyte/s	455	100	455	100	58	13	154	34	250	55
1 kbyte Out	kbyte/s	455	100	455	100	53	12	154	34	250	55
Average	kbyte/s	732	100	937	128	98	13	324	44	340	46
4 kbyte In	kbyte/s	800	100	1000	125	117	15	343	43	**20**	**2.5**
4 kbyte Out	kbyte/s	800	100	1000	125	100	13	333	42	**20**	**2.5**
Empty Call	ms/Call	1.4	100	1.4	100	11.4	10	4.9	29	2.1	67

Table 6. CPU time used in the experiment, shown in Table 2

Tool	process	CPU time	sum	comparison	Average from Table 2
DCE RPC	client	380 sec			
	server	391 sec	sum = 771 sec = DCE-time / 1.00		100 %
DFN-RPC[6]	Server	168 sec			
	client	168 sec	sum = 336 sec = DCE-time / 2.29		263 %
PVM 3.0	server	363 sec			
	client	362 sec			
	daemon	494 sec	sum = 1219 sec = DCE-time / 0.63		72 %
SUN RPC	client	365 sec			
	server	391 sec	sum = 756 sec = DCE-time / 1.02		99 %

range of input and output quantities larger than 3.88 kbyte, e.g. see values in
Table 5 printed bold. We have tested it too on a SUN and have obtained similar
results.

PVM is a message passing library. It was examined because it is also a tool to
distribute scientific-technical applications. At the moment, PVM is outstanding
because of its good functionality for parallel applications, but it is very slow,
because it uses daemons for data transfer. Although there was an increase of
performance of a factor of 3 between PVM 2.4.1 and PVM 3.0, as shown in
Table 5, there must be done a lot to obtain full performance.

A further indicator is the consumption of cpu time, as shown in Table 6.
Obviously, there is a correlation to the performance shown in Table 2.

---

[6] With a buffersize of 2400 bytes.

4 Functionality

Fortran application interfaces consisting of subroutines, entries, and functions of type INTEGER, REAL or DOUBLE with arguments of type INTEGER, REAL, DOUBLE, COMPLEX and arrays (with fixed lengths) of these types can be distributed without problems with DCE RPC. DCE RPC has the following problems with other language elements of Fortran [5]:

- The application interface (function names and argument list) defined in Fortran has to be redone in C, so that a corresponding Interface Definition File can be written as the input for the DCE RPC stub generator. The language transition from Fortran to C depends on the manufacturer, but it is documented in most cases, products as fidl [7] may also help here.
- If this manufacturer dependent language transition is different and therefore a different RPC protocol arises on client and server, the direct use of DCE RPC for Fortran applications isn't possible anymore. Examples for this are functions or arguments of type LOGICAL or CHARACTER. On computers with a different length of a *numerical unit* (e.g. workstation 4 byte, compute server 8 byte) the type REAL*8 (or equivalent Fortran 90 definitions) is changed to double in C on the workstation and to float in C on the compute server. In this case, DCE RPC doesn't find a proper network presentation between client and server, so this type can't be transmitted. This is also true for COMPLEX*16. On the contrary, different language transitions of the function names in Fortran to names in C aren't a problem, because only the position of the function in the IDL file is transmitted.
- For the Fortran language element *alternate return* no transition into C can be found and *function name arguments* are not supported by DCE RPC. ·

In these last two cases, the application programmer either has to change the Fortran interface or has to write additional stubs which put his interface into an interface that can be distributed with the DCE RPC.

Besides this, the possibilities with arrays that have variable dimensions and different or separated input and output areas are very limited. This can cause the situation that more elements than the application needs have to be transmitted.

Therefore, looking at functional aspects, in most cases, tools with a Fortran interface (e.g. DFN-RPC, PVM) are the better choice for distributing scientific-technical applications programmed in Fortran.

5 Conclusion

Looking at the three requirements, that such tools should be easy to use, should have a fortran interface and that they must be efficient, it is desirable that the DCE RPC gets a better performance without weakness in particular environments. It should get also a Fortran interface like the DFN-RPC and an additional Fortran message passing library like PVM.

References

1. Allrutz R., Rabenseifner R.: Der DFN-RPC, ein Remote Procedure Call Tool. Proceedings, 15. DECUS München Symposium (1992) 523–532
2. Geist, A. et al.: PVM 3.0 User's Guide and Reference Manual. ORNL/TM-12187, Oak Ridge National Laboratory, Tennessee (2/1993)
3. Johnson, D. B., W. Zwaenepoel: The Peregrine High-performance RPC System. Software-Practice and Experience 23(2) (1993) 201–221
4. Jones, A. V., Shepard, I.: ESTER - a European Source Term Evaluation System. CEC Joint Research Centre, Safty Technology Institut (6/1991)
5. Kollak, W.: Distribute Fortran Applications using DCE RPC. White Paper. Rechenzentrum Universität Stuttgart, March 5, 1993.
6. Kollak, W., R. Rabenseifner, H.D. Reimann: RPC Tools im Benchmark-Vergleich: DFN-RPC, SUN-RPC, DCE RPC, sowie PVM. White Paper. Rechenzentrum Universität Stuttgart, 31.3.1993.
7. Laifer, R., A. Knocke: fidl, Ein Werkzeug zur einfachen Verteilung von Fortran-Anwendungen. Benutzeranleitung, Universität Karsruhe, Rechenzentrum, 31.3.1993.
8. Open Software Foundation (OSF): OSF DCE Version 1.0, DCE Application Development Guide, Part 3: DCE Remote Procedure Call (RPC). Revision 1.0, Dec. 31, 1991.
9. Rabenseifner, R., H.D. Reimann: Verteilte Anwendungen mit dem DFN-RPC. DFN Mitteilungen 31, Berlin (3/1993)
10. Rabenseifner, R., H.D. Reimann: Verteilte Anwendungen über Hochgeschwindigkeitsdatenkommunikation, der DFN Remote Procedure Call. Benutzerhandbuch, Rel. 1.0, Rechenzentrum Universität Stuttgart, 23.11.1992.
11. Rabenseifner, R.: Distributed Applications between Workstation and Supercomputer using ISO/OSI Protocols. Proceedings, Twenty-Seventh Semi-Annual Cray User Group Meeting, London. April 22-26 (1991) 80–84
12. Schmidt, F., Schuch, A., Hinkelmann, M.: Der Europaeische Quellterm-Code ESTER - Grundideen und Werkzeuge zur Kopplung von ATHLET und ESTER. Abschlussbericht BMFT-Vorhaben 317-4015-1500945, Universität Stuttgart, IKE 4-136 (4/1993)
13. Schuch, A.: Die Anwendung von Remote Procedure Calls für die Verteilung eines Anwendungsprogramms. Diplomarbeit. Institut für Kernenergetik und Energiesysteme, Universität Stuttgart (11/1991)
14. SUN microsystems: Network Programming Guide. Part Number 800-3850-00 (1990)

Some DCE Performance Analysis Results

B. Dasarathy, Khalid Khalil, David E. Ruddock

Bellcore, RRC, 444 Hoes Lane, Piscataway, NJ 08854, U.S.A.

Abstract. This paper explores the performance behavior of two core services of the OSF DCE, RPC (Remote Procedure Call) and threads. The RPC performance is gauged as a function of the length of argument(s) passed. We show that:

- DCE RPC performance behavior with or without security features is linear with the length of the messages and is comparable to that of a commonly available RPC technology once the client and server are fully bound to each other,

- authentication on RPCs is inexpensive, and

- encryption and integrity on messages do not come cheap.

We also demonstrate that multi-threading increases throughput even on a single processor system and how much the throughput is improved in comparison with multiple single-threaded processes. The effect of multi-threading a client process on throughput and response time as a function of the number of threads is brought out.

1. Introduction

We describe in this paper a performance analysis study of some core OSF™ DCE services in DCE 1.0.1, a pre-production release of DCE. Experimentation with DCE has been an ongoing effort since April 1992 in a distributed system testbed environment at the Computing Technology Integration (CTI) Laboratory at Bellcore. The testbed environment, as the name implies, is intended to facilitate analysis of emerging distributed computing platform, transaction monitor and distributed system management technologies from the perspective of developing inter-operable telephony applications. DCE in our testbed environment currently runs on several types of platforms. The study reported in this paper has two major goals: to quantify the cost or overhead associated with the remote procedure call (RPC) feature of DCE, annotated with different levels of security, and the impact of its multi-threading feature, a feature for achieving concurrency/performance enhancement in applications layered over DCE.

1.1 What is DCE?

DCE is a collection of services for the development, use and maintenance of transparent distributed systems using the client/server architecture. Enabling application-level inter-operability (among heterogeneous platforms) is the essence of DCE. The communication paradigm supported by DCE is synchronous RPC across address spaces in conjunction with multi-threading within an address space for concurrency. Transparency is provided by a directory service/name server. The security features of DCE include authentication of servers and clients to each other and to the system, support for resource authorization by an application server in providing services to its clients, and various levels of message integrity (at different levels of cost) and encryption. For an overview of DCE, see [1], [2], [3] and the introductory chapter of these proceedings.

1.2 Why DCE Performance Analysis?

DCE has industry-wide support and is, or will become, available as a product on a variety of platforms. It is intended to provide interoperability of an application on heterogeneous platforms regardless of distance between application components and type of physical connection. DCE, moreover, hides the complexity of distribution. Its RPC mechanism, which behaves functionally more or less like procedural calls in a sequential program, permits development of distributed programs as if they were centralized, i.e., no major paradigm shift is required on the part of a programmer, unless the use of threads is employed for higher throughput.

Since our experimentation began in April '92, we have found DCE to be usable and to be working in conformance with its documentation [4]. This report provides information regarding DCE performance characteristics. From the performance viewpoint, distribution has both negative and positive consequences. On the positive side, distribution provides processing concurrency. On the negative side, distribution involves network delay.

Our performance analysis can be characterized as latency- (response time-) based and from an application or a client perspective. An alternative approach is a throughput-based analysis, often carried out at a high utilization rate of a resource. It is our view that the latency-based analysis is more suitable than throughput-based approach for measuring performance from an application perspective and the throughput-based approach is more appropriate for the analysis of a server.

The performance of DCE RPC is analyzed as a function of the length of argument(s) passed over the network. Most secure features of DCE are associated with its RPC. The overhead associated with various forms/aspects of security —authentication, authorization, and message integrity and protection —on DCE RPC is analyzed. To provide a perspective on the performance of DCE RPC, the "vanilla" form of DCE RPC, i.e., one with no secure features, is contrasted with that of a commonly available RPC technology from a vendor.

We also report here on our performance analysis of the threads feature of DCE. Multi-threading within an address space has the potential for increasing performance even on a single processor system as a result of the low context switching associated with threads. We demonstrate how multi-threading a client address space with n threads (doing identical work) improves throughput/response time in comparison with n (identical) single threaded client processes. We also report our analysis of the effect of multi-threading a single address space on throughput and response time, as a function of the number of threads.

In Section 2, we describe our performance analysis of RPC and various forms of secure RPCs. Section 3 deals with performance analysis of threads. In Section 4, the Concluding Remarks Section, we summarize our findings and outline the future directions for this work.

2. RPC Performance

2.1 Test Environment

All our experiments, except the one reported in Section 2.4, were carried out on a homogeneous set of RISC workstations running DCE 1.0.1, a pre-production release of DCE. The MIPS-rating and the SPECint-rating of these machines is 28.5 and 22 respectively.

All our experiments were carried out in an Ethernet LAN, in a typical, every day, operating environment.[1] Purposely, no traffic/load was added on or removed from the network or the individual machines hosting the client and server processes. This is because our main goal was to study how DCE behaves in a typical environment (from an application perspective) and not to study how well DCE behaves under optimal/ stress conditions. In all our experiments, the application client and server were on separate machines and these machines were different from the machine that hosted the DCE server processes for Cell Directory Service (CDS), security and DTS so as to simulate typical application configurations. Moreover, if a client and server were to be on the same (single processor) machine, the RPC time will be overshadowed/colored by the context switching time (of the CPU) between the server and client processes. Although this RPC performance between two processes on the same machine might be of interest, it does not shed much light on the RPC efficiency or lack of it. All our experiments were carried out with UDP/IP as the network protocol. Finally, in all our experiments, neither the client nor the server process carried out computationally intensive tasks and the single-threaded client process submitted serial requests. (See Section 3 for the performance analysis of multi-threaded clients.) The effect of concurrent requests on the application server was not a focus of study, although application servers are automatically multi-threaded (to a default maximum of ten) in DCE.

2.2 DCE Vanilla RPC and Secure RPC Performance Analysis

In this set of experiments, we studied the DCE RPC performance as a function of the length of the message passed across the wire. The data type was restricted to ASCII character (idl_char) strings. Since the client and server machines were of the same type, there was little data marshalling/unmarshalling overhead in our experiments/test

---

1. The network utilization of our operating environment is normally about 5% and about 10% during the high activity periods. Thus, our Ethernet LAN is a "well behaving" one. Although several utility programs (e.g., mail, clock), word processors and editors were running and many windows were being displayed on our application clients and server machines, while our experiments were being conducted, they were often in a dormant state. Neither these machines nor the DCE server machine acted, for instance, as a file or print server for other machines and, thus, did not have any significant background load on a sustained basis.

results. The client in our RPCs made use of CDS for server identification. Once the binding to the server was obtained, a client made 20 RPCs to the server. (We repeated the experiments ten times for each length of message studied and each type of security annotation.) A statistically accurate picture, we felt, required 10 to 20 RPC calls. A lot more than 20 —50 for instance — would have skewed the RPC time appreciably upward, as elapsed time for some of the RPCs would include context switching and/or swapping time on either or both client and server processes. (This was especially true when the message was long and integrity/encryption was required on the parameters passed.) We separated the behavior of the first RPC from subsequent ones, because the first RPC from a client to the server (and back) took appreciably more time than the subsequent RPCs. Subsequent RPC times stabilized and did not differ significantly. (Occasionally, we saw a few peaks, perhaps due to context switching/swapping.) The first RPC (before the client and server were fully bound to each other) took more time (about 30 ms; see the constant factors in Figure 1 and Figure 2 below) because of the involvement of the *rpcd* daemon (the endpoint mapper) for allocating/finding the end points (ports) for the client/server communication.

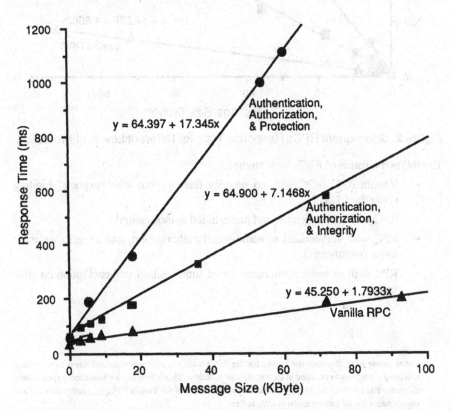

Figure 1: First RPC Response Time for Different Levels of Protection

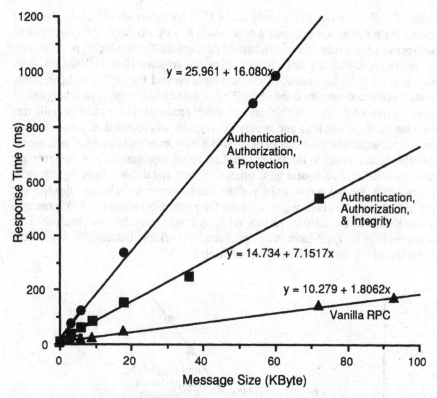

Figure 2: Subsequent RPCs Response Time for Different Levels of Protection

The following forms of RPCs were studied:

- Vanilla RPC (RPC with no security features, but with "explicit" binding using the CDS)
- RPC with authentication and name-based authorization[1]
- RPC with authentication, name-based authorization, and integrity on messages (parameters)
- RPC with authentication, name-based authorization, and encryption on messages

---

1. The response time characteristic curves for the RPCs with just authentication and name-based authorization are not, however, listed in the two figures to follow. This is because we found the response time characteristic for this case to be (statistically) same as that of the vanilla RPC, i.e., authentication and simple name-based authorization is almost free.

52

The DCE authentication service is done with software[1] and is based on DES (Data Encryption Standard). It is a modified version of the Kerberos™ Network Authentication Service, Version 5. In our experiments with authenticated RPCs, both clients and servers authenticated to DCE. The client took on the login context of the user on whose behalf it ran and the server authenticated using a password file specified by the server. In the case of name-based authorization, the DCE RPC runtime passes the login id and other privilege information to the server. It is entirely up to the server to allow resource authorization based on the login id of the client. The implication of this is that performance of resource authorization is very much application-dependent. In our experiments, the part of the server program that performs authorization is about 150 lines long, with no iteration, for validating client-provided data such as desired protection level by the client and for granting access to a requested operation based on the client's login id. The highest form of protection that DCE provides for the arguments on its RPCs is encryption. The second highest form of protection is integrity which ensures none of the data transferred between client and server has been modified. (Other levels of protection/integrity at low(er) costs include assurance that all packets received by the server are from the expected client and protection only at the beginning of an RPC.)

In Figure 1 and Figure 2 above, we capture the performance of first and subsequent RPCs, as a function of the length of the argument(s) of the RPC, respectively. In these figures, response time is the elapsed time between just before the RPC is made (on the client side) and just after the RPC is completed (also on the client side). As the figures indicate, message integrity and encryption are not free.

Moreover, as can be seen from the figures, the DCE RPC performance is predictable and linear with the length of the RPC arguments/messages, i.e.,

- 2 ms (about) per kilobytes of message for the vanilla RPC and for the RPC with just authentication and name-based authorization
- 7 ms per kilobytes of message for the RPC with authentication, name-based authorization, and integrity on messages
- 17 ms per kilobytes of message for the RPC with authentication, name-based authorization and encryption on messages

Finally, a word about constants or null-length RPC time quantities. The constants and the slopes in the figures are generated by a curve fitting software program which tends to favor smaller slopes and larger constant values to larger slopes and smaller constant values. Moreover, as the length increases, our RPC times are skewed upwards as the result of context switching which in turn has the tendency to exaggerate constant and/or slope factors as a whole for a given curve. To be more specific, for instance (See Figure 2.), we clocked null vanilla RPCs (the subsequent ones) at 6 to 7 ms (rather than at 10 to 11ms) and authenticated RPCs with message integrity at 9ms (rather than at 14 to 15 ms).

---

1. The use of a DES hardware chip could improve encrypted RPC performance.

2.3   DCE RPC in Comparison To Another RPC Technology/Implementation

Here we provide a perspective on the performance of DCE RPC by contrasting the vanilla form of DCE RPC with a commonly available RPC technology from a vendor on
many platforms. The interface definition language compiler program of this RPC technology generates client/server stubs just as the DCE *idl* compiler does for marshalling
and unmarshalling data. Just like the DCE RPC, this technology hides communication
complexities by generating stubs that interface to its run-time facilities. This commonly available RPC technology using the interface definition compiler program does not,
however, provide location transparency through a directory service and/or support
message protection/integrity and resource authorization support. Moreover, it is also
restrictive in its argument passing. No more than one parameter can be specified for
either input or output. (If more parameters are needed, one must create a structure and
pass it as the single parameter.) We were also hampered by the size restriction imposed
by this RPC mechanism. The largest size of the message we could pass is around 8000
characters/bytes[1]. Finally, to our knowledge, no industry-wide secure RPC technologies exist, i.e., Kerberos-like technology integrated with the RPC technology, against
which we could compare secure RPC features of DCE.

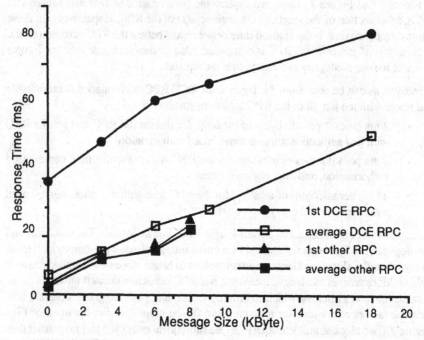

Figure 3: Response Time: DCE RPC Vs. Another RPC Implementation

---

1. According to a representative of the vendor of this RPC implementation, this is a restriction imposed
   by the UDP protocol and that there is no length restriction in their RPC implementation over TCP/IP.
   However, a developer does not encounter any message length limitation with DCE RPCs over UDP.

In Figure 3, we contrast the performance of the two RPC implementations. As in Section 2.2, we separate the performance of the first RPC between a client and a server from subsequent ones. It should be noted that this commonly available RPC has a faster response time. However, as the length of the message increases, the difference between the response time of this RPC implementation and that of DCE RPC remains constant or decreases slightly. Thus, as the length of the message(s) increases, the performance advantage of this RPC technology over DCE RPC becomes less significant.

2.4   RPC Performance Across Heterogeneous Platforms

The client and server machines involved in this experiment were RISC machines with the MIPS rating of 37 and 28.5 respectively. Their SPECint ratings, perhaps a better measure of CPU, are about the same at 22. As in other experiments, the data type of the arguments passed over the wire was restricted to ASCII character (idl_char) strings. The response time behavior characteristics for both first RPC and subsequent ones are given Figure 4. It appears that heterogeneity does incur some performance penalty (both in constant and slope factors), even when there is little marshalling and unmarshalling of data.

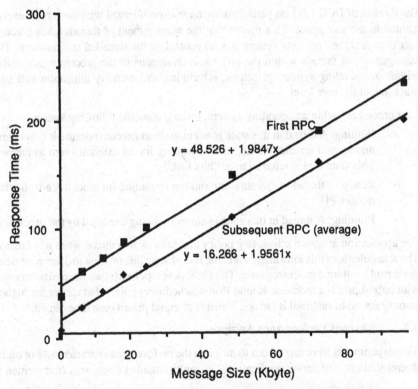

Figure 4: RPC Response Time Across Heterogeneous Platforms

3. Thread Performance

3.1 Threads: An Overview

A thread is a single, sequential flow of control within one process.The DCE multi-threading service allows multiple threads, that is, multiple flows of control within a single process or address space.

We shall demonstrate that the main advantage of multi-threading is the increased speed of computation due to parallelism even when there is only one processor involved. This is because the context switching[1] overhead required to execute a different thread is less than the context switching overhead to execute a different process.

By using threads, server applications can service multiple clients concurrently. A client can use threads to make multiple simultaneous requests to a server or multiple servers. Each thread progresses independently. Some threads continue processing while other threads wait for services such as disk I/O.The benefit of multi-threading is increased throughput, except when the CPU utilization is very high.

Thread Implementation

The threads of DCE 1.0.1 on platforms we have experimented with have been implemented in the user space. This means that the management of threads takes place in user time and the operating system has no control of the threaded environment. The management of threads within the process is analogous to the process management within an operating system: priorities, scheduling and memory allocation still take place, but at the user level.

Like processes within an operating system, threads have the following states:

- Waiting: A thread in this state is not eligible to execute because it is synchronizing with another thread, or it is waiting for an external event to happen. This state is also referred to as "blocked."
- Ready: A thread in this state can run but is waiting for other threads to relinquish CPU.
- Running: A thread in this state is currently being executed by the processor.

The application assigns a scheduling policy and priority to a thread when it is created. The scheduler uses this information and the thread state information to determine when the thread is allotted processor time. The DCE developer kit(s) we have experimented with only supports a modified Round Robin Scheduling policy that allows the highest priority thread to run until it blocks. Threads of equal priority are time-sliced.

3.2 Threads Performance Analysis

Two experiments were carried out to measure the performance characteristics of multi-threaded client and server applications. A multi-threaded client was first written to

---

1. On a uniprocessor machine, the computer runs one process for a short period of time and then switches to another. Changing from one process to another is called a "context switch".

send 1000 small RPC messages to the server and wait for each reply. (As in our experiments in Section 2, the client and server programs were also not compute-intensive.) The same program was then modified to send the same 1000 short messages to the server using multiple single threaded processes. The intent of doing this was to gauge the performance of:

- a multi-threaded client relative to the number of threads used, and
- a single multi-threaded client doing the same tasks as performed by multiple single threaded clients.

As in experiments in Section 2, testing was done on a Ethernet LAN (using only the UDP/IP protocol) during normal business hours to obtain typical results. To minimize transient environmental conditions that may have occurred during testing, each test was performed twelve times and the results averaged (minus the high and low extreme times before the results were merged).

Testing was performed using single CPU client and server machines. Different test results would be obtained on a multi-processor machine using an operating system that supports system level threads (e.g., threads scheduled by the operating system and not by the user level threads scheduler).

Client efficiency was measured in terms of:

- Average time to complete an RPC.
- Average time in real seconds (elapsed time for n RPCs divided by n) to complete the task.
- Average number of voluntary context switches[1] performed on the client.
- Average time in seconds the client spent in user mode.
- Average time in seconds the client spent in system mode.

In all these experiments, regardless of whether the client side consisted of a multi-threaded single process or single threaded multi-processes, the server was multi-threaded up to a maximum of ten, i.e., up to ten threads could be spun off to process client requests on an as needed basis. The number of threads on the client side was varied from one to ten in our experiments.

Round Trip RPC Time

The first metric analyzed is the average time to complete a single RPC. The results of the experiment are shown in Figure 5. This figure shows that the average time to complete a single RPC call increases almost linearly as the number of client threads or processes increases. This increase in latency per RPC is to be expected because increasing

---

1. Voluntary context switches are done when the application performs some task that blocks the process. The application is not allowed another time quantum until the blocking condition is resolved. Involuntary context switches are performed as normal course of events such as when a program time quantum has expired.

the number of concurrent activities decreases the time allotted to any single activity. This increase in latency is attributed to (but not limited to):

- Server loading: A multi-threaded server can process serialized requests faster than multiple simultaneous requests. In other words, the server can process individual requests faster if there are no other requests pending. This is because the server multiplexes time allotments between multiple threads which cause the total time to complete all threads to increase.

- Client loading: As RPC replies are received by a multi-threaded client, the number of threads ready to execute increases. Since the client can process only one thread at a time, the amount of time spent processing each thread in the ready state decreases in a given time period.

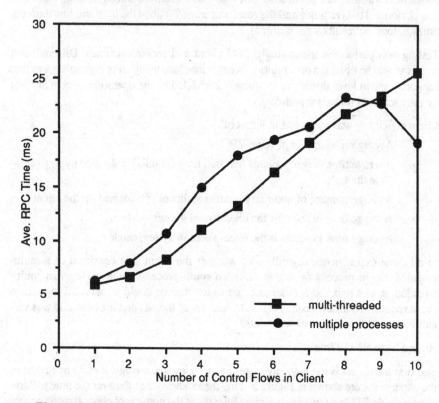

Figure 5: Average RPC Time Versus No. of Control Flows in Client

The average RPC time for a multi-threaded single process application is lower than that of the single-threaded multi-process application. This is due to fewer context switches in the former case than in the latter. Further study is required to determine if client or server loading is the major controlling factor leading to the increase in round-trip time and the drop of the multiple process curve as the number of processes increases.

Multi-Threaded RPC Throughput

Figure 6 charts the amount of average real time required to complete a single RPC using multiple threads and multiple processes. The average real-time is the elapsed time taken by n concurrent control flows on the client side, (each making an RPC) to the same server divided by n. As noted before, neither the client(s) nor the server were compute-intensive. The graph demonstrates that a single multi-threaded process performs much better than multiple single-threaded processes.

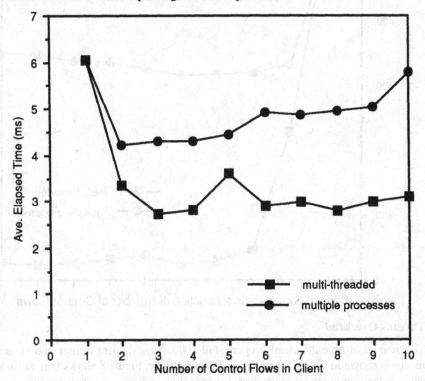

Figure 6: Throughput as a Function of Number of
Concurrent Processes & Threads

One reason for this striking increase in multi-threaded efficiency is shown in Figure 7. This graph shows a dramatic decrease in the number of voluntary context switches performed on the multi-threaded client program. It comes about because the client thread that initiated the RPC blocks while the other threads continue processing using the remainder of the time quantum. The remainder of the time quantum would have been forfeited by a block in a single threaded program.

Figure 6 and Figure 7 show that there is an optimal number of threads for this particular client/server arrangement. This means that there is little if any performance gain when more than three threads are used. We stress that three threads turned out to be optimal for this application in our environment; it may or may not be optimal for others. Other studies are needed to show how varying the message size and adding security to the RPC affect the optimal thread count in an application.

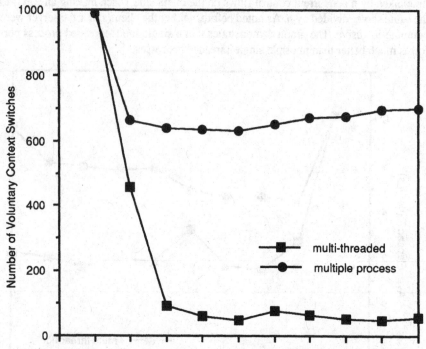

Figure 7: Context Switches as a Function of Number of Control Flows

Threads Overhead

The amount of time the client program (all 1000 threads) spent in user and system modes is shown in Figure 8 and Figure 9, respectively. Figure 8 shows that the time spent in the user mode for multi-threaded or multiple process clients varies little with the number of control flows, i.e., the amount of user level time needed to do the same tasks is independent of the number of control flows in both the schemes. We conclude that DCE thread management routines add little user time overhead to the completion of the same operations.

Figure 9 shows that the time spent in system mode decreases slightly for threaded clients and linearly increases for multiple process clients. These results are expected because the multi-threaded client has fewer voluntary context switches, reducing the amount of time the system dedicates to managing the program. Conversely, the system mode time increases with the number of processes because the operating system must manage more programs that have more voluntary context switches.

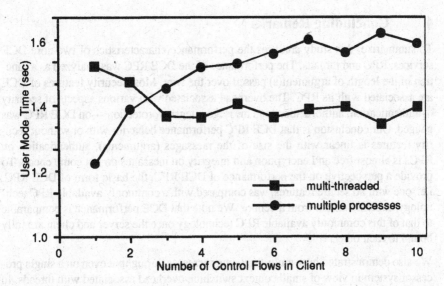

Figure 8: Time Spent in User Mode as a Function of Number of Control Flows

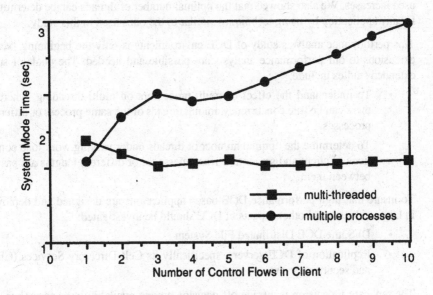

Figure 9: Time Spent in System Mode as a Function
of Number of Control Flows

4.   Concluding Remarks

To summarize, this study analyzes the performance characteristics of two core DCE services, RPC and threads. The performance of the DCE RPC was analyzed as a function of the length of argument(s) passed over the wire. Most security features of DCE are associated with its RPC. The overhead associated with various aspects of security —authentication, authorization, and message integrity/protection —on DCE RPC was gauged. Our conclusion is that DCE RPC performance behavior with or without security features is linear with the size of the messages (arguments), authentication on RPCs is almost free and encryption and integrity on messages do not come cheap. To provide a perspective on the performance of DCE RPC, the basic form of DCE RPC, i.e., one with no secure features, was compared with a commonly available RPC technology/implementation from a vendor. We note that DCE performance is comparable to that of this commonly available RPC technology once the server and client are fully bound to each other.

We also demonstrated how multi-threading increases throughput even on a single processor system in view of small context switching overhead associated with threads. In particular, we demonstrated how multi-threading a client address space with n threads, 1<=n<=10, the n threads doing identical work, improves throughput/response time in comparison with n (identical) single threaded processes. We also demonstrated that multi-threading a client address space increases throughput as the number of threads used increases. We also showed that the optimal number of threads can be determined for any application by using techniques similar to the ones used in this study.

This performance analysis study of DCE environments is only the beginning. Many extensions to our performance analysis are possible and needed. The goals of such extended studies include:

- To understand the effect of multi-processors on multi-threading, whereby there can be true concurrency among threads of the same process or different processes.

- To determine the optimal number of threads under varying work load conditions of client and server and when messages of different lengths are passed between them.

To insure that high performance DCE-based applications are designed and deployed in large scale, several other aspects of DCE should be investigated:

- DFS, the DCE Distributed File System
- Replication of DCE servers, specifically its Cell Directory Services (CDS) and security servers.

The replication decision is a trade-off decision among availability, performance and consistency parameters.

5. Acknowledgments

Our appreciation to Terry Barrett, David Bauer, Alan Dickman, Joel Fleck, John Kaminski, Dennis Mok, Bob Robillard, Diane Ruddock, Suresh Subramanian and John Unger, all of Bellcore, and Transarc Corporation for their review of this paper.

References

[1] Open Software Foundation, *Introduction to OSF DCE*, Prentice-Hall, 1992.

[2] W. Rosenbury, and D. Kenney, *Understanding DCE*, O'Reilly & Associates, Inc., June 1992.

[3] J. Shirley, *Guide to Writing DCE Applications*, O'Reilly & Associates, Inc., June 1992.

[4] B. Dasarathy, *Experience with OSF™ DCE: A Perspective*, Panel Discussion on the OSF DCE: User Experiences and Perspective, Proceedings of the UniForum 1993, San Francisco, 1993, pp. 723-724.

Trademarks

Kerberos is a trademark of the Massachusetts Institute of Technology.
OSF is a trademark of the Open Software Foundation, Inc.

A Performance Study of the
DCE 1.0.1 Cell Directory Service:
Implications for Application and Tool Programmers

Joseph Martinka, Richard Friedrich, Peter Friedenbach, Tracy Sienknecht

martinka@nsa.hp.com, richf@nsa.hp.com
peterf@nsa.hp.com, tracy@nsa.hp.com
Hewlett-Packard Company - Networked Systems Architecture
Cupertino, California U.S.A.   95014

Abstract. This paper summarizes performance results of a systematic evaluation of the Open Software Foundation (OSF) Distributed Computing Environment (DCE) Cell Directory Service (CDS). The CDS is a distributed name database which is used to locate servers and objects within a DCE cell. We designed and built a systematic CDS performance test system and then characterized and projected the performance of important CDS operations with the primary focus on the RPC Name Service Independent (NSI) interface. These results should assist customer application modeling as well as CDS porting and performance tuning by developers using DCE. We believe CDS in its present form has performance tuning opportunities and we provide several recommendations for users of the CDS.

1 Introduction

We conducted a systematic study of the performance characteristics of the Cell Directory Service. This paper discusses some of our performance measurements of basic CDS services, how and why these measurements were made, and implications for the design of DCE applications using CDS.

The CDS provides distributed applications with the ability to access servers without *a priori* knowledge of the server's physical location. This server location transparency enhances availability by connecting clients with currently available servers.

A distributed application will use the directory service the same way we use a telephone book. The predominate service it provides is the lookup of a server by name: where is the network location of a requested service? Name lookups are a frequent operation in distributed applications and must execute efficiently. These requests need a true distributed and reliable server for which there are few alternatives other than CDS.

The CDS also provides uniform naming mechanisms for distributed applications, supports higher application availability by providing for the read-only replication of the name space, provides client side caching and provides X/OPEN Application Program Interface (API) support.

1.1 Overall Conclusions

We worked closely with HP DCE's developers during our investigation in Fall 1992 to provide performance improvements to CDS. Our performance improvements were on the order of 30-80% and will be made available through OSF to other vendors of DCE.

For small to medium cells (tens to hundreds of nodes), where the access to the CDS is infrequent, the performance of the CDS makes it a viable distributed name server. The CDS functions adequately and is viable for the short term. In the longer term it may be a performance bottleneck for certain classes of applications that depend on CDS in a critical performance path (such as some OLTP or applications with high CDS access frequencies). This paper will provide insight into how to use CDS efficiently.

1.2 Paper Organization

In section 2, the CDS test system is explained. We describe our methodology and cautions for data interpretation in section 3. The performance data for binding import measurements is presented in section 4, while the performance data for binding exports is in section 5. In section 6 we briefly describe results for the low level response times for the *cdsclerk* and *cdsd*. The final sections discuss future CDS performance improvements, recommendations, and areas for future research.

Figure 1   Description of Test System Boundary

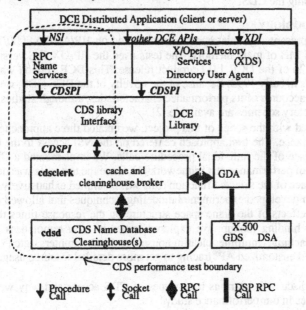

2   System Description

This section describes the boundaries of the tested subsystems within DCE.

There are two external APIs that DCE application developers can access CDS: the Name Service Independent (NSI) and X/Open Directory Interface (XDI) [11]. A third API called the Cell Directory Service Programming Interface (CDSPI) exists. The CDSPI interface is not available to application programmers as it is an internal DCE library interface used by NSI and XDI library functions. CDSPI was important for us to investigate since it represents quantifiable units of work delivered to the CDS daemons.

Figure 1 illustrates the relationships among these APIs. NSI calls are made directly by application developers, or indirectly from within the IDL-generated stub code and

DCE libraries. NSI calls present DCE-knowledgeable access to the name service database. By DCE-knowledgeable, we mean that the DCE/NSI library knows about the CDS attributes which characterize objects as profiles, groups, or server entries[10]. This functionality is not found in the XDS or lower level CDSPI interfaces.

The DCE library makes all its accesses to the CDS through the CDSPI interface. There is nearly a one-for-one correspondence of the CDSPI interface calls within the DCE library to the socket calls actually made out of the library to the *cdsclerk*.

As shown in Figure 1, the other external API interface to CDS, XDI, is outside the boundary of our study. However, the programmer using XDS has the choice to use the GDS X.500 database or CDS through the Directory User Agent (DUA). If the DUA references the CDS, it generates the accesses to the *cdsclerk* using the same CDSPI interface as does the NSI requests. The results of this report (section 6) which address the primitive response time costs to retrieve and modify attributes as well as to create and delete objects, can be taken as the minimum bounds for XDS response times for operations using the CDS.

3   Methodology

The data presented in this report was measured on HP/Apollo 9000/720 workstations with 64 MB of main memory. The tests used the HP-UX O/S version 8.07, and OSF's build 26 of the DCE 1.0.1 product release. This DCE version was released to HP customers in early 1993. Because of the novelty of the DCE CDS, we are unaware of published accounts of its performance characteristics, although studies of other distributed directory schemes are available [2].

When faced with the scope of this project, we created three approaches to evaluate CDS performance. The first approach centered on the NSI access to the CDS and the parameter space of the individual procedure calls. We implemented a CDS test suite using a custom performance test framework [1]. Once the test suite was developed, the parameter space of the selected function calls was examined exhaustively [6]. The second approach developed experimental modeling techniques that allowed us to explore some of the effects of the name space structure on the response times that would be expected for binding lookup. We explored issues of *cdsd* remoteness, nested CDS structures, caching, multiple clearinghouses, softlink pointers, etc.[7]. The third approach used customized API tracing to get more detailed resource usage across CDS daemons [9].

We now discuss the various basic types of CDS access and why we emphasized these activities in our performance study.

3.1   Importing RPC Bindings from the CDS

We believe the retrieval of binding information from the distributed name service is the predominant mode of CDS access by applications using the CDS service[1].

We were interested not only in the costs to retrieve a single binding, but multiple bindings as well. The reason to import multiple bindings is that the client application may need to retrieve several protocol stacks to a server, for load balancing or reliability.

3.2   Exporting Bindings to the CDS

Binding export (or any name space modification) is a function that we estimate will not be as frequent as binding import discussed in the previous section. The objective

---

1. There is supporting empirical evidence for this assertion based on performance workload measurement work from DEC on their own Domain Naming Service[4].

of any distributed name service is that it should contain information which is neither static nor rapidly changing. If it were static, the data should be in some configuration file somewhere, not cluttering up the name space. If it were rapidly changing, that is, binding exports and other name space manipulation represent a large majority of all transactions on the name space, it will cause havoc with the distribution algorithms for replicas and other clearinghouse housekeeping.

Export performance will be important to some users of CDS. The expectations of rapid binding export may be part of the performance start-up path. We cannot forget that CDS may also be used through XDS where modifications of the name space could be a much more important part of the usage of CDS. In cases of managed objects and client instrumentation, the export of a client's location to the name space may need to be efficient.

3.3 Caveats for Direct Application of Results

The reader of this report is advised that the performance data discussed herein does not necessarily represent the exact performance a real application will experience. The differences are:

- Much of the performance data presented is the running average of multiple, repetitive operations to the RPC Name Service. Because of the nature of the CDS, these tests avoid the larger costs associated with initial calls to the name space and maximize the positive impact the CDS clerk cache has on the results. Actual applications will typically not exhibit the same repetitive retrieval patterns as our test environment.

- Our measurements were performed on a DCE cell linked over an isolated IEEE 802.3 LAN. The CDS directory server was always within a 2 to 3 millisecond (msec) RPC to the local node's *cdsclerk*.

- Local non-CDS tasks requiring computations or contested network bandwidth may lengthen the response times in a more typical real world scenario.

- The performance test bed used in this report is a synthetic structure, systematically generated for purposes of this study. Real name spaces will actually evolve over time, growing in size and complexity.

- The DCE CDS is a recently released service which is expected to change and improve.

4 RPC Binding Import

The response times for the importation of server bindings in DCE 1.0.1 fall in a wide range depending on whether the attribute information is cached, the number of bindings requested, whether it was the first or subsequent binding lookup, and the kinds of group and profile structures encountered.

4.1 Test Case Descriptions

The import binding tests that we want to discuss in this paper are listed in Table 1. The letters in the first column are the index keys to the graph which follows it.

In Table 1, we used both cached and uncached trials, nested groups and profiles, and multiple binding lookups to give the reader a sampling of the variety of tests that we conducted.

4.2 Local Node Binding Retrieval Results

We plot in Figure 2 the first and subsequent response times for each of the import tests discussed in Table 1. The First Response time includes an Access Control List (ACL) check to ensure that the user has the permissions to reference the CDS entry.

This time also includes preparing DCE library memory structures and other house-keeping. The Mean Response is the average response times of subsequent imports of the same CDS objects.

Table 1 Binding Import Test Names

Index	Action taken in test
bI	Single binding **import** from a server entry
bL	Single binding **lookup** from server entry
c1	The *cdsclerk* cache hits for server attributes
c2	The *cdsclerk* cache miss on first attribute read
c3	The *cdsclerk* cache is disabled (high confidence)
b1	One binding lookup from a server entry
b2	Two binding lookups from a server entry
b5	Five binding lookups from a server entry
g1	One binding lookup starting from a group entry
g2	Two binding lookups starting from a group entry
g5	Five binding lookup starting from a group entry
p1	One binding lookup starting from a profile entry
p2	Two binding lookups starting from a profile entry
p5	Five binding lookups starting from a profile entry
ng1	One binding lookup from a single nested group entry
ng2	One binding lookup from a 2 deep nested groups
ng5	One binding lookup from a 5 deep nested groups
np1	One binding lookup from a single nested profile entry
np2	One binding lookup from a 2 deep nested profiles
np5	One binding lookup from a 5 deep nested profiles

Figure 2 Binding Retrieval from Local Clearinghouse

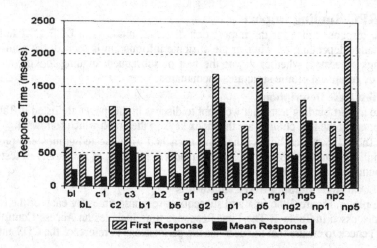

For name space lookup satisfied by the *cdsclerk* cache (all tests except bars *c2* and *c3*), first response times are between 44 milliseconds to over one second. Subsequent lookups have better response times. Simple non-cached name space lookups requiring *cdsd* involvement (tests *c2* and *c3*) have response times range between 550 msecs to over a second, more than three times longer than the cached counterparts. The non-cached responses for the more complex tests are not shown, but have similar increases in response times. Note that since the test clearinghouse was local to the same node, there were no network latencies in the non-cached response time.

Servers that are found through groups or profiles (tests *g1* through *np5*) have response times for binding lookup from 600 msecs to 2 seconds. Simple modeling shows that these response times increase markedly when attributes are not cached and the server *cdsd* is located at network delays greater than 20 msecs.

4.3 Binding Import Conclusions

Other observations that we made from the binding import measurements include:

- CDS Clerk caching has a major impact on performance. Those measurements which accessed entries that were not already in the CDS Clerk cache took four times longer to complete. DCE nodes which do not have application sets that request repetitive retrievals to identical objects may experience low hit rates to the CDS Clerk cache. In addition, environments with complex or slower network topologies will experience greater performance increases than documented in this report.

- The CDS name server exhibits linear increases in performance proportional to the increase in the complexity of a CDS object entry for:
  - number of binding handles retrieved per entry.
  - number of members accessed per group or profile
  - number of attributes accessed per group or profile.
  - level of nesting of groups/profiles.

  While these growth patterns, by themselves, are not a problem for simple uses of the CDS, it may be of concern when using complex name searches.

- The CDS name server exhibits increasing processing behavior when searching through lists of object UUIDs and profile elements with multiple interfaces or versions. This is a problem for name bindings that are long-lived and are subject to numerous updates.

- Binding retrievals using *rpc_ns_binding_import_** can produce very unpredictable performance results because the operation is actually implemented as calls to *rpc_ns_binding_lookup_** with a fixed vector size of five. Among the behavior we have seen is:
  - Simple single binding imports are 25 to 35% higher with *rpc_ns_binding_import_** than they are with *rpc_ns_binding_lookup_** using a vector size of one.
  - Import performance from a server entry can vary as much as 25% depending on the number of handles in the entry. Surprisingly, the best performance is achieved when there are 5 or more handles in the entry.
  - Importation tests using group and profile entries experienced up to three times the response time for single binding retrievals based upon the number of qualifying handles in the compound structure. This phenomena was particularly evident in a profile structure where multiple elements existed with different, but compatible minor version numbers.

- Object identifiers, while having minimal impact on the retrieval of binding handles from a server entry, can cause significantly slower performance response times if used to differentiate server entries within group and profile structures.

4.4 CDS Structure Affect on Response Times

We used experimental design techniques to understand the primary factors which affect CDS access response time. Several 2-factor combinations (interactions) have statistically significant effects on binding import response times.

Primary factors that affect average response time (neglecting the cost of the first CDS response time cost) are listed below. Note that these effects can be multiplicative for objects with multiple components (e.g., groups, profiles).

- The basic cost to retrieve a binding for a server from the name space is 15 to 20 msecs.
- A significant incremental response time increase occurs if the server entry is not found in the cdsclerk cache. This effect is on the order of 40 to 50 msecs.
- The number of softlinks traversed to find a server entry increases response time incrementally per softlink-indirection level. This affect is on the order of 1 to 2 msecs per softlink.

The only significant 2-factor interactions occurred in the presence of multiple clearinghouses. These results have not been fully examined. All of the interaction factors are on the order of 3 to 4 msec per lookup.

- Number of clearinghouses in the search path interacts with softlink depth.
- Number of clearinghouses in the search path interacts with entry read from cache.
- Directory depth of server entry interacts with softlink depth.
- Number of entries per directory interacts with softlink depth.
- Number of entries per directory interacts with entry read from cache.

Our measurements and analysis suggest that there are several CDS access and structures that do not appear to affect response time.

- The size of the name space (up to 1200 directories and objects) did not significantly alter the response time as compared to the case of 100 directories and objects.
- The directory depth of a server entry shows no significant effect on response time in our test environment. This was tested for a server entry at the root of the tree and 5 levels deep.
- The number of other entries in the name space at the same directory as the server entry shows no significant effect on response time in our test environment. This was measured for up to 10 objects in the same level in the directory.
- A "remote clearinghouse" containing the server entry (i.e., a clearinghouse that is one LAN hop away from the client node) has no significant effect on response time. Intuitively, this result seems surprising since the network delay should cause accesses to a remote clearinghouse to be longer than for the local node. However, as confirmed by earlier measurements of DCE RPC performance, the difference in response times between local and remote RPC is negligible in a local LAN environment. MANs and WANs, on the other hand, demonstrate a significant deleterious effect since the WAN delay is additive to response time.

4.5 CDS Access Times Across High-Latency Networks

There are network costs that are not part of these measurements where the *clearinghouse* is located remote from the local node on which the client runs. In fact, this is a likely real-world situation. Here, we model typical network delays for each RPC to the remote *clearinghouse* based on our trace measurements. We measured the underlying resource demands for various retrieval modes for DCE 1.0.1. We also know the cached and non-cached behavior of the retrieval mechanisms.

If we assume several network delay scenarios, we can construct a simple model of the effects. In Table 2 we have modeled different degrees of "remoteness" for the clearinghouse and its *cdsd* by choosing typical network delays as a model parameter.

- LAN - Local Area Network - *cdsd* is on the same LAN as the client application. Assumed a 2 msec round trip time.
- MAN - Metropolitan Area Network - *cdsd* is in the same metropolitan area as the client application. Assumed a typical 40 msec round trip time.
- WAN - Wide Area Network - *cdsd* is on the same continent as the client application. Assumed a typical 80 msec round trip time[1].

Table 2   Modeled Binding Lookup Response Times for Remote Servers (msec)

	Binding Operation to be Performed	cache	LAN	MAN	WAN
--	Single Attribute Read	yes	3	3	3
--	Single Attribute Read	no	16	55	95
b1	One Binding Retrieval	yes	14	14	14
b1	One Binding Retrieval	no	45	160	280
p1	One Binding through Profile Retrieval	yes	37	37	37
p1	One Binding through Profile Retrieval	no	120	425	750
g5	Bindings from 5 Servers through a Group	yes	126	126	126
g5	Bindings from 5 Servers through a Group	no	400	1430	2500
p5	Bindings from 5 Servers through a Profile	yes	130	130	130
p5	Bindings from 5 Servers through a Profile	no	450	1600	2800
np2	One Binding from 2 nested Profiles	yes	62	62	62
np2	One Binding from 2 nested Profiles	no	195	700	1200

The column group header above "LAN MAN WAN" reads "Round trip Time (msec)" and above "cache" reads "Remoteness of *cdsd:*".

Table 2 presents the modeled response times for various binding lookups for cached and non-cached situations. This table estimates the response times on HP9000 S720 *cdsd* servers including the assumed networked delays.

The lines with *yes* as cache status in the table are from our direct measurements on DCE 1.0.1. The lines marked *no* as cache status are generated from a simple model based on the number of known attribute reads which occur for each of the test cases multiplied by the round trip RPC time to the *cdsd*. Our estimates do not include any additional delays for RPC pings on the longer transactions.

Of course, we expect some of the attributes are cached on a retrieval lookup. Therefore, the response time is bounded by the cached and uncached results for each of the test cases.

1. We measured 100 msec DCE RPC round-trip time from Cupertino, California to Chelmsford, Massachusetts. Results can vary based on network topology and distance.

Response times grow very large when CDS servers are not local. This problem has motivated the clearinghouse replica capability of CDS. Replicas are not always available locally to every user, nor are they useful for binding exports which must go to the master replica. For some users, binding lookup could experience a long wait. For example, servers that are found through groups or profiles can have response times for binding lookup on the order of several seconds when attributes are not cached and the server *cdsd* is located at network time delays greater than 20 msecs round trip time.

4.6 An Application's Binding Response Time

To determine a particular application's CDS response time, one cannot use these results without modification. In order to estimate the probability of communicating with the *cdsd* for binding lookup, one needs answers to workload characterization which were **not** addressed as part of our initial investigation. These questions include:

- What percentage of the binding lookups are designated by the application designers to proceed with high confidence, bypassing the *cdsclerk* cache? Of the remaining proportion of binding lookups, some will hit the *cdsclerk* cache and some will not. What is the probability in a typical client that the binding lookups actually are found in the *cdsclerk* cache? This can be highly variable. It may be based on the default value for attribute time-outs in cache, frequency or rate of repeated attribute access by clients on a node, the multiple workload composition on the node, the design of the running client applications on the node.

- What is the probability that binding handles found in CDS server entries point to network ports that have no server's manager currently active?

- What is the number of distinct CDS clearinghouses which need traversal before the retrieval can occur?

The network delays are added in for a miss in the *cdsclerk* cache for every attribute read which occurs. The number of attribute reads is highly dependent on the structure of the binding lookup parameters and name space structure, but can be as few as three to as much as dozens of read attribute requests.

5 RPC Binding Export

We turn now to the area of binding export. This function must be completed as the server readies itself to accept RPC calls for its services. The export activity requires that the CDS object be updated (or created) with the correct binding handle information.

5.1 Test Case Descriptions

The investigation using API tracing analysis looked at a wide variety of name space binding [9]. This paper discusses a few of those parameter combinations which appear to be more interesting from a performance or frequency of occurrence standpoint.

Four classes of assumptions about the aspects of the name space object are made prior to export. These are:

- **new object** - the server object does not yet exist.
- **new intfc** - the server object exists but does not have the specific interface registered in the object.
- **new version**- the server object exists and has the interface registered, but does not yet have a protocol stack with the correct major version number.
- **existing** - the server object with the correct protocol stack already exists prior to the export.

In each of the above classes the test registers from 1 to 5 protocol stacks. Each protocol could represent a different network protocol offered (UDP, TCP, etc.) or concurrent interface IDs[1]. Object attribute caching in the *cdsclerk* was enabled.

We traced each API call repeatedly. This allows us to examine both the first response time, and the subsequent response time exporting to the same name under the same conditions. These times are rarely the same. This repetition required the test program to undo any operations if necessary to put the object back in the same state between tests. The resulting API traces were examined as well as the measured response times.

5.2 Simple Export Results

Figure 3 shows the DCE 1.0.1's first and subsequent response times for exported names. First response times are more variable than the subsequent response time in our measurements. Measuring the response time of the first binding export by a server, many components enter into the operation. To isolate some of the long-term CDS code effects, we also measured the response time average of subsequent exports to the same object by the same client. We wanted to distinguish between the two because the average response time of subsequent exports is influenced less by some of the factors that increase the variability of the first response time. Details of the first response time incremental costs are beyond the scope of this paper [9].

5.3 Disk I/O Operations for Name Space Changes

For reliability, the CDS changes are written to a log file on the compute node running *cdsd*. This log file grows until it exceeds a non-configurable maximum size or a configurable checkpoint time interval has elapsed. At this time a checkpoint will occur.

The response time of simple CDS object updates are roughly stable at about 70 to 80 milliseconds. The CPU was 25% idle during export operations when the *cdsd* is on the same node as the requesting application and the database is relatively young[2]. Simple calculations based on the I/O rate, service times, and CPU utilization suggest that the I/O cost is around 18 msecs as expected on the internal disk drives of the tested workstation.

Figure 3 Binding Export Response from Local Clearinghouse

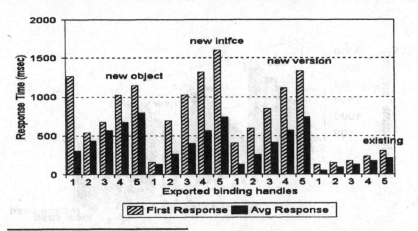

---

1. The test changed the RPC port number to distinguish the various binding handles.
2. There is an import and export response time degradation that occurs as a CDS object are modified, which increases response time as well as lowers I/O rates and CPU idle.

We conclude that *cdsd* performs a single disk I/O per name space modification, object creation, or object deletion. It appears that this transaction log I/O is synchronous. The log record is written out before the *cdsd* can return the RPC. Since multiple attributes must be written, several synchronous disk I/O's are required. There is no apparent concurrency permitted while the CDS is logging. We observed a 170 byte increase in log file length per modify_attribute call. About 11 000 bytes on average is logged for a create and a delete of a name space object. At this file growth rate, 600 to 700 update operations can occur before a checkpoint is started.

5.4 Adjusting for Network Delays

We caution the reader that these measurements were made with the *cdsd* on the same node as the test application. The measured response times is higher if the *cdsd* is not local to the node.

These basic response times include the full RPC call operations from *cdsd* to the *cdsclerk*. In this test, both processes resided on the same node so the network delay was zero. Earlier analysis of RPC performance discovered that the overall response time for both of the processes is roughly equivalent whether or not an actual local LAN network was used. In [8] we traced the packets for typical RPC calls. In the case of UDP protocol transactions, we expect that at least two packets are exchanged per RPC call. Thus if the *cdsd* was on the other end of a LAN or WAN network, the response times will be increased by the node-to-node packet transmission cost multiplied by the number of packets that make up each RPC.

The best case is two packets for each RPC. In the case of TCP/IP protocol connections between DCE servers (a possibility in the near future for DCE 1.0.1 or DCE 1.0.2), 5 packets are needed to set up a connection, 2 packets to transfer the data, and 4 packets to take down a connection. The connection setup and takedown costs will probably be amortized across the numerous concurrent communications between a *cdsd* and its *cdsclerk* on an active system, so in both cases, a two packet delay is more likely to be added to the average response time per *cdsclerk* to *cdsd* communication.

Figure 4 Remote Clearinghouse Effects on Binding Export

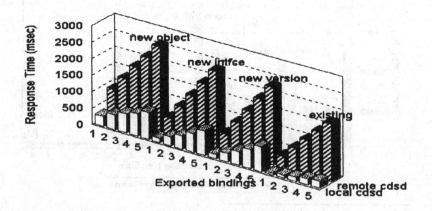

5.5 Remote Clearinghouse Model

We can use our knowledge of the underlying communication packet requirements to model the export timings for a *cdsd* server which is remote to the local node. In Figure 4, we have graphed the measured local *cdsd* node response times as the white bars. These test categories are the same as described for Figure 3.

Plotted in dark bars are the results of our modeled response times if the *cdsd* clearinghouse server has a large round trip latency. This latency could be related to distance, slow-speed communication, routers, or a combination of the three. In this case, we used a 80 millisecond round-trip time. The response time costs are two to four times more expensive for the first three test cases, and significantly more expensive for the last test case when the object's binding already exists in the CDS name space. Very few export cases are less than one second in response time.

If the application wishes to update a group or profile object as well, the response time costs to update a second object will double the total costs to several seconds.

6 Basic CDS Attribute and Object Operations

We turn briefly to the underlying services being performed at the CDSPI on behalf of these binding imports and exports. We instrumented a custom version of a *cdsclerk* in order to trace its operations during various test suites. We used the traces produced with HP DCE toolkit facilities to measure the important *cdsd* and *cdsclerk* functions.

From the analysis of API traces, we could determine the basic response time costs of the *cdsclerk*'s operations that were needed to handle the incoming DCE CDSPI library request; check the caches for attributes, clearinghouses, directories as needed; get the authenticated binding handle from the cache; if a read attribute from *cdsd*, place the attribute into the common cache (shared memory); CMA thread processing; and other kernel operations (sockets or DCE RPC).

Similarly, the basic response times of calling *cdsd* via RPC calls from the *cdsclerk* were analyzed. In Table 3, we summarize some of the basic measurement comparisons which do not include network delay. The basic costs for certain canonical CDS operations are listed for the *cdsd* and the *cdsclerk*. We used measurements such as these to model the performance and improvements for more complex NSI operations.

Table 3 Basic response times for primitive name space activities[1]

Primitive Activity	cdsd		cdsclerk
	Typical Measured RespTime	Estimated Non-I/O RespTime	Typical Measured RespTime
Read Attribute (cached)	not used	not used	3 msec
Read Attribute (non-cached)	13.4 msec	13.4 msec	4 msec
Test Attribute	12.8 msec	12.8 msec	4 msec
Create Object (existing)	11.2 msec	11.2 msec	3 msec
Create Object (not existing)	81 msec	63 msec	5 msec
Modify Attribute of Object	75 msec	57 msec	3 msec
Delete Object	71 msec	53 msec	4 msec

1. These measurements were taken on a HP Series 9000/720. The CPU speed is estimated as 28 million HP-PA instructions per second for this workload based on instruction pathlength tracing measurements of the DCE library code using H-P internal tools.

7 Future CDS Performance Potential

We worked closely with HP developers porting the OSF DCE release to improve the performance of the CDS during our investigation. There remain substantial potential for future improvement. These changes may or may not be implemented by a participating OSF technology supplier. For example:

- Further binding lookup response time improvements could be achieved, conservatively estimated between 13% to 30%, on binding lookups through group or profile objects if the NSI library is made aware of which attributes exist for an object. Non-existing attribute reads are often 1/4 to 1/3 of the total attribute reads made by these more complex lookups.

- Three additional levels of specific performance tuning steps were defined, providing response time improvements of 20% to 50% for multiple binding handle exports to local *cdsd*, and up to 70% for *cdsd* clearinghouses that are remote (80 msec network round trip).

- A large number of unnecessary attribute reads could be saved. In most cases a quarter to a third of all attribute reads involve lookups that use groups and profiles are for non-existent attributes. Enumeration of attribute data can be 'piggy-backed' on the ubiquitous *CDS_ClassVersion* read. This enhancement could yield measurable performance savings in future releases.

Other examples exist of CDS performance improvements, some may occur from a overhaul of some of the underlying architecture. While no promises should be inferred from this paper, the authors continue to believe that the performance of CDS can be improved in the coming releases from DCE vendors.

8 CDS Recommendations for Applications

Based upon these observations, we can offer the following advice for developers using the RPC Name Service[1].

In general, access to the name space should be minimized to prevent unnecessary CPU consumption and response time.

- Avoid using *rpc_ns_binding_import_** to retrieve binding handles. Use *rpc_ns_binding_lookup_** directly. Binding importation is a trade-off between performance and the size of the pool of handles from which the name service randomly selects a server. Unfortunately *rpc_ns_binding_import_** hides this trade-off from the developer, making an arbitrary choice of a vector size of five. *rpc_ns_binding_import_** appears to offer simplicity, but is actually only one of an array of choices available with *rpc_ns_binding_lookup_**. As the data in this report shows, mixing *rpc_ns_binding_import_** with the wrong name space configuration can lead to some serious performance problems.

- Avoid the use of object identifiers to differentiate server entries within group and profile structures. Because of the nature of the search algorithms, mixing object UUID based lookups with these groups and profiles result in an extensive and slow search of the name space to retrieve the requested server information.

- Clean up obsolete server and binding information from the name space when an application rolls major and minor version numbers.

- Because servers tend to stop and start, the name service provides an application the capability to overlay the binding and server information stored in the name space for a specific interface identifier. This capability allows the application to

---

1. Other CDS recommendations are found in [5].

avoid un-exporting the old information and therefore saving on the overall number of changes to the name space. Unfortunately as application interface versions are created, this obsolete information can remain orphaned in the name space. As the data in this report suggests, leaving this information in the name space will degrade the performance of the name space.

- Be careful when using profile and group structures in binding retrievals. Groups should contain only identical interface ID's. Especially be aware of binding retrievals that search profiles or nested profiles that encompass an extensive range of disparate servers in a name space. If an *rpc_ns_binding_import_** uses such a structure, the name server can end up traversing the entire structure looking for a minimum of five compatible binding handles. This result could also occur if *rpc_ns_binding_lookup_** is called with a vector size larger than the currently available bindings in the requested structure.

- Disabling of Clerk Cache - avoid setting the *cdscp* confidence level to HIGH or setting NSI attribute cache time-out to zero so that NSI lookup routines are unable to take advantage of the caching capability of the *cdsclerk*.

- Use Softlinks carefully — In a complex environment with more than one clearinghouse, the incremental cost to traverse a softlink is 1.7 msecs per softlink in the search path.

- CDS transaction log file size - We observed on several occasions that the cost of the CDS recovering its name space from the transaction log file (e.g., after a crash or *cdsd* interruption) can delay any pending CDS requests for many minutes. The application designer or system administrator cannot control the growth of the checkpoint log file. However, one can minimize the exposure to long recovery times by setting the configured intervals between CDS checkpoints to a value which keeps the transaction log file small using *cdscp*.

9 Future Research

Although the scope of this project was large, it still represents only a portion of the performance aspects of CDS. Among the interesting areas of future performance evaluation work are:

- Name service update times during CDS *skulks*, or direct update propagation around a large, extensive DCE cell with multiple replicas of clearinghouse.

- Performance of *cdscp* commands or other name service administrative activities such as directory, group, or profile creation.

- Exhaustive treatment of the security aspects of the name service except as described within this document.

- Global naming services (GDS), intra-cell naming services, X.500, or cross-cell caching.

- Background, asynchronous, solicitation/advertiser costs on network and CPU bandwidths.

- Local endpoint mapping or protocol stack selection with run-time libraries.

- Exception handling, errors and failures of the CDS naming retrieval code.

- Differences in client and server nodes' processor speeds effect on retrieval.

- Extensive instruction pathlength tracing of any of the test CDS calls.

- How well *cdsclerk* caching performs in a dynamic environment. Specifically, offering the expected hit rates to a cache in a "real" loaded client environment with the average name lookup response time measurements.
- The XDS name service interface performance. We have made only indirect measurements for XDS by looking at basic CDSPI operations.
- Understand the cost of CDS updates in the presence of many replicated clearinghouses for the directory in which the update takes place.

Acknowledgements

We wish to acknowledge the consistent support of HP's NSA management during this and prior projects as they recognize the value of a strong performance organization and the commitment of resources to do a credible, useful analysis. John Grober from HP CSSL-Chelmsford was especially helpful in patient explanations, prototyping, and review of this work.

References

1 *Basic Systems Services Performance Measurement Suite - User's Guide*, Networked Systems Architecture, Hewlett-Packard Company, Internal Document: NSA-92-016, August 1992.
2 Bolot, J., et al, *Evaluating Caching Schemes for the X.500 Directory System*, The 13th International Conference on Distributed Computing Systems, May 1993, 112-119.
3 Box, G., et al., *Statistics for Experimenters*, John Wiley and Sons, Inc., New York, 1988.
4 *Distributed Name Service Workload Case Study*, Digital Equipment Corporation, released to HP, August 1989.
5 Dilley J., *Practical Experiences with the DCE Cell Directory Service*, Networked Systems Architecture, Hewlett-Packard, International Workshop OSF DCE, Karlsruhe, Germany, October 1993.
6 Friedenbach, P., et al., *Performance Characterization of the DCE 1.0.1 RPC Name Service*, Networked Systems Architecture, Hewlett-Packard, Internal Document: NSA-92-018, December 1992.
7 Friedrich, R., et al., *Performance Characteristics of the DCE 1.0.1 Cell Directory Services using Experimental Design Techniques*, Networked Systems Architecture, Hewlett-Packard, Internal Document: NSA-92-019, December 1992.
8 Martinka, J., *Pathlength Measurements of DCE's RPC on HP-UX*, Information Architecture Group, Hewlett-Packard Internal Document: IAG-92-004, March 1992.
9 Martinka, J., et al., *CDS API Tracing: Performance Tuning and Models*, Networked Systems Architecture, Hewlett-Packard, Internal Document: NSA-92-020, December 1992.
10 *OSF DCE 1.0 Application Development Guide*, Revision 1.0, Open Software Foundation, December 31, 1991.
11 *OSF DCE 1.0 Application Development Reference*, Revision 1.0, Open Software Foundation, December 31, 1991.
12 Sienknecht, T., et al., *A Critical Evaluation of the DCE-CDS Architectural Design as it Relates to Directory Naming Service Performance*, Networked Systems Architecture, Hewlett-Packard, HP Internal Document: NSA-92-022, December 1992.

fidl - a tool for using DCE from Fortran

Roland Laifer, Andreas Knocke

University of Karlsruhe, Computing Centre
Zirkel 2, D-76128 Karlsruhe, Fed. Rep. of Germany
E-mail: laifer@rz.uni-karlsruhe.de

Abstract. A tool, called **fidl**, has been developed which gives the
Fortran programmer an easy access to the Remote Procedure Call
(RPC) of the Distributed Computing Environment (DCE). It supplies
a Fortran application interface by defining a Fortran-like interface
definition language and facilitates the creation of distributed applications
by generating the additional code automatically. As a result, the Fortran
application programmer does not have to learn much about the DCE
RPC system, the programming language C, or the peculiarities between
Fortran and C.
The experiences gained in developing **fidl** have been collected in the first
part of the article. These experiences will give general hints how to use
DCE RPC from languages other than C.

1 Introduction

In a distributed application, different computers work together and parts of the
application are running on different machines. Reasons for creating distributed
applications include the use of special properties of computers (e. g. compute
power, graphics), the common usage of resources (e. g. data, software, printers),
and the distribution of the load to different computers in a network.

Nowadays, there are different systems that support the program developer
in generating distributed applications. Some message passing systems (e. g.
Parallel Virtual Machine PVM, see [1]) can be used to communicate between
machines in a heterogeneous network instead of nodes on parallel computers.
For communication, the programmer has to write code to marshall, unmarshall,
send, and receive messages. On the other hand, Remote Procedure Call (RPC)
systems use the 'natural' separation of programs into procedures. The system
usually derives the code for marshalling and unmarshalling the parameters and
sending the call over the network from an interface description.

The RPC of the Distributed Computing Environment (DCE) has a number
of advantages compared with other RPC systems and message passing systems.
First, DCE is a proven technology agreed upon and supported by many members
of the computer industry. Most manufacturers of UNIX based systems provide
DCE products, and even on other platforms DCE is and will become available.
Secondly, the DCE RPC is tightly connected with other DCE components: the
DCE Directory Service, the DCE Threads, and the DCE Security Service (see [2]
to [5]), for example. With the help of the DCE Directory Service an RPC client

does not have to know where a server is located. Thus, the server can be started on another computer to distribute the load or if a computer has crashed down. The DCE Threads support the parallelization within a process. A client can call multiple servers at the same time and a server can handle multiple requests. The DCE Security Service, among other things, provides secure communication for the DCE RPC.

A disadvantage of the DCE RPC is that it does not support yet the distribution of *Fortran* programs. However, the code for the solution of many scientific and engineering programs is written in Fortran. Therefore, the first part of this article discusses how to use the DCE RPC from Fortran. In the second part the tool fidl is described, which preserves the Fortran programmer from writing C code and code calling the DCE library.

2 Using DCE RPC from Fortran

This section describes how the DCE RPC can be used to distribute Fortran applications. The following subsections show the experiences gained in developing fidl which have been incorporated into the tool. In the first subsection, some concepts how to use DCE from Fortran will be discussed. Thereby, general hints show how to distribute applications from languages other than C. The second subsection presents the interface between Fortran and C, and the third subsection shows problems in using DCE from Fortran.

2.1 Fundamental Decisions

In order to distribute an application DCE library calls have to be added to the application. The main tasks of the library functions are to store the interface of a server and to bind to an appropriate server. At first sight, one could simply try to call the library from Fortran instead from C. But this is not practicable because in Fortran it is not possible to define new data types and nearly all DCE library functions have such newly defined types as arguments in their parameter list. Furthermore, Fortran only supports call by reference.

As a second attempt one could try to write intermediate routines in C which are called from Fortran and which call the DCE library. However, some library functions need output parameters of other library functions as input parameters. Therefore, these parameters have to be declared as global variables which will produce complex and incomprehensible code.

For this reasons, it is the best to combine the code for the distribution in two additional C routines. The server routine consists of the server main program which can be nearly the same as for a C application. Only one entry (the manager entry point vector which contains the names of the callable Fortran routines) has to be adapted to Fortran because it has to use the compiler dependent spelling (see Sect. 2.2). The application part of the server – the manager routines – can be written in Fortran and need not contain any DCE library call.

On the client side, the additional C routine handles the binding. It is possible to omit this routine by using the automatic binding method, but it is more flexible to write one's own binding routine. Since it is not possible to define the data type of a binding handle in Fortran, the favourite binding method is explicit customized binding.

To use customized binding for a specific function, the type of the first parameter must have the **handle** attribute in the interface definition. Furthermore, the programmer has to supply a bind and an unbind routine for every first parameter type (example in Sect. 2.2). These routines are called automatically from the client stub. If the programmer wants to use different routines for functions with the same first parameter type, he can use a **typedef** in the interface description to define a new name for that data type. Even if the first parameter of the RPC is passed to the bind routine, there is no need to specify the binding depending on this parameter! For example, every function could use a different global string variable to specify a server name, and this variable could be set at runtime in the client application code.

As a result, the appropriate concept for the distribution in a language other than C is the separation of the additional code for the distribution and the application code. The code for the distribution is contained in the server main program and in the customized bind and unbind routines and is written in C. With this concept even the exception handling can be included for client *and* server side. Since DCE header files are only necessary in the distribution code, their inclusion is no problem, contrary to the results of [4]. Another advantage of the concept is that there is no additional layer between the Fortran application code and the stubs. Therefore, the performance does not decrease.

2.2   The Interface between Fortran and C

In order to write an interface definition in the C-like Interface Definition Language (IDL) and to derive stubs that are suited to the Fortran application, the programmer has to take notice of the interface between Fortran and C. However, if he uses the tool fidl there is no need to know the following peculiarities:

1. In Fortran all parameters (except the internally passed lengths of strings) are passed by reference. Therefore, the parameters in the idl-file (except arrays and string lengths) must be declared as pointers.
2. Arrays in C are stored in row-major order, whereas Fortran stores arrays in column-major order. Because of this, the dimensions of arrays in the idl-file must be given in reverse order.
3. Fortran passes character strings by using two parameters internally: a pointer to the first character and an integer (passed by value) specifying the length of the string. These two parameters have to occur in the parameter list of the IDL for every Fortran character string.
4. For each Fortran data type equivalent C data types must be declared. Table 1 shows this transformation for HP-UX 8.05 on the series 700. It is machine-dependent but it should apply to most UNIX workstations. Notice that

Table 1 only shows the corresponding data types. In a parameter list the C types must be declared as pointers and for a character (even if it has the length 1) there are two corresponding arguments.

5. Some Fortran compilers change the spelling of external names, e. g. `FUNCTION` or `SUBROUTINE` names or names of external variables, by appending underscores or converting to lowercase letters. The IDL must be suitable; if necessary it has to differ on client and on server side.

6. External variables have to be declared as names of `COMMON` blocks in Fortran. For example, the global variable `server` in C

```
char server[80];
```

has to be declared in Fortran as

```
    CHARACTER*80 SERV
    COMMON /SERVER/ SERV
```

In this example the Fortran compiler converts the external name `SERVER` to lowercase letters. If a Fortran programmer wants to assign a value to `SERV` he has to append a null byte (`SERV = 'text'//CHAR(0)`) explicitly, because C strings are terminated by a null byte.

Section 3.3 shows an example how fidl converts the Fortran-like interface description into the C-like IDL.

Table 1. Data type transformation for most UNIX Workststions

Fortran 77	C
INTEGER X	long x;
LOGICAL X	long x;
REAL X	float x;
DOUBLE PRECISION X	double x;
COMPLEX X	struct {float re, im;} x;
CHARACTER X	char x;

2.3 Problems in Using DCE from Fortran

There are a number of problems in using DCE in a heterogeneous system which occur only in Fortran. They arise from the way Fortran programs are usually written, from the non-uniform interface between Fortran and C, and from missing features in the IDL.

One of the most important problems is that a lot of existing Fortran programs communicate via `COMMON`-blocks. In the case of distribution this is not possible, because the address spaces of client and server are separated. Therefore, the needed variables inside the **COMMON**-blocks must be added to the parameter list, i, e. changes in the existing code are necessary.

Another problem may occur not only in Fortran but also in C: if the internal length of a **REAL** is 4 bytes on one computer and it is 8 bytes on another, the programmer has to change all **REAL**s into **REAL*8** (if the Fortran compiler allows this data type) or the 4 byte **REAL**s into **DOUBLE PRECISION**. Data types with fixed length (like the IDL data types) do not exist in Fortran and therefore it is difficult to write portable code. The **KIND** attribute of Fortran 90 may help in this case.

Additional problems may arise if the interface between Fortran and C differs in a heterogeneous system. For example, the arrangement of the length parameter of **CHARACTER** variables, invisible in Fortran, may differ depending on the compiler. If one Fortran compiler arranges these lengths at the end of the parameter list and the other after the **CHARACTER**-parameter (and if there is no appropriate compiler option), the programmer must write an intermediary C routine that changes the arrangement of the parameters.

Some Fortran and C compilers do not share a common definition of true and false. Moreover, the internal representation for false may differ between Fortran compilers. If the Fortran compiler on the client side uses 1 for false and on the server it is −1, a logical parameter which is false on the client becomes true on the server.

Other problems are inherent to the IDL. There are some missing features, and it is not obvious why they are absent:

- It is not possible to specify more than one dimension of an array dynamically, i. e. to give the **length_is** attribute for more than one dimension (see Sect. 3.3). This is particularly a restriction in Fortran, since arrays in Fortran are often defined very large and only a small range is actually needed.
- There is another limitation for passing arrays dynamically. The variables for the **length_is** attribute must occur as an argument of the parameter list, i. e. they cannot be an expression or a constant. If an existing program has to be distributed and the desired **length_is** variable is not in the parameter list, the program code has to be changed and an additional integer value must be transmitted.
- If the explicit customized binding method is used (which is recommended for Fortran users), the first parameter must have the **in** attribute. But sometimes it would not be necessary to send this parameter to the server.

Similar problems have been described in [6]. But it is possible to overcome several restrictions described therein. For example, it is not necessary to use implicit binding for a RPC from Fortran (compare Sect. 2.1).

The above listed problems can be solved by making changes in the existing code, writing intermediate C routines or simply accepting a lack of performance. Nevertheless, some problems could be solved, if only the compilers supplied appropriate options. These options are not only necessary for a distributed program, but also to port easily a program which is written in Fortran and C.

Above all it should be possible to control optionally the arrangement of the character lengths and to change the spelling of external names. The optional conversion of all REALs to DOUBLE PRECISION and vice versa would be very helpful, too.

3 The Tool fidl

A Fortran programmer who wants to use DCE RPC must write an interface description in the C-like Interface Description Language. Therefore, he must know the peculiarities between Fortran and C. Moreover, he must write the additional code for the distribution, such as the server main program, in the language C. This is why a tool called fidl has been developed (see [7]). It was designed to give the Fortran programmer an easy access to and to facilitate the use of DCE RPC.

3.1 Benefits of the Tool fidl

The first aim – to facilitate the access from Fortran – was met by defining and converting a Fortran-like interface description language. A Fortran-like interface definition, based on Fortran 77 syntax with extensions taken from Fortran 90 whenever possible, was defined (as recommended in [8]). fidl converts this interface definition to the IDL. Useful error messages and syntax diagrams help the programmer to correct errors in the Fortran interface description.

The second aim – to facilitate the use of the DCE RPC – was reached by taking information from the interface description and generating the additional C code for the distribution automatically. It takes some time to get used to DCE which could be an essential drawback for the use of DCE. Therefore, fidl automatically generates server main programs and binding routines, which call the DCE library. As one result, the programmer does not have to call any routines of the DCE library, and thus saves the time of getting used to DCE. As a second result, the Fortran programmer does not need to have any programming knowledge in C since all necessary C files are generated by fidl.

But the tool fidl provides still more support: for linking and compiling the distributed application, it generates 'makefiles'. With the information of these makefiles, the UNIX tool make can be used to compile and link the necessary files and libraries automatically.

Of course, fidl does not offer all features included in DCE. But if a programmer wants to use additional features, he can use the fidl-generated files and add the desired code.

Figure 1 shows how the tools fidl, make, and the IDL compiler collaborate to create a distributed application. IF stands for the interface name. fidl can also generate code for an application with multiple interfaces, but this is not shown in this figure. The file 'IF.fdl' has to be identical on client and server side. The generated files 'IF.idl' are nearly identical, too; only the function names may differ (see Sect. 2.3). 'IF.uuid' contains an automatically produced interface identification (UUID), and therefore it has to be generated only on client side and copied to the server. It is included into the files 'IF.idl'. The information of 'IF.fdl' is not only used to generate 'IF.idl', but also to generate the files 'IFserver.c', 'IFbind.c' and 'makefile'. The application code of the client and server is contained in the files 'client.f' and 'IFmanager.f'.

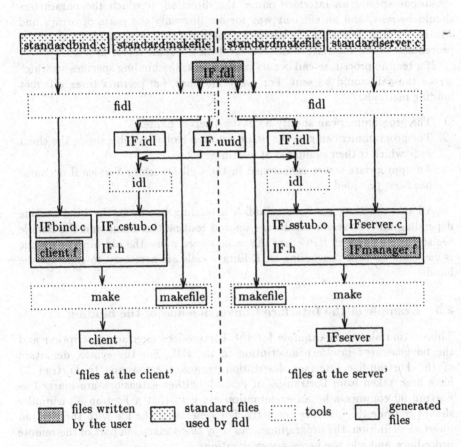

Fig. 1. Creating a distributed application with fidl, idl and make

3.2 The Programmer's Remaining Work

The programmer's remaining work is to deliver the originally non-distributed code which has been separated into client and server parts, the Fortran-like interface description, and little additional information for the binding.

For the separation, a purely procedural interface must be used: COMMON-blocks between client and server are not allowed because of the separated memory.

Function names as parameters and alternative returns from the distributed function are forbidden, too. Since the network between client and server is often the bottleneck in an application, the programmer should use a depression of data for the separation with as few as possible data transfer.

The Fortran-like interface description consists of the declarative part of the remote procedures with few extensions. Similar to the C-like IDL, these extensions specify an interface name, the direction in which the parameters should be sent, and an efficient way for sending only the parts of arrays and strings actually used over the network. The programmer must combine all the procedures to one interface which should form the same server process.

If a remote procedure call occurs in the client, the binding specifies to which server the call would be sent. For every interface, fidl permits three different binding methods:

1. The programmer can specify a constant server name.
2. The programmer can give the name within a global variable inside the client code which is then evaluated at runtime.
3. An appropriate server is searched in the Cell Directory Service if no name has been provided.

All three binding methods establish a binding handle in the bind routine depending on a server name. In the unbind routine this name and the handle are stored. If the next RPC uses the same server name the old binding handle is used and no time-consuming DCE library calls are necessary to generate the handle.

3.3 Example of the Interface Conversion and of the binding

This section shows an example for the Fortran-like interface description and the fidl-generated interface description in the IDL. For the syntax definition of the Fortran-like interface description language extensions to Fortran 77 have been taken from Fortran 90, if possible. Other extensions are marked as Fortran 90 comments by an exclamation mark so that a Fortran 90 compiler should compile the interface correctly. For generating the file with the Fortran interface definition, the programmer can copy the declaration part of the remote procedures and add the necessary declarations.

In the example the remote subroutine QREV calculates eigenvalues and eigenvectors of a hermitian matrix. The complex matrix EV holds the input matrix and the eigenvector matrix on output. The real vector EW returns the eigenvalues and N stores the dimension. The contents of the file 'QR.fdl' are as follows:

```
INTERFACE !QR
SUBROUTINE QREV( N, EV, EW )
INTEGER DIM
PARAMETER ( DIM = 200 )
INTEGER, INTENT(INOUT):: N
```

```
      COMPLEX*16, INTENT(INOUT):: EV(DIM,DIM) ! LASTDIM(N)
      REAL*8, INTENT(OUT):: EW(DIM)  ! LASTDIM(N)
      END
      END INTERFACE
```

The fidl-generated file 'QR.idl' includes the file 'QR.uuid' which contains the interface UUID (generated by the DCE tool uuidgen). A **typedef** defines the first parameter **N** as customized handle. The subroutine **QREV** is translated according to the description in Sect. 2.2.

```
[
#include "QR.uuid"
,version(1.0)
]
interface QR
{
typedef struct dcomplex { double re, im; } dcomplex;
typedef [handle] long hidce;
void qrev(
[in] hidce *N,
[in,out,length_is(*N)] dcomplex EV[200][200],
[out,length_is(*N)] double EW[200] );
}
```

In this example it can be seen, why it is a problem that IDL cannot specify more than one dimension of an array dynamically. If the number of elements in each dimension is $10, 2000 (= 200 * 10)$ elements of the matrix **EV** are transmitted while only 100 elements contain the necessary information.

In the following an extract of the fidl-generated binding file 'QRbind.c' will be listed. It is an example for a customized binding which uses the name of a server contained in the global variable **QRSERVER**. How to set this variable is described in Sect. 2.2. The status check calls have been omitted in order to shorten the listing.

```
#include <dce/rpc.h>
#include <pthread.h>
#include "QR.h"

#define LSTRING 80
unsigned_char_t nils[] = "";

char qrserver[LSTRING] = "";
static rpc_binding_handle_t old_handle;
static int old = 0;
static char old_server[LSTRING] = "";

rpc_binding_handle_t hidce_bind(dummy)
```

```
hidce dummy;
{
  unsigned_char_t           *string_binding;
  unsigned32                st;
  rpc_binding_handle_t      rpc_handle;

  /* if first call or server name was changed */
  if (old == 0 || strcmp(qrserver,old_server) !=0) {
    rpc_string_binding_compose(nils, (ndr_char *)"ncadg_ip_udp",
        (ndr_char *)qrserver, nils, nils, &string_binding, &st );
    rpc_binding_from_string_binding(string_binding, &rpc_handle,
        &st);
  }
  else  rpc_binding_copy(old_handle, &rpc_handle, &st);
  return rpc_handle;
}

void hidce_unbind(dummy, rpc_handle)
hidce dummy;
rpc_binding_handle_t rpc_handle;
{
    unsigned32            status;

    old = 1;
    /* store the handle */
    rpc_binding_copy(rpc_handle, &old_handle, &status);
    strcpy(old_server, qrserver);
    rpc_binding_free(&rpc_handle, &status);
}
```

For subsequent calls with the same server name in the global variable, the old fully bound binding handle will be used. Therefore, the execution of the bind routine and the call of the server will be essentially faster.

4 Conclusions

It has been shown that it is possible to use DCE from Fortran. The tool fidl gives the Fortran programmer an easy access to DCE and facilitates the generation of distributed applications.

Nevertheless, there are problems that arise only in a heterogeneous distributed environment. Some of the problems could be solved if the interface between Fortran and C would be standardized and if the compilers offered appropriate options (see Sect. 2.3).

In future the support for parallelization and secure communication will be included into fidl by the use of the DCE Threads and the DCE Security Service. Additionally, fidl will be accomodated to heterogeneous systems.

Acknowledgement

This work has been sponsored by the project distributed applications of the research network BelWue of the state of Baden-Württemberg and by the ODIN cooporation of the University of Karlsruhe and Siemens Nixdorf Informationssysteme.

References

1. Al Geist, Adam Beguelin, Jack Dongarra, Weicheng Jiang, Robert Manchek: PVM 3.0 - User's Guide and Reference Manual. Oak Ridge National Laboratory, Oak Ridge, Tennessee (1993)
2. Open Software Foundation: OSF DCE 1.0 - Introduction to DCE. Prentice Hall (1992)
3. Open Software Foundation: OSF DCE 1.0 - Application Development Guide. Prentice Hall (1992)
4. Ward Rosenberry, David Kenney, Gerry Fisher: OSF Distributed Computing Environment: Understanding DCE. O'Reilly & Associates Inc., 136-140 (1992)
5. John Shirley: OSF Distributed Computing Environment: Guide to Writing DCE Applications. O'Reilly & Associates Inc. (1992)
6. Werner Kollak: Distributing FORTRAN applications using DCE RPC. Report, Computing Centre, University of Stuttgart (1993)
7. Roland Laifer, Andreas Knocke: fidl - Ein Werkzeug zur einfachen Verteilung von Fortran-Anwendungen. Users' Guide, Computing Centre, University of Karlsruhe (1993)
8. Paul Buis, Wayne Dyksen, John Korb: Fortran Interface Blocks as an Interface Description Language for Remote Procedure Call. Proceedings of the Conference 'Programming Environments for High Level Scientific Problem Solving' in Karlsruhe, Computer Science Department, Purdue University, 119-120 (1991)

Converting Legacy FORTRAN Applications to Distributed Applications

T. Marll McDonald

Digital Equipment Corporation

Mail Stop LKG2-2/Z7

550 King Street

Littleton Massachusetts 01460, USA

e-mail address is M_MCDONALD@TERSE.ENET.DEC.COM

Abstract.

The standard Distributed Computing Environment (DCE) offering from the Open Software Foundation implies that the client side of a distributed application, the server side of the application, and the remote procedures in the server side must be written in C. Digital Equipment Corporation has enhanced its DCE product so that the client side of a distributed application and the remote procedures in the server side can be written in FORTRAN. This enhancement means that, within certain limits, existing FORTRAN applications can be converted so that compute-intensive subprograms execute on fast server machines. This paper explains the conversion process and its limits based on a comprehensive example.

1 Introduction

The DCE was designed for creating distributed applications and with no consideration for converting legacy (that is, existing) applications. Furthermore, the DCE documentation uses C as the only language for its examples of developing distributed applications. The examples always show the following high-level language components written in C:

- The client side of the application

- The server side of the application

- The remote procedures that reside within the server side of the application

Note

The interface definition language (IDL), that creates a network contract between the client and server sides of the application, closely resembles the C language.

An advantage of writing these three components in C is that they have full access to the routines in the remote procedure call (RPC) runtime library. For example, a client can call routine **rpc_binding_free( )** to free the memory used by a binding handle. The client can also call security routines in the DCE runtime library.

All of Digital Equipment Corporation's DCE products allow programmers to create distributed applications using the C and IDL languages.

Additional DCE documentation from outside the Open Software Foundation (see [1] and [2]) emphasizes using the C and IDL languages. However, Rosenberry and Kenney and Fisher [1] summarily answer the questions "Do I really have to use C?" and "Can I write DCE application programs in languages other than C? Please?".

2 Using FORTRAN—Overview

Digital adds considerable value to its DCE products. One addition allows developers of distributed applications to use, with relatively few exceptions, FORTRAN for the following high-level language components:

- The client side of the application

- The remote procedures that reside within the server side of the application

As of October 1993, Digital's DCE and FORTRAN combinations are:

- Digital DCE Developers' Kit for OpenVMS VAX and VAX FORTRAN (a superset of FORTRAN 77)

- Digital DCE for DEC OSF/1 AXP and DEC Fortran

The full Digital documentation for creating distributed applications with FORTRAN is in the product guides for these two DCE products (see [3] and [4]). (The README file, mentioned in the FORTRAN chapter of each product guide, is also helpful.) This paper goes beyond the product guides to summarize converting legacy FORTRAN applications. You should read the product guide for your Digital DCE product and this paper to obtain all available information.

This paper assumes the combination of VAX FORTRAN applications running on OpenVMS systems. All the principles in this paper apply to DEC Fortran applications running on DEC OSF/1 AXP systems.

A small number of C routines form the server side of an application. In fact, programmers frequently use the same C routines, with small changes to some arguments, as the basis of any server side.

As a result of this FORTRAN capability, programmers can both convert many existing applications to distributed ones and create new distributed applications. If much of a program's computations occurs in its subroutines, programmers can move the subroutines to a fast server machine. The result will be a distributed application that, overall, can execute much faster than the original nondistributed application.

2.1 Assumptions

The distributed FORTRAN applications assume that a name service database exists. They will always have automatic binding between client and server processes. The binding portions of the applications might execute a little slower than the binding portions of applications that use RPC runtime library routines to establish implicit or explicit bindings. Also, distributed FORTRAN applications cannot be multithreaded.

The distributed FORTRAN applications have no DCE security because of automatic binding selection and because the client sides, written in FORTRAN, cannot easily call routines—specifically including **rpc_binding_set_auth_info( )**—in the RPC runtime library. The applications can have DCE security if programmers establish implicit or explicit bindings and modify the client FORTRAN modules to call routines in the RPC runtime library. The modification could include a C module, callable from FORTRAN, that in turn calls routines in the RPC runtime library. The details of such a modification are beyond the scope of this paper.

2.2 Example

For an introductory example, consider the following skeleton of a FORTRAN program in source file MATH1.FOR.

```
      PROGRAM MATH1          ! In file MATH1.FOR
      REAL*4     A, B, C, D, E, F, G, P, Q
      INTEGER*4  M
      REAL*4     R, S, T, U, V, RESULT1, RESULT2
C     Assign values to the subprograms' arguments.
      CALL SUB1(A, B, C)
      CALL SUB2(D, E)
      CALL SUB3(E, F, G, M)
      CALL SUB4(P, Q)
C
      RESULT1 = FUNC1(R, S, T)
      RESULT2 = FUNC2(U, V)
C
      STOP
      END
```

Compiling separate source files MATH1.FOR, SUB1.FOR, SUB2.FOR, SUB3.FOR, SUB4.FOR, FUNC1.FOR, and FUNC2.FOR followed by linking their object files creates the traditional nondistributed application completely contained within executable file MATH1.EXE.

Suppose that subroutine subprograms SUB2 and SUB3, and function subprogram FUNC2, require much computation. Their execution time is almost all of the time MATH1.EXE requires.

You can convert this nondistributed application to a distributed application. It is based on the three source files MATH1.FOR, MATH1_IF.IDL, and MATH1_SERVER.C. The first file already exists; you must create the second and third files.

In the distributed application, source file MATH1.FOR and the six .FOR files containing the six subprograms remain unchanged with one exception. MATH1.FOR needs the additional statement

```
INCLUDE 'MATH1_IF.FOR'
```

(MATH1_IF.FOR is an interface (IF) file created by the IDL compiler from file MATH1_IF.IDL.)

MATH1_IF.IDL is the second source file in the distributed application. It contains the names of the three subprograms SUB2, SUB3, and FUNC2 plus descriptions of their arguments D, E, F, G, M, R, S, and T.

Its skeleton is next.

```
[
uuid(...)
version(1.0)
]
interface MATH1_IF
{
        /* The next four lines correspond to
           "CALL SUB2(D, E)" in MATH1.FOR.    */
        void SUB2(
                [in]   float D,
                [out]  float E
        )
        /* Two more subprogram names (SUB3 and FUNC2)
           and argument descriptions are here.           */
}
```

The third source file in the distributed application is MATH1_SERVER.C. Its skeleton is next.

```
/* This is file MATH1_SERVER.C                           */

#include "MATH1_IF.FOR_H"     /* Interface file created by
                                 the IDL compiler from
                                 source file MATH1_IF.IDL  */
main ()
{
        rpc_server_use_all_protseqs(...)
        rpc_server_register_if(...)
        rpc_server_inq_bindings(...)
        rpc_ep_register(...)
        rpc_ns_binding_export(...)
        rpc_server_listen(1,...)    /* First argument is
                                       always 1 to specify
                                       1 thread (= no
                                       multithreading).    */
}
```

In reviewing the three important files that comprise the distributed application, you can see that:

- The original source program file, MATH1.FOR, remains unchanged except for the addition of one statement. All files containing the local subprograms (SUB1, SUB4, and FUNC1) remain unchanged. These four files are part of the client side. All files containing the remote subprograms (SUB2, SUB3, and FUNC2) remain unchanged. These three files are part of the server side.

- The new interface definition file, MATH1_IF.IDL, reflects the subprograms that will execute on a remote computer and the arguments in the subprograms.

- The new server program file, MATH1_SERVER.C, remains largely the same, regardless of what the client program is. The major changes to the server program, as the client programs change, are the name of the .C source file and the #include statement for the generated header file.

Therefore, converting a legacy FORTRAN application to a distributed application often involves no rewriting of the statements in the application's source program files.

Note: One small change to the syntax of the command that invokes the IDL compiler enables much of Digital DCE's support for FORTRAN applications. The change is the addition of:

- option **-lang fortran** (universal syntax)
- qualifier /LANGUAGE=FORTRAN (OpenVMS DCL syntax)

  In the case of IDL file MATH1_IF.IDL, the respective commands that invoke the IDL compiler are:

- $ idl math1.idl -lang fortran
- $ IDL/LANGUAGE=FORTRAN MATH1.IDL

  Either command generates files MATH1_IF.FOR and MATH1_ IF.FOR_H for the FORTRAN client and C server source program units, respectively, to include.

3 Restrictions and Data Types

Two major restrictions apply to converting legacy FORTRAN applications to distributed ones.

COMMON blocks (labelled and unlabelled) cannot appear in both the main program and any of its remotely executed subprograms. This is because a COMMON block is one area of memory in one address space that separate program units address. In the model of remote procedure calls, two address spaces exist and a program unit can address only one of them. However, program units can contain a COMMON block if it is contained within the client process's .EXE file or within the server process's .EXE file.

The distributed program units must be in separate files. In terms of the previous example, individual files (with reasonable names) MATH1.FOR, SUB1.FOR, SUB4.FOR, and FUNC1.FOR existed. However, single file MATH1.FOR could contain the statements for MATH1, SUB1, SUB4, and FUNC1.

Similarly, the statements for SUB2, SUB3, and FUNC2 could be in individual .FOR files or in one .FOR file. The statements for SUB1 and for SUB2 must be in different .FOR files because SUB1 executes on a client computer and SUB2 executes on a server computer.

Digital's DCE product guides (see [3] and [4]) list all the restrictions.

Digital's DCE product guides also list the correspondence between FORTRAN data types and the data types in an IDL file. For example, a single-precision, floating-point number is declared in a FORTRAN program with a REAL*4 statement; it is declared in an IDL file with a float statement. You can see this by locating single-precision, floating-point variable D in file MATH1.FOR and in file MATH1_IF.IDL.

4 Overview of the Program Conversion Process

To begin a program conversion, look closely at the files comprising the application that you want to distribute. Make sure that none of the aforementioned restrictions applies. For example, you might have to extract program units from a .FOR file that contains more than one program unit and place them into separate files.

If you have an application with much of its communication between program units occurring by means of COMMON blocks, it could take an unreasonable amount of time to change it. For example, consider the following communication structure:

```
PROGRAM FOO
COMMON /COLD/ A, B, C
...
CALL FOO1()
...
END
```

```
SUBROUTINE FOO1()
COMMON /COLD/ X, Y, Z
...
RETURN
END
```

You cannot make subroutine FOO1 a remote procedure because it and main program FOO have the same COMMON block. You would have to rewrite the application based on the following communication structure:

```
PROGRAM FOO
...
...
CALL FOO1(A, B, C)
...
END

SUBROUTINE FOO1(X, Y, Z)
...
...
RETURN
END
```

Once your source files meet the restrictions listed previously, you can begin building the application. The following sections summarize the process in terms of the overview example. The summary is based on the traditional VAX FORTRAN program MATH1.FOR that runs on the OpenVMS operating system.

You can easily adapt the example's case of one main program, four subroutine subprograms, and two function subprograms to meet your specific needs.

5 Creating Distributed Source Program Units

This section presents the source program units that result at runtime in the creation of a client process based on MATH1.EXE and in the creation of a server process based on MATH1_SERVER.EXE. Remote procedures SUB2, SUB3, and FUNC2 execute within the server process in response to calls from within the client process.

The source program units are in three groups. They are the interface definition file MATH1_IF.IDL, the original seven .FOR files, and the server side of the distributed application in file MATH1_SERVER.C.

5.1 Interface Definition File

You must create the interface definition file—in this case, MATH1_IF.IDL. It usually changes considerably from one distributed application to another.

File MATH1_IF.IDL begins with the creation of a universal unique identifier (UUID). This number is an electronic fingerprint that identifies the interface across all time and space. A utility program creates a UUID. One version of the command, using OpenVMS DCL syntax, follows.

$ IDENTIFIER/GENERATE/OUTPUT=MATH1_IF.IDL

(Adding the qualifier /FORMAT=IDL would create a more complete version of MATH1_IF.IDL.)

MATH1_IF.IDL contains ASCII text such as

```
d1b14182-6544-11cb-ba12-08002b17908f
```

Editing MATH1_IF.IDL according to the current application can result in the following final version of the file. Note that argument G of subroutine SUB3 is both input to and output from this remote procedure.

```
[
uuid(d1b14182-6544-11cb-ba12-08002b17908f)
version(1.0)
]
interface MATH1_IF
{

void   SUB2(
[in]   float D,
[out]  float E
)

void   SUB3(
[in]   float E,
[in]   float F,
[in,out] float G,
[out]  long  M
)

float FUNC2(
[in]   float U,
[out]  float V
)
}
```

5.2 Original .FOR Files

The seven .FOR files remain unchanged with one exception. You must add the following statement to file MATH1.FOR:

```
INCLUDE 'MATH1_IF.FOR'
```

5.3 Server Program File

You must create the server program file—in this case, MATH1_SERVER.C. It usually changes little from one distributed application to another.

Creating MATH1_SERVER.C according to the current application can result in the following final version of the file. Note that the names of the subprograms for the three remote procedures and the names of the subprograms' arguments do not appear in the file. The information becomes part of MATH1_SERVER.EXE from MATH1_IF.IDL and from the commands to the FORTRAN compiler and the Linker. Locate the seven occurrences of the string "math1_if" (including upper case and comments) in MATH1_SERVER.C. The string has this value because of the name of the IDL file, MATH1_IF.IDL.

```c
/* This is file MATH1_SERVER.C                              */
#include <stdio.h>
#include <file.h>
#include <dce/dce_error.h>
#include "math1_if.for_h"  /* The IDL compiler created this
                              file from file MATH1_IF.IDL.  */

main()
{
error_status_t st;
rpc_binding_vector_p_t bvec;

/* Register all supported protocol sequences with the
   runtime.                                               */
rpc_server_use_all_protseqs(
    rpc_c_protseq_max_calls_default,
    &st
);
if (st != error_status_ok)
{
    fprintf(stderr, "Can't use protocol sequence - %s\n",
                    error_text(st));
    exit(1);
}
```

```
if (st != error_status_ok)
{
    fprintf(stderr,"Can't establish protocol sequences - %s\n",
                   error_text(st));
    exit(1);
}

/* Register the server interface with the runtime.         */
rpc_server_register_if(
    math1_if_v1_0_s_ifspec, /* From the IDL compiler; "v1_0" */
                            /* comes from the statement      */
                            /* "version(1.0)" in file        */
                            /* MATH1_IF.IDL.                 */
    NULL,
    NULL,
    &st
);
if (st != error_status_ok)
{
    printf("Can't register interface - %s\n", error_text(st));
    exit(1);
}

/* Get the address of a vector of server binding handles.  The
   call to routine rpc_server_use_all_protseqs() directed the
       runtime to create the binding handles.              */
rpc_server_inq_bindings(&bvec, &st);
if (st != error_status_ok)
{
    printf("Can't inquire bindings - %s\n", error_text(st));
    exit(1);
}

/* Place server address information in local endpoint map. */
rpc_ep_register(
    math1_if_v1_0_s_ifspec,
    bvec,
    NULL,
    (idl_char*)"FORTRAN Math1_Interface Test Server",
    &st
);
if (st != error_status_ok)
{
    printf("Can't register ep - %s\n", error_text(st));
}
```

```
/* Place server address information into the name service
   database. */
rpc_ns_binding_export(
    rpc_c_ns_syntax_default,
    (idl_char*)".:/FORTRAN_math1_if_mynode",
    math1_if_v1_0_s_ifspec,
    bvec,
    NULL,
    &st
);
if (st != error_status_ok)
{
    printf("Can't export to name service - %s\n",
            error_text(st));
}

/* Tell the runtime to listen for remote procedure calls.
   Also, FORTRAN cannot support multiple execution threads.   */
rpc_server_listen((int)1, &st);
if (st != error_status_ok)
    fprintf(stderr, "Error listening: %s\n", error_text(st));
}
```

6 Creating Executable Distributed Program Units

The previous section presented the three sets of source program files. This section explains how you use these files to create client .EXE and server .EXE files. At runtime, these files form the two processes that comprise the executing distributed application that relies on remote procedure calls.

6.1 Interface Definition File

You use the IDL compiler to create four files based on MATH1_IF.IDL. The command, using OpenVMS DCL syntax, is:

$ IDL/LANGUAGE=FORTRAN MATH1_IF.IDL

The four files that the IDL compiler creates are:

MATH1_IF_CSTUB.OBJ   (Client stub; for input to Linker)

MATH1_IF_SSTUB.OBJ   (Server stub; for input to Linker)

MATH1_IF.FOR   (For inclusion by client, MATH1.FOR)

MATH1_IF.FOR_H   (For inclusion by server, MATH1_SERVER.C)

6.2 Client Program File

The following commands, using OpenVMS syntax, create the client
.EXE file, MATH1.EXE. This file has the same name as the original
nondistributed executable file. Note that the subprograms that remain
local procedures appear in the commands.

```
$ FORTRAN MATH1.FOR
$ FORTRAN SUB1.FOR, SUB4.FOR, FUNC1.FOR
$ LINK MATH1.OBJ, SUB1.OBJ, SUB4.OBJ, FUNC1.OBJ, -
_$ MATH1_IF_CSTUB.OBJ, SYS$INPUT:/OPTIONS
SYS$SHARE:DCE$LIB_SHR/SHARE
<Ctrl-z>
```

6.3 Server Program File

The following commands, using OpenVMS syntax, create the server .EXE
file, MATH1_SERVER.EXE. Note that the subprograms that are remote
procedures appear in the commands.

```
$ CC MATH1_SERVER.C
$ FORTRAN SUB2.FOR, SUB3.FOR, FUNC2.FOR
$ LINK MATH1_SERVER.OBJ, SUB2.OBJ, SUB3.OBJ, FUNC2.OBJ, -
_$ MATH1_IF_SSTUB.OBJ, SYS$INPUT:/OPTIONS
SYS$SHARE:DCE$LIB_SHR/SHARE
<Ctrl-z>
```

7 Running the Distributed Application

The previous two commands to the Linker created client executable
file MATH1.EXE and server executable file MATH1_SERVER.EXE. The
following commands, using OpenVMS syntax, create the two processes
that, running together, form the distributed application.

```
$ ! Start searching for bindings in the name service database.
$ DEFINE/NOLOG RPC_DEFAULT_ENTRY -
_$ "./FORTRAN_math1_if_mynode"
$ ! Create the server process.
$ SPAWN/NOWAIT/INPUT=NL:/OUTPUT=MATH1_SERVER.LOG -
_$ /PROCESS=MATH1_SERVER RUN MATH1_SERVER.EXE
$ WAIT 00:00:10 ! Wait for the server process to start.
$ RUN MATH1.EXE ! Create the client process.
$ STOP MATH1_SERVER ! Stop the server process;
$ ! the client process has already stopped itself.
```

8 Summary Figure

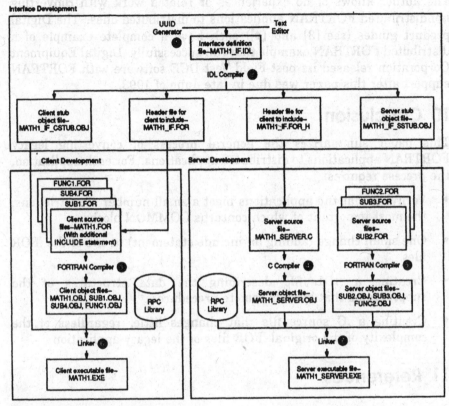

1. $ IDENTIFIER/GENERATE/OUTPUT=MATH1_IF.IDL

2. $ IDL/LANGUAGE=FORTRAN MATH1_IF.IDL

3. $ FORTRAN MATH1.FOR
   $ FORTRAN SUB1.FOR, SUB4.FOR, FUNC2.FOR

4. $ CC MATH1_SERVER.C

5. $ FORTRAN SUB2.FOR, SUB3.FOR, FUNC2.FOR

6. $ LINK MATH1.OBJ, SUB1.OBJ, SUB4.OBJ, FUNC1.OBJ, -
   $ MATH1_IF_CSTUB.OBJ, SYS$INPUT /OPTIONS
   SYS$SHARE:DCE$LIB_SHR/SHARE
   <Ctrl-z>

7. $ LINK MATH1_SERVER.OBJ, SUB2.OBJ, SUB3.OBJ, FUNC2.OBJ, -
   $ MATH1_IF_SSTUB.OBJ, SYS$INPUT /OPTIONS
   SYS$SHARE:DCE$LIB_SHR/SHARE
   <Ctrl-z>

ZK-6260A-GE

9 Experiences and Related Work

The author knows of no experiences or related work with converting nondistributed FORTRAN applications to distributed ones. The Digital product guides (see [3] and [4]) each have a complete example of a distributed FORTRAN example that ran successfully. Digital Equipment Corporation released its post-Field Test DCE software with FORTRAN support after this paper was due in late June of 1993.

10 Conclusion

This paper summarizes the general process of converting legacy FORTRAN applications to distributed applications. For each application, the process requires:

- Verifying that the applications meet a small number of restrictions, the most important of which concerns COMMON blocks

- One small change (adding an include statement) to one of the .FOR files

- Creating a .IDL file describing the data structures of the subprograms that become remote procedures

- Creating a .C source file that changes little, regardless of the complexity of the original .FOR files of the legacy application

11 References

1. Rosenberry, Ward, and Kenney, David, and Fisher, Gerry. *Understanding DCE*, Sebastopol, California, USA: O'Reilly and Associates, Inc., 1992.

2. Shirley, John. *Guide to Writing DCE Applications*, Sebastopol, California, USA: O'Reilly and Associates, Inc., 1992.

3. Digital Equipment Corporation. *Digital DCE Developers' Kit for OpenVMS VAX Product Guide*: 1993. Part number is AA-PV4FA-TE.

4. Digital Equipment Corporation. *Digital DCE for DEC OSF/1 AXP Product Guide*: 1993. Part number is AA-PZK4A-TE.

Using Standard Tools to
Build an Open, Client/Server Prototype

Bernard S. Hirsch

Hewlett-Packard Company
930 East Campbell Road
Richardson, Texas 75081 USA
(214) 699-4197
bernie@bsh3185.ssr.hp.com

Abstract. This paper will benefit software developers, MIS managers, and end users because it will help explain some of the practical benefits and implications of the Open Software Foundation (OSF) Distributed Computing Environment (DCE) in the context of a prototype application environment that was developed using the OSF DCE. The environment, a Financial Desktop, consists of a series of OSF Motif and MicrosoftWindows based clients which obtain information and resources transparently from a series of DCE based services, that reside on a range of heterogeneous computing hardware and software, including multivendor operating systems, networks, architectures, and databases. This paper will explain how DCE was used to implement this Financial Desktop in such a way that installed assets were leveraged, new technologies were integrated, and the focus of control for this environment has shifted away from a single hardware or software vendor. The use of the DCE remote procedure call (RPC) is discussed with respect to the role that it plays in this environment.

1 Introduction

The seemingly elusive goal, whereby the wealth of information and services in an enterprise is transparently accessible to end users on demand, is one about which much is written and discussed. Furthermore, there is an ever accelerating requirement to accomplish this in an open, distributed computing environment.

The first requirement that the computing environment be distributed is due to several ongoing trends in which an organization's business units, functions, data, users, and computing equipment are all now more and more distributed. The second requirement that the computing environment be open is resulting due to the need for these enterprises to control their own destiny. That is, they do not want to be reliant on a single hardware/software vendor when using information technology to help meet business goals. With the frantic pace at which new technologies, products, and methodologies are introduced nowadays, an enterprise would like to be in control to incorporate these to increase its competitive advantage, while still leveraging its many existing computing investments.

This paper describes how a prototype of an open, distributed application environment for stock brokers was created in which financial information and services are transparently accessible across a range of heterogeneous computing hardware and software, including multivendor operating systems, networks, architectures, and databases. Further, it is shown how this environment, the "Financial Desktop" (or FDT), was created using standard, off-the-shelf tools and technologies including the Open Software Foundation (OSF) Motif graphical user interface and components of the OSF Distributed Computing Environment (DCE). Using this open approach it is shown how installed assets are leveraged, new technologies can be integrated, and how the focus of control for the environment has shifted away from a single hardware or software vendor.

First the FDT user interfaces and services are described in detail, and the tools and technologies that were selected to implement the prototype are presented. Next, implementation details and experiences are discussed, followed by a summary of the prototype development. Finally, conclusions are drawn on the prototype environment and related work is introduced.

2 Description of the Prototype Environment

2.1 User View: Graphical User Interfaces

The setting for the prototype is an application environment for a stock broker, that consists of a series of hardware and software components working together in unison, so that the stock broker can very efficiently and transparently get his or her job done, by having presented at their desktop all of the needed information and services. The software components that come into play in this environment are a collection of services (or servers) and user interfaces (or clients).

From the stock broker's perspective, four (4) user interfaces "drive" the entire application (see Figures 1, 2). That is, all interaction with the system is done by simply entering some information -- such as the customer account number -- and then pressing a button in the graphical user interface (GUI). All of the information that the stock broker needs to know about that customer, for example, and the status of his or her investments are then automatically and transparently presented to the stock broker in the same unified interface. The four GUIs (e.g., clients) are described below. [1]

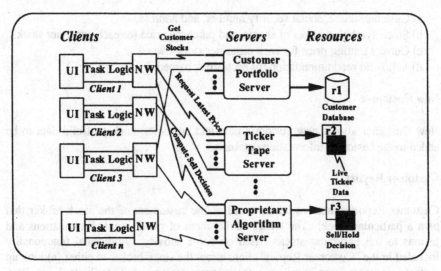

Fig. 1. FDT Client/Server Architecture

Marketminder

Using a "real-time" feed to the Dow Jones, Marketminder simultaneously presents the NYSE and NASDAQ ticker tape data (e.g., latest stock prices) and allows the stock broker to query the latest price for a particular stock. Specific information on each stock presented to the stock broker includes:

a) Stock Name.
b) Current, High, and Low stock prices for the current trading period.
c) Stock price change between the current and the previous trading periods.
d) Volume.

Financial Desktop (FDT)

FDT allows the stock broker to query a customer information database for individual customer and portfolio data. A heuristic function analyzes various data and suggests whether the time is right to sell particular customer stocks. Specific information presented to the stock broker includes:

a) Customer name, social security number, and address.
b) Stock symbol, number of shares, and purchase price for each customer stock.
c) Current trading price for each customer stock owned.
d) Sell/Hold recommendation for each stock owned.

New Customer

New Customer allows new customer data and customer stock portfolio data to be added to the customer information database.

Customer Report

Customer Report generates letters to all of the customers of the stock broker that own a particular stock. The letters advise them of pending recommendations and actions to sell particular stocks based on some activity. Additional functionality included in the "Customer Report" client allow the stock broker to either (a) look up a stock company name based on a Dow Jones stock symbol, or (b) look up Dow Jones stock symbol based on the company name.

2.2 Resource View: Backend Services

From a functionality perspective, a significant amount of processing is transparently occurring to be able to present all of this information to the stock broker within each of these four GUIs (see Figures 1, 2). A description of the various server data andoperations in this environment will help explain some of this processing. Five (5) servers provide access to all of the information and services within this prototype envirnoment. The five servers are described below. [2]

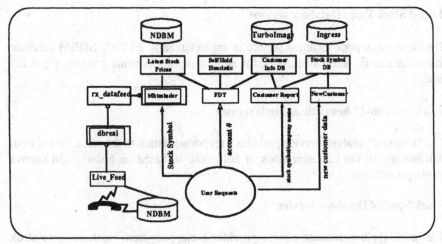

Fig. 2. FDT System Architecture

Customer Information Database service

The customer information database service is implemented as an MPE/iX TurboImage proprietary network database of customer information that manages the following data:

a) Customer account number, customer name, social security number, address, and number of stocks owned.
b) Stock symbol, number of shares, and purchase price for each customer stock owned.

Its server operations include:

i.) "Get customer data" retrieves all of the data in (a) above, given a customer ccount number.
ii.) "Get customer portfolio data" iteratively retrieves all of the stock information in (b) above for each customer stock held.
iii.) "Add new customer" adds the new customer and customer portfolio data [specified in (a) and (b) above] to the database.
iv.) Get customer owning stock" iteratively retrieves all of the customers that own a particular stock, given a specific stock symbol.

Dow Jones ticker tape service

The Dow Jones service provides a real-time feed to the latest NYSE and NASDAQ stock prices. Either the Telerate or Prodigy dialup services can be used as underlying services.

Latest Stock Price Database service

The latest stock price database service is implemented as a UNIX NDBM database that maintains the latest stock price for each of the stocks coming across the ticker tape.

Stock "sell/hold" heuristic analysis service

The "sell/hold" analysis service provides a recommendation to the stock broker as to whether to sell the customer stock or hold onto it, based on historic and current market conditions.

Stock Symbol Database service

The stock symbol database service provides a mapping from stock name to stock symbol, or from stock symbol to stock name, for each of the stocks in the NYSE and NASDAQ. This database service is implemented as a relational database using Ingres.

The following server operations are supported:

i) "Get stock symbol" retrieves the Dow Jones stock symbol, given the company name.

ii) "Get company name" retrieves the company name, given the Dow Jones stock symbol.

2.3 Hardware, Operating Systems, and underlying Network

The customer information database service is implemented using an existing TurboImage network database on a HP 3000 Series 900 business computer running the MPE/iX operating system.

The Dow Jones ticker tape service, latest stock price database service, and the "sell/hold" analysis service are all implemented on the following hardware and operating systems:

a) HP 9000 Series 700 workstations and Series 800 servers running the *HP/UX* operating system.

b) IBM RS/6000 Model 320 workstation running the *AIX* operating system.

c) DEC DecStation 3100 workstation running the *OSF/1* operating system.

d) DEC VaxStation 3100 running the *VMS* operating system.

e) DEC DecStation 5000/200 workstation running the *Ultrix* operating system.

f) Siemens-Nixdorf workstation running the *SINIX* operating system.

g) Groupe Bull workstation running the *BOS* operating system.

h) Stratus fault-tolerant minicomputer running its variant of the *UNIX System V Release 4* operating system.

The stock symbol database service is implemented using the Ingres relational database on the HP 9000/730 workstation running the HP/UX operating system.

The clients are implemented on the following platforms:

a) HP 9000 Series 700 workstations running the *HP/UX* operating system.

b) Intel 80386 PC's running Microsoft *DOS 5.0* and *Windows 3.0*.

The clients and servers are networked together using both Ethernet and IEEE 802.5 token ring, using TCP/IP and UDP/IP protocols.

4 Selected Tools and Technologies

The technologies and tools that were selected to be used to implement the Financial Desktop application environment are briefly discussed.

4.1 User Interfaces

Motif 1.1 using UIMX interface builder

It was decided that OSF Motif 1.1 was the primary GUI technology to be used to implement the client user interfaces. The familiar and intuitive appearance and behavior of an interface that complies with the Motif style guide empowers end users to be productive immediately. Further, UIMX (also called Interface Architect) from Visual Edge was selected as the interface builder for the Motif GUI, due to its ease of use, quick prototyping capability, and ability to generate pure Motif C code, so that portability to future client platforms can occur very easily. In addition, since very efficient C source code is generated, the prototype interface code can also be deployed quite appropriately in a production environment. [2]

Microsoft Windows 3.0 SDK

The Microsoft Windows 3.0 SDK was used as a secondary, supplemental GUI technology to develop MS Windows interfaces for two of the FDT clients that are to run natively on the PC platforms. Although MS Windows is not standard or open, it is the most popular GUI in use today on PCs, and thus it is strategic to many users.

4.2 Application Interoperability

DCE Remote Procedure Call (RPC)

It was decided that the OSF DCE RPC would be the enabling technology to be used to achieve application interoperability between the four FDT clients and the five FDT servers. The primary decision criteria here was the openness of DCE, as an enormously popular consortia-sponsored interoperability standard, and as such, the expectation that it will be increasingly available on almost every computing platform. For the prototype, early versions of DCE were used for x386 Windows-based PCs, Series 700 HP/UX workstations, and MPE/iX minicomputers, to achieve interoperability across the various FDT clients and servers.

Other decision criteria also affected the selection of the DCE RPC. First, the transparency, and scalability afforded the application developer and end users is much greater for applications architected with DCE RPC than with some of the less robust, pure messaging technologies. The familiar and intuitive local procedure call semantics empower software developers to be productive developing distributed applications with minimal training. Second, DCE RPC greatly simplifies the development of the clients and servers by automatically generating client and server stub (or "glue") C code. Most distributed computing complexities are taken care of automatically by the DCE RPC tools, generated stub code, and the DCE RPC library. Finally, DCE RPC can just as easily be used to implement a production worthy implementation as it can to achieve the prototype described in this paper, since this third generation technology was designed with these goals in mind. [3, 4]

5 Implementation Details and Experiences

5.1 Background

The FDT prototype was originally developed in early 1991 at HP Dallas using Network Computing System (NCS) 1.5.1 RPC and directory services on HP Domain/OS, HP/UX, and MPE/XL operating systems. NCS 1.5.1 supports a non-threaded distributed computing environment with a non-hierarchical name space with no additional security. [5] This technology was used because DCE, even in snapshot form, was not yet available from OSF. In addition, the UIMX Motif prototyper tool was used to generate the client user interfaces. Since one of the purposes of the prototype was to demonstrate heterogeneous distributed application interoperability and data access, some rudimentary visual feedback was added such that the screens of the various RPC servers "light up" green whenever an RPC request is serviced.

DCE Implementation

In July of 1991, OSF decided to use this prototype environment as the basis for its DCE demonstration to the support the September 17, 1991 worldwide availability announcement of DCE. As such, the FDT client and server code was reengineered o use DCE RPC and DCE threads, so that any DCE licensee can utilize the prototype environment for demonstration purposes, by building it with their DCE implementation. At the time of the implementation, the latest version of the DCE code was Snapshot 5, and the CDS security services were not yet mature enough to be used. The FDT code was ported to OSF/1 on the DECstation 3000 workstation and the HP PA-RISC 720 workstation, as the two primary development environments.

5.2 Utilization of DCE Core Components

RPC and Threads

The DCE remote procedure call was heavily utilized throughout the FDT environment to accomplish both distributed data access and distributed computation. Idempotent call semantics were used throughout, since read only access was he only requirement for the initial implementation. The new DCE RPC context handle feature was also utilized in the data access interfaces so that servers can maintain client state and clean up if necessary. The endpoint mapper daemon (rpcd) was not utilized since well-defined endpoints were used in the Interface Definition Language (IDL) files. This is poor implementation practice, in general, but was used here due to the infancy of the DCE software. Finally, the broadcast attribute was specified for the *send_tick()* procedure of the Dow Jones Ticker Tape Service, so that multiple MarketMinder clients/servers are instantly informed of new ticker tape activity.

Threads were not used explicitly in any client implementation except for a workaround that was required for some initializations that were not occurring in early DCE code. Threads were used implicitly by every FDT application server so that multiple clients are serviced simultaneously. It was for this same reason that context handles were also required. The manner with which multi-threaded servers are created in DCE is very straightforward and thread complexities are transparent to the developer.

Cell Directory Service Emulation

Part of the source code port from NCS to DCE included porting NCS location broker (*lb_$*) calls to the DCE NSI calls to register services into and lookup services from the Cell Directory Service (CDS). The original goal was to utilize the new automatic binding feature in DCE, whereby with no explicit programming on the part of the application developer, clients will automatically and seamlessly connect with their appropriate servers, and if those servers should fail, the clients will then automatically reconnect with other equivalent servers.

However, since the CDS portions of DCE were not ready at that time, a C library was created which emulated CDS (actually, RPC NSI) functionality and behavior. Conditional compilation allowed use of either the native DCE CDS or the emulation library, while providing transparency to the application. In addition to emulating the automatic binding and rebinding on server failure, the library randomly picks a server to which the client will connect, if there are multiple equivalent servers available. This will, in effect, amortize the various RPC calls -- and thus the RPC load -- across the various RPC servers, creating a simple form of RPC load-balancing.

The additional step of emulating CDS required the static definition of server locations (e.g., hostnames) for each interface definition in a configuration file. This is sufficient for a small, static prototype environment, but this methodology will not scale up to a larger, more dynamic, and more realistic environment.

What worked well here, in addition to the transparency to the application source code, is that clients compiled with the emulation library will interoperate with both servers compiled with the emulation library as well as with servers compiled with the true RPC NSI interface -- in effect, creating two namespaces. The converse is not true, however.

5.3 Demonstrating DCE Interoperability

Demonstrating distributed application interoperability and data access is not an intuitive concept. If application components are interoperating correctly, user requests are processed and results are presented. However, it is not obvious where events and actions are happening. As such, a not insignificant amount of effort went into providing visual feedback as part of the FDT environment, such that one is able to discern where distributed computing is occurring.

Specifically, the lighting up of screens was expanded to display specific vendor logos on both client and server machines. To accomplish this, an additional RPC parameter was added to each function signature in the FDT IDL files to denote either from which machine an RPC is being called or where it is being serviced:

```
[idempotent] void  db_stocks_open([in]     handle_t      h,
                          [in,out] long            *vendor_id,
                          [out]    file_handle_t  *fh);
```

The background of the server machine's screen, for example, will display a bitmap of the client's vendor logo (i.e., the HP or IBM logo) when the RPC is serviced. And the client GUI will display a bitmap of the server's vendor logo when the RPC completes. In this way, it is easy to determine between which machines an RPC is being rocessed. The user can then press a toggle button which alternates between visual feedback mode and "live" mode, in which RPCs can complete at full speed with no visual feedback.

5.4 Replicated Application Servers

FDT application servers were replicated to demonstrate the concepts of utilizing DCE for high availability, load balancing, and multiple custom server implementations in a distributed computing environment. High availability is demonstrated by unplugging the network connection from an FDT server during a series of RPC calls. Then, when the ensuing RPC is requested on that now unavailable server, the client delays slightly and then rebinds to another equivalent server, with its new server vendor logo displayed in the client GUI. In the FDT clients, the default RPC timeout was changed from about thirty-two (32) seconds to either four (4) or eight (8) seconds. Depending on which application server to which a client connects, a different server implementation is executed. For example, on a customer database lookup, either a Unix flat file is sequentially searched or an HP MPE TurboImage network database is searched.

In the prototype environment, the general replication problem is scaled down and some assumptions are made so that only application servers with no update interface can be replicated. If no assumptions are made -- which in a real application environment cannot be done -- either a replicated database or a distributed transaction processing (TP) monitor would be required for an application server managing a database. Since the former solution requires a monolithic, single database vendor implementation, the latter TP monitor solution would have been preferred, and the Transarc Encina technology would have been selected since it is already integrated with OSF DCE. In this scenario, an update is no longer a non-idempotent (i.e., at most once) operation, but instead is transactional (i.e., exactly once), in which each replicated database is updated with the scope of that single transaction. In effect, the Encina TP monitor solution is used to keep heterogeneous databases in synchronization by utilizing a two-phase commit across the various databases. [6]

5.5 Developers' Skills and Roles

Three developers were intially involved in the building of the FDT prototype. Each had different backgrounds and skillsets that were effectively utilized in creating different portions of the FDT clients and servers. It was found that a high degree of concurrent development was achieved in large part due to the inherent requirement to first define the client/server interfaces in the DCE IDL files. This is somewhat akin to defining an object in object-oriented analysis and design methodologies. DCE encourages the view of resources and their services as objects and methods, and the requirement that this definition be done first allows the DCE client and server developers to proceed independently once an IDL file is agreed upon.

The developer with legacy database management skills proceeded to create the customer database schema, load the database, and develop the interface routines (e.g., methods) that comply with the service's IDL file. In effect, this developer was encapsulating the legacy database with a layer of openness that any client developer could then access once given the IDL file -- and could access it without knowing its underlying implementation or even being knowledgeable about that implementation. A customer database object has now been created.

The developer with a background in GUI design was given the liberty to create a GUI that the user would be comfortable with, and as such dealt primarily with ergonomic and style-related issues. The third developer, in effect, acted as an integrator between the user interface object and the customer database object. This developers' role was to translate user interface messages (e.g., callbacks) into customer database messages (e.g., business transactions) and to create the necessary application logic to have the DCE client perform as desired.

These three roles are prevalent throughout the FDT clients and servers. When an object and its method already exists, it can simply be reused. This is the case, for example, in the Latest Stock Price Database with the *request_price()* method used by both the Marketminder client and again later by the FDT client. This reusability of server operations is one of the primary benefits achieved through thoughtful and generalized IDL design.

6 Summary of Prototype Development

Before the summary of the steps involved in developing the FDT prototype application environment is presented, it should be emphasized again that the selected tools and technologies promote parallel development of the application. The benefit of this approach is not only that the prototype will be produced more rapidly since it is produced in parallel, but also that the learning curve is minimized since current skillsets can be partitioned into these three pieces. That is, user interface experts can concentrate exclusively on building GUIs, and specific technology experts can deal solely with providing access to an underlying technology/service by developing the server and server operations. An expert on the TurboImage database can provide access to TurboImage data by implementing the previously agreed upon server operations, and a client developer can then access TurboImage data without having to know anything about the TurboImage database, by simply invoking the appropriate server operation.

The primary steps, then, that were followed to create the FDT prototype are outlined below:

1. **Client/Server Interface Definition:** For each service, the client and server software developers need to agree upon the client/server interface definition and its supported server operations. These server operations include the operation name, input and output parameters required by the operation, and possibly some additional, optional attributes. This information is specified in a DCE IDL file. These server interfaces and server operations were discussed above in "2 Description of the Prototype Environment". One of the server operations for the customer information database service is specified as:

   [idempotent] void get_customer_data(*[in]*   handle_t   h,
                                        [in]   char   acctNum[4],
                                        [out]   customer_t   *custData,
                                        [out]   long   *numStocks,
                                        [out]   long   *status);

2. **Interface Compilation:** For each interface, the DCE IDL compiler is executed taking the DCE IDL file as input and producing as output the respective client and server side stub code.

3. At this point, the client and server software developers can start their parallel developments, since their interface has now been formally defined.

   3a. **Server Implementation:** The server software developer will develop the implementation for the server operations agreed to in Step 1, above. In the implementation of each server operation, the server developer needs to manipulate the underlying resource as specified by the operation. This entails using TurboImage system calls, for example, in the customer information database server, to query or update this database. In the stock symbol service, the server developer needs to issue imbedded SQL statements to retrieve the requested stock symbol or company name.

   3b. **Client Implementation:** Development of the client application can also be done in parallel here, by first specifying the formal interfaces between the GUI and the application logic. What needs to be agreed to and specified up front are (1) the callback function names and parameters, so that the appropriate function can be called when the user presses a button, and (2) the names and types of the GUI objects/widgets so that the client software developer can read from and write back to the appropriate user interface elements.

3b-i. **GUI Development:** The user interface developer will create the appearance and behavior of the GUI and will link the user requests for action (e.g., button presses) with client application "callback" functions. The information presented in the user interfaces was discussed above in "2 Description of the Prototype Environment". UIMX was used here to create the Motif GUIs, and the Microsoft SDK was used to create the MS Windows GUIs.

3b-ii. **Client Application Logic:** The client software developer will develop the necessary "callback" functions and client application logic, and will call the server interface operations as needed. Also, the client software developer needs to read from and write to the appropriate graphical user interface elements. Some pseudo-code for the FDT client shows a sample of the flow of processing that occurs when the stock broker enters a customer account number and presses the "*OK*" button:

```
void ok_callback();
{
...
/*
 * First read the customer account number from the GUI.
 */
acctNum = XmTextGetString(textWidget);
...
/*
 * Next invoke the customer data "query" operation.
 * Note: This is an RPC call.
 */
get_customer_data(bindingHandle, acctNum, &custData,
                  &numStocks, &status);
...
/*
 * Then, put the customer data just obtained to the screen.
 */
XtSetValues(firstNameLabel, data1, count1);
XtSetValues(lastNameLabel, data2, count2)
XtSetValues(ssnLabel, data3, count3);
XtSetValues(addrLabel, data4, count4);
...
}
```

7 Conclusions

A prototype client/server financial application for stock brokers was developed using standard, off-the-shelf technologies and tools -- OSF Motif and OSF DCE. The technologies and tools that were used to develop the application were selected primarily due to their openness, standards compliance, and their capability to also be deployed in a production environment. By prioriting openness as the highest decision criteria, it is shown how installed assets can be leveraged, new technologies can be integrated, and how the focus of control for the environment can be shifted away from the vendor and back to the customer, where it belongs. By using standard compliant APIs that are portable to many different systems (PCs, MPE/iX, and Unix), by using standard compliant protocols that are interoperable with other vendors' tools, technologies, and implementations, by using tools and technologies that are widely available by tens and hundreds of vendors, and by using tools and technologies that scale well from a prototype application to a fully deployed application, an enterprise can start to regain control of its computing destiny.

Specifically, it is seen that by using these open technologies, the investment in installed assets, such as the TurboImage database, can be protected, and in fact enhanced, by opening up access to the data to the entire enterprise. In this fashion, where the enterprise's business units can use this technology to methodically open up the access to their business data and services to anyone who needs to use them, business processes can start to be better optimized and reshaped.

It is also seen how new technologies, such as the Ingres relational database (and in the future, object-oriented databases and audio and video), can then also be easily added to the environment for the additional benefits of those latest technologies.

Finally, the client/server development process has demonstrated to lend itself very nicely to rapid and effective systems development, in part by allowing the capability for parallel software development, in part because the development tools (the DCE IDL compiler and the UIMX interface builder) automatically generate much of the source code, and in part because if the services are developed in a generalized manner, they can be reused many times over by many new clients.

8 Related Work

The FDT prototype is currently being used as an educational tool to help demonstrate some of the features and benefits of OSF DCE. An HP customer education course entitled "Hands-On With Open, Client/Server Technologies" (HOW) has been developed to give information technology professionals a hands-on exposure on what is involved in developing a client/server solution using true, standards-based tools and technologies, such as OSF Motif and OSF DCE. The class is four (4) days long -- half lecture and half lab -- and utilizes the FDT prototype for the lab exercises. Two new clients and one new server have been added to the FDT environment in the development of this class to allow students to be added as customers, to allow customer reports to be generated, and to allow a two-way mapping between stock symbol and company name. [7]

Several other enhancements to the FDT prototype are currently planned or are already completed. The first enhancement is introduced in "5.4 Replicated Servers" in which the Transarc Encina TP monitor will be used to keep the replicated FDT application servers in synch with each other by the XA-compliant two-phase commit protocol. If it is determined that this significantly degrades interactive performance, then the Encina RQS technology will also be used to batch transactions into persistent queues for later processing. [6]

Another enhancement request is for better use of the DCE core components including rpcd, cdsd, and secd (for authentication, integrity, and privacy). Better illustration of the distributed computing is also planned, in particular with the use of multimedia features such as audio on the clients and servers. Additional functionality such as the ability to track and analyze specific stocks or customer portfolios over a period of time is planned with the purpose of better illustrating the benefits of reusability of DCE server interfaces.

References

1. Hirsch, B.: Building an Open, Client/Server Application, Interact, Volume 12, Issue 10, 100-115 (October 1992)
2. HP Interface Architect 2.0 Developer's Guide, Hewlett-Packard Company (1993)
3. OSF DCE Application Development Guide, Volumes I and II, Open Software Foundation (1993)
4. OSF DCE Application Development Reference, Open Software Foundation (1993)
5. Lyons, T.: Network Computing System Tutorial, Prentice-Hall (1991)
6. Spector, A.Z.: Preparing for Distributed Computing and Open OLTP, Transarc Corporation (1992)
7. Hands-On with Open Client/Server Technologies, HP Computer/Instrument Systems Training Course (1992)

Pilgrim's OSF[1] DCE-based Services Architecture[2]

J. David Narkiewicz   Mahesh Girkar   Manoj Srivastava
Arthur S. Gaylord   Mustafizur Rahman

Project Pilgrim[3]
University of Massachusetts
Amherst MA 01003

Abstract

Within a heterogeneous distributed computing environment, it is necessary to integrate services, such as printing and mail, that are scattered throughout the environment and which perform single logical tasks. This paper discusses a general purpose architecture which provides a framework for designing complex multi-user systems capable of interfacing with these services. The merits of this generalized approach are reflected in the following two case studies of applications being developed by the University of Massachusetts' Project Pilgrim: PIMS (Pilgrim Interface to Mail Systems) and PIPS (Pilgrim Interface to Print Systems). These designs incorporate the principles of this architecture and utilize OSF DCE.

PIPS permits the uniform access of a heterogeneous system's printing facilities and provides support for printing complex multi-document jobs. This interface is platform independent, supports flexible mappings between logical and physical printers and permits all printing resources to be visible throughout the cell. ISO DPA is used for specifying print job attributes and non-DCE systems are also supported. PIMS similarly allows distributed mail clients to work directly with a set of uniform, system independent primitives. This interface remains consistent regardless of the mail environment/system-architecture native to the client or that used to store a given user's mailbox and folders. These primitives allow multiple mailboxes to appear as a single unified (coherent) postbox. This enables operations to be performed on individual messages or folders residing on several different machines regardless of underlying mail protocol, the user's present host, hardware or operating system. PIMS supports variable format messages (multimedia) including executable code, alternate display/audio forms, and message indirection. Various levels of mail access are supported on clients ranging from laptop PCs to supercomputers.

1   Introduction

A computing environment which is distributed introduces a new paradigm for designing applications. At the same time, managing such applications poses new challenges for the designer. Techniques for handling these issues are being developed and should reflect

---

[1] OSF is a trademark of Open Software Foundation

[2] Developed at Project Pilgrim, University of Massachusetts, Amherst

[3] Project Pilgrim is partially funded in part by Digital Equipment Corporation, Hewlett-Packard Company, and University of Massachusetts

the fact that such environments are likely to be heterogeneous in nature. Services on these heterogeneous platforms have traditionally relied on proprietary standards and hence frequently do not facilitate interoperability. Additionally, these services have not been designed to utilize DCE, nor can they be replaced with equivalent, DCE-aware services without substantial modification. Given the importance of these services, a primary task in a distributed environment is to insure their integration and also to provide a means of managing these (now distributed) applications in a standard conformant fashion. By its very nature, DCE is designed to provide a means by which to simplify access to services within a heterogeneous environment, otherwise it would not fulfill its purpose.

A consistent architecture allows a number of applications to pool knowledge and techniques for addressing issues associated with a distributed environment. There are numerous ways that an application designer can choose to resolve these problems. As is usually the case, there is a tradeoff between the generality of a solution and the number of issues that it can address.

This paper addresses the previously discussed issues by reviewing the basic client/server model within the context of a distributed environment (Section 2). Section 3 presents the Pilgrim Services Architecture, which is a uniform approach to developing complex client/server applications. Following this section the PIPS (Section 4) and PIMS (Section 5) case studies are presented. Utilities developed by Project Pilgrim and lower level DCE design issues are disscussed in Section 6. The conclusion (Section 7) evaluates both case studies within the context of the other tools and utilities being developed at Project Pilgrim.

2 Beyond the Basic Client/Server Model

Project Pilgrim has been developing OSF/DCE applications at the University of Massachusetts for the last three years. This suite of tools provides services to users in a distributed environment and the facilities the administration of these tools. Furthermore, the integration of legacy applications and personal computers into the OSF DCE environment are also goals for the project. Pilgrim's environment includes PCs, mainframes, workstations and super-computers. Nodes are connected by LAN's and are organized in a loose knit hierarchy based on administrative, departmental and research group. The University is a diverse environment (as is any 5000+ computer shop) in that system management must address the restrictions associated with the business-oriented, heavily security conscious administrative community while adapting to the flexibility and openness inherent in an academic/research-oriented institution. In this section, we describe our experiences with working in such a computing environment, and the common methodology, or architecture, that has evolved as we developed some of the more complex applications.

The basic client–server model as described in [1, 2, 3] works very well for simple applications. However, for complex applications, especially those which attempt to connect multiple service providers to several users, this model is inadequate. Furthermore, under this scheme, managing such an application would be difficult. If we had n users and m services, this would potentially require $n \times m$ client–server connections. However, if we simply introduce a single extra layer, then this number reduces to $n + m$. Extending applications by adding a new service is simpler in the latter scheme that is, it requires just one new connection instead of the m connections required in the former scheme. Managing the application and the services it interfaces to is also simplified, since the new layer could provide a management API as well as information caching and logging.

By adopting the basic Client/Server model, the Server module has to cater to the disparate access methods required by the different services. This constitutes the access method dependent part of the Server. The Server also contains a common application specific portion that remains independent of the service being accessed. Similarly, the client module needs to provide various styles of user–interfaces, and it also contains an application specific (i.e., user–interface independent) part. This motivates us to consider partitioning the Server as well as the Client, into two components — one of which deals with the intricacies of accessing the service or a particular style of user–interface, and the other more stable component, which is dependent upon the needs of the application.

For example, printers may be available at different locations, and accessing them from a VMS machine differs considerably than accessing them from a UNIX machine. Furthermore, even different flavors of UNIX, such as BSD or SYS V, have different print interfaces, lpr and lp respectively. Similarly, electronic mail poses similarly complexities. RFC 822 specifies a format for Internet text messages as [4] does for multimedia style messages. Such standards can conflict with proprietary mail environments (such as certain PC and mainframe based systems). Mail access can also vary from being system-based (VMS) to file/directory-based as are most Unix variants. Thus application design has to account for such diversity, and provide a homogeneous interface to access these services. A similar diversity is present in designing a user interface to the application. The style of the interface can vary widely, often on a platform or in a site-specific manner, and regardless of graphical capabilities inherent in an architecture, a command-line interface (CLI) to an application is an important consideration. Whether an interface is graphical or command-line in nature, this module should be small and lightweight in order to enable small machines to interact with the application.

For some applications, context has to be maintained between user requests, and some applications need a common context to be maintained for all users. In the latter case and especially if this common context is modifiable, maintaining it in the user–interface module would cause inconsistency. Further more, this context may contain local information, that is, information that may not be accessible from any one point in the environment. Any transient Client (*e.g.*, a command line interface) may not be able to maintain this context even for subsequent user requests. Thus, for certain complex applications, a single layer in between the two modules (obtained by splitting the Client and Server as described above) is inadequate (for example, the single layer proves to be a bottleneck, or the information that needed to be cached may not have been available at any one location in the environment).

There were a number of other issues of concern, such as integrating security, ease of management and control, flexibility and configurability, and the potential for providing as well as accessing services on platforms that did not support OSF DCE. All the issues previously discussed are addressed by the Pilgrim Services Architecture.

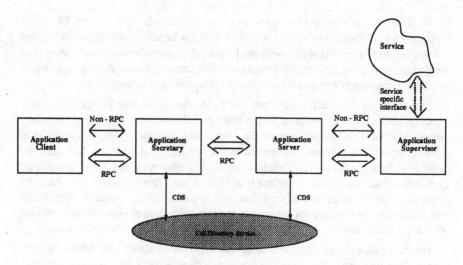

Figure 1: Components of the Architecture and their Interaction

3 Pilgrim Services Architecture

The services architecture adopted by Project Pilgrim is general enough to accommodate most of the applications that seek to provide an interface for existing services to multiple users. This architecture consists of four components — *Client*, *Supervisor*, *Secretary* and *Server*. It should be noted, that Client and Server components are not to the same as those referred to using DCE terminology in [1, 2, 3]. Any of these components may be DCE Servers of Clients in their own right. The Client and Supervisor form the *outer layer* of the applications while the Secretary and Server comprise the *inner* or *core layer*.

A particular application may choose to collapse one or more of these components as per their individual requirements. More over, the architecture does not impose any restriction on the number of instances of any component of an application, leaving those considerations to the application designer and site administrator. It is envisaged that the most common configuration of an application will be a single (or small number of) Server; a number of Supervisors (dependent on the accessibility and the number of services available); multiple Clients (typically a small number per user); and a number of Secretaries depending upon various factors (such as, complexity of the application, local site configuration, etc).

3.1 Inner Layer

The inner layer components are designed to be system independent, relatively stable and robust, and may provide various levels of caching. Additionally, a management API should be provided by these components.

The Server is the core of the application and represents the primary mechanism in an implemention. If necessary, it should cache any global information pertaining to the application. The Server should receive requests from one or more Secretaries and dispatch it to one or more Supervisors, possibly returning the results of the transction back to the Secretaries. The dispatching needs to be done only if the service needed is not local to the host running the Server. Additionally, the server interacts with the Supervisor using an application specific common protocol, thus avoiding host specific dependencies needed to access the service. The Server should implement all the dynamic aspects of an application, such as dispatching requests to Supervisors according to their priorities (if any); choosing the best Supervisor to service every request if more than one is available; and implementing an application specific queueing mechanism for the requests.

The Secretary acts as the liaison between the Client and the Server. Unlike the Server, the Secretary may cache *local* information that may not be accessible to the Server or Client specific information, which could help provide a context between subsequent Client calls or in between calls from different Clients. It is meant to take over some of the mundane tasks such as authenticating a Client thus relieving the Server from these duties. The Secretary may be responsible for setting up the Client request. It should handle any translation, if required, to and from the internal application specific common protocol to the format required by the Client.

Note that no assumption is made regarding the nature of the Clients which interface to a Secretary; these need not be just users, but could be parts of a different application. For example, in a mail application, its Server could connect to a local Secretary of a print application in order to print a mail message on behalf of a mail user. This makes it easier for the mail application to use the print services in the environment, as it obviates the need to know the locale of a Server responsible for printing, thereby leaving that job to the Secretary of the print application.

In summary, dividing the inner layer into a Secretary and a Server is essential for the following fundamental reason: The task load of several complex applications can be partitioned into a static and a dynamic part. The static part could vary depending upon the site. By making the Secretary responsible for the static portion, and the Server for the dynamic part, a flexible organization of the application can be achieved in the environment.

3.2 Outer Layer

The outer layer should encapsulate all the operating system or environmental dependencies. The components of this layer should be small and lightweight, hence enhancing the portability of the application. The communication between the inner and outer layers should use non-DCE transport.

The Supervisor acts as a liaison between the Server and any external service that the application interacts with. It is essentially a wrapper around the host specific interface to the service, hiding the intricacies of accessing this service from the rest of the application. If required, the Supervisor can translate the information provided by the service to an application specific common protocol and vice-versa.

The Client serves as the user interface to the application and should use the interface provided by the Secretary to request a service. Using this interface, a Client may be designed to provide a variety of user interfaces that are as simple as a command line interface or as complex as a graphical user interface.

4 Case Study: PIPS

PIPS, Pilgrim Interface to Print Systems, is a system designed to uniformly interface with the various facilities for printing within a distributed environment. The fundamental premise is not to rewrite the existing print systems, but to provide a homogeneous interface to them. PIPS therefore fits the profile of applications that could benefit from this architecture.

4.1 PIPS: Pilgrim Interface to Print Systems

The fundamental object processed by PIPS is a "job". By definition a job is a collection of documents (files) to be printed. For example, a teacher in a school might use a job in order to print a set of materials needed for a class. This job could consist of documents such as exams or a syllabi. PIPS allows users to print these materials while maintaining a permanent list of jobs.

Using PIPS, the user can specify ISO DPA (*ISO DP10175 Document Printing Application (DPA) Draft Service and Protocol Standard*) options for the job as a whole or for any of its individual documents thus hiding the vagaries of the individual print system commands from the user. The ISO DPA options, as well as their translations to the format of the print system specified is performed by storing this information in the Cell Directory Service.

PIPS provides a notion of logical printers. A number of logical printers may map to a single physical printer. Information of this map is also stored in the Cell Directory Service. Access control for each of these logical printers is implemented as part of PIPS.

4.2 PIPS Design

PIPS has four components a prescribed in the architecture description in Section 3. We begin with a description of the outer layer components. The supervisor in PIPS dispatches pre–formatted print requests to the print system. It queries the print system upon request from the server about the status of the print system queue, parses the output, and returns it in a format understood by the server.

The client connects to a secretary to send a job for printing, or to find the status of submitted jobs, or the status of a logical printer. Currently, using the interface provided by the secretary, two clients have been developed — one is a simple *tty* client, and the other is a complex client which uses Motif [4].

The server manages jobs submitted for printing. It performs printer or queue specific translations needed to print the documents in a print job. For example, if the number of copies for a document to be printed is "2" (specified by ISO DPA option *copy–count*), and the logical printer for this document is provided by print system "lpr" of UNIX, then the

---

[4] Motif is a trademark of OSF.

server translates this option to the lpr option "-#2". In lpr, "-#" is an option for printing several copies of a document. The server also keeps track of the progress of the information and statistics regarding jobs on a queue.

The secretary manages static description of the jobs belonging to a singe user. It also aids a user in creating new jobs and modifying existing ones. It reads valid job and document ISO DPA options from the Cell Directory Service and caches this information, which could be used to validate requests from any client that connects to it.

The secretary authenticates the user submitting the request and sends the user's identity to the server with this and every request. The server verifies that all requests to it come from an authenticated secretary. Once it authenticates the secretary, it trusts the user identity provided to it, and uses that information to implement access control on the logical printers. Similarly, the supervisor verifies the server before dispatching the request. PIPS uses OSF DCE Security core component to perform authentication and implement the access control.

Thus, a print request from a client, undergoes some preliminary checking at the secretary (validation of ISO DPA options), is sent to the server, which expands the job into its constituent documents and provides printer specific translations for each document. These documents in turn are sent to the corresponding supervisor which submits them to the underlying print system. The progress of this job is monitored by the server and the final status is sent back to the user. Pilgrim Event Notification Service[5] is responsible for returning this status.

PIPS simplifies the management of the print services within a given environment. For example, to allow or remove access to a new printer, the administrator adds a logical printer in the Cell Directory Service. The printers is then mapped to the new printer by storing such information as the print system to be used, the translations (or pointer to these) from ISO DPA options to the print system specific options, the supervisor that needs to be contacted for this printer, etc. Then, by using the server management API, the server is refreshed, so that any new request to this printer can now be serviced.

5 Case Study: PIMS

PIMS, Pilgrim Interface to Mail Systems, is designed to simplify mail access within a distributed environment. Each user is no longer described as a "username/address" pair but simply by the user's principal name – this despite an extensive host environment with decentralized control and policy enforcement. The principal name maps directly to their *primary mailbox* which is stored in the Cell Directory Service. For a given user, this mailbox represents where all PIMS mail is delivered as well as mail from outside the cell. This mailbox specification can be changed only by the system administrator. Given the loosely structured nature of the University's LAN hierarchy, which is similar to that of any compartmentalized corporation or organization, mandating a policy of a single mailbox per-user is unenforceable. Within the environment, PIMS allows the typical user (such as the 15,000 undergraduates at UMass) to simply receive all mail at their *primary mailbox* and hence literally have a centralized mail repository.

Also associated with each user is a pointer to a set of configuration files which includes the PIMS setup file. This file allows configuration information to be standardized across all platforms, allows all incorporated mail environments to fully support folders and aliases, and provides a locale in which users can store mailbox locations in addition to their *primary mailbox*. This later feature allows transparent folder/message migration across platforms and mail systems. Setup information of a more general nature is also stored at this configuration file.

Given PIMS's generic representation, entire sets of user mailboxes can be migrated to new hosts/mail-formats without the user's knowledge or being affected; thus backups, system upgrades, maintenance and fault-tolerance are readily supported. Related to this, privacy issues exist in the event of an underlying mail system storing folders in "user-space" as opposed to "system-space," but these are political rather than technical. PIMS use of certain aspects of the MIME standard saves disk space in that messages to multiple users (especially broadcast style messages) can be shared through indirect addressing. Also a policy of user transparent data compression can be instituted. Image and graphical messages can similarly be retrieved from a set of such libraries or user space such as when a user's picture is included with each message they may send. This feature will be further advantageous given the development of special purpose architectures, storage devices and algorithms for handling such data.

5.1 Rationale

Regardless of their size, many computing environments inevitably support legacy mail systems. The reasons for maintaining multiple mail protocols and access tools are numerous – most notably the cost of retraining personnel and user resistance to change. Obviously ensuring that individual mail systems can intercommunicate with each other and the maintenance of user interfaces is itself expensive. Resolving misaddressed mail sent within the local environment, insuring that a diverse set of mail systems are properly backed-up and user migration given system modifications can be daunting tasks given the diversity and backwards compatibility requirements inherent in supporting legacy mail systems. With messages potentially arriving for a single user at multiple locales and under separate protocols, a variety of *ad hoc* schemes have been introduced in order to provide some sense of system coherency. Users seeking to maintain access to their preferred mail reader often use "forwarding" or simply "login" to each host where their mail resides. Forwarding requires constant maintenance and is susceptible to cyclic forwarding, while users who maintain multiple mailboxes face both the possible task of mastering multiple interfaces as well as the reality that crucial messages can be left unread in infrequently accessed mailboxes.

Additionally, mail setup information must be maintained independently on each platform and must be changed with each system upgrade. A policy mandating a single-user/single-mailbox is often too restrictive considering it is difficult to compartmentalize certain anomalous classes of users and that users have traditionally utilized their mailboxes as folders or as temporary file storage depending on such factors as the quota allotted them on a given system. It is recognized that certain environments can maintain site-wide aliases, but this assumes that a single mailbox is enforceable and that the entire environment is capable of accessing alias tables.

Pilgrim Interface to Mail Systems (PIMS) addresses and offers solutions to the previously mentioned shortcomings inherent in many current computing environments' mail systems. Additionally, its use is not precluded within environments either supporting only a single mail protocol/accessing-tool or where users are associated with only a single mailbox. Using the Distributed Computing Environment (DCE), PIMS provides a set of primitives designed to enable system independent access to numerous mail systems. It is neither another new mail protocol nor yet-another-graphical-interface to mail, rather PIMS is a generic representation that masks mail locale and format from the user. Within this environment, each mailbox appears as if it resides on the host the user is accessing without requiring the user to log into remote hosts. Similarly the folders associated with each mailbox are also visible and appear as if they reside on the present host. Mail setup information is also represented by this general format and hence regardless of the underlying mail environment this information is consistent and requires no modification in the event of system modification or upgrading.

From the system managerial level, PIMS provides a logical methodology and framework for organizing the potentially thousands of mail users within a cell and allows for enforcement and "persuasive" migration toward a truly centralized single mailbox. A single-mailbox/single-user environment is preferable for many reasons: it more readily facilitates fault-tolerance through replication; simplifies many mail addressing formats and hence reduces misaddressed mail; decreases the chance of stale messages; makes indirectly referenced message bodies and shared message bodies simpler to implement; and can aid in backing up procedures and enforcing quotas for various mail systems.

The benefit of PIMS's independent representation is that only a single translator is required in order to incorporate a new mail format into the environment. This is because once a message has been converted to its PIMS representation, a translator for any mail format can be used to convert it into that representation. PIMS performs the lowest level mail manipulations using the local mail environment and hence can rely on lightweight translators making conversion all the simpler. Once in the PIMS general form, any mail system can communicate with any other supported by the PIMS environment by simply converting between generic and native formats. This approach is superior to translating directly between each format because for accessing N mail systems only N translators are required compared with N^2. Furthermore, this generic representation is designed to handle non-text (multimedia) mail messages sent under the MIME protocol[4]. Facilitating this is that message bodies are not viewed as a single entity but are composed of multiple parts and text need not be necessarily 7-bit American ASCII, but can be any width representation. The generality inherent in PIMS insures that in the future, it will be capable of handling alternate multimedia standards once they are established.

PIMS is further enhanced in that the Application Programmer Interface (API) provided for communicating with mail system front- ends is asynchronous. This non-blocking nature greatly enhances any mail client's ability to optimize it's performance through multi-threading. In order to achieve coherency certain objects (mailboxes, folders and messages) are locked and restrictions placed on write, rename and delete operations. Despite these requisite constraints, a significant amount of low-level parallelism can be exploited.

5.2 The PIMS Architecture

PIMS unifies mail within its diverse environment through a three level architecture: *mail client*, *communications server* and *mail server*. It should be recognized that mail differs from printing in that, except for sending an individual message, accessing electronic mail typically involves a multi-command session and that in order to unify scattered mailboxes, potentially three RPC layers are required. In order to reduce the number of levels requiring communications across the network the client and secretary portion have been combined into a single module, the *mail client*. The client portion accesses the secretary (acting as a local secretary) through the PIMS provided API. The *communications server* acts as a global secretary for multiple clients. It accesses *mail servers* which are composed of an applications server and an applications supervisor. On a lower level, each of the three fundamental PIMS components acts as both a DCE client and server. This asynchronous architecture allows data requests to be spawned by the *mail client* and hence allows continued operation rather than the synchronous waiting for data or status to be return. This organization is specific enough to suit this particular application's needs and general enough to be applied to other client-server based applications.

A "typical" PIMS session sees a user access their preferred mailer/mail-reader which has been modified to interface with the PIMS API, hence providing seamless access to a distributed mail environment (see Figure 2). This action activates a PIMS *mail client* which accesses the Cell Directory Service (1). This globally accessible database provides a profile on the user and a binding handle to a *communications server* (2). The *mail client* then initiates a session with the *communications server* by passing it a list of *auxiliary mailboxes* a user seeks access to (3). This server is responsible for determining the validity of a user and determining their *primary mailbox* by accessing the Cell Directory Service. The Cell Directory Service also provides binding handles so that the *communications server* can access the *mailbox server* associated with each mailbox a user seeks access to. Once this information has been determined, the *communications server* requests information pertaining to each mailbox (4). Each *mailbox server* contains a set of back-end interfaces which translate between PIMS's generic representation and the local mail format (5) (e.g. Unix, X.400, VMS). These back-end interfaces provide the requested information which is passed back to the *communications server* (6) followed by to the *mail client* that initiated the request (7).

5.3 Fundamental Components

5.3.1 Mail Client:

A typical *mail client's* access to the Cell Directory Service allows it to interpret multimedia messages. Host profiles contain each host's abilities in system independent form. Using this information each multimedia message can be accessed based on the constraints placed on it due to the viewing/audio environment it is accessed from. In support of this information source, a set of interfaces exist between the *mail client* and the local host, which permits generic queries as to each host's capabilities to be made, this augments the information stored in the Cell Directory Service.

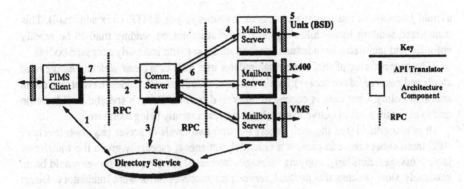

Figure 2: PIMS Overview

The standard *mail client* is multi-threaded, with a client portion making *command* requests to the *communications server*. Such commands are detached from the main thread through a threadpool (a virtually infinite pool of threads). Each *mail client* also contains a server portion "listening" for messages sent by the *communications server* (e.g. client requested data, new mail or error/warning status).

5.3.2 Communications Server:

Unlike potential *mail clients*, *communications servers* are required to be deployed on powerful hosts with a full access to each DCE component. This allows such servers to access any required *mail server* and act as a caching service and Cell Directory Service liaison for *mail clients* with limited resources. Information retrieved from the Cell Directory Service is cached primarily because such entries as a user's primary mailbox are for all intensive purposes static at the *communications server* level. Similarly binding handles associated with *mailbox servers* are cached. In the event of such a server's graceful termination, the *communications server* will be informed directly and hence only the initial access to the Cell Directory Service is required for each *mail server*.

Although the entire system is designed to perform asynchronously, it is recognized that user's can potentially be blocked waiting for data/status to be returned. In order to circumvent this, the sending of mail and informing the user of the arrival of new mail are designated as low priority tasks while processing requested information and commands are designated as higher priority task.

5.3.3 Mail Server:

Mail servers are divided into two categories: send and access. A send server's primary role is to handle the sending of mail and hence contains a local cache of user addresses resolved. Their back-end interface interfaces to the local mail system (e.g. Unix mail, VMS mail, X.400) in order to "send" mail within the cell while other interfaces provide access to mail gateways or routines that access such gateways (e.g. SMTP, Unix sendmail). This centralized sending locale allows quotas and restrictions on sending mail to be readily enforced and facilitates such features as mail messages with indirectly accessed bodies.

The access flavor of this server manipulates user mail data (*read, delete, change read status* and *general folder access*). Again this centralized controller aides in enforcing quota and mail policy. User data is cached in order to determine a user's specific mail location and to maintain a list of active users whose mail is currently being monitored.

It is recognized that the mail access through two levels of server (e.g. two levels of RPC interconnection) can present a potential bottleneck, especially given the transfer of large messages. Similarly, copying messages from *mail server* to *mail server* would be an extremely slow process if a *postbox server's* interaction/control were mandatory. Direct communications between *mail servers*, and *mail servers* and clients is permitted and facilitated by passing the appropriate binding handles with each operation performed. This allows the *postbox server* level to be bypassed and thus streamlines network communications.

5.4   Client Support and Server Interaction

As stated previously, a *mail client* host can vary from laptop to super-computer. Given the various levels of power associated with each potential client host, a spectrum of client performance must be supported. The optimal client machine (a workstation or larger host) will have complete DCE access, have the ability to store a full caching of a user's mail environment locally (either in memory or on disk) and possess a graphics/audio capable terminal. Restricting mail to only such hosts is an unrealistic limitation; therefore each client contains a snapshot of the user's mail and the remaining messages operated on are stored over the network. Local caching of messages is handled at a level behind the PIMS provided API as are cache-misses which are resolved over the network.

Clients are configurable based on each host's power, current load and the accessibility of each DCE component. The most restrictive form of client is the *batch-client*. Such a client might be a remote PC seeking to access their mail over a limited baud rate modem and with none of the DCE components available. Such a client would be required to login to a DCE accessible host and establish security credentials. Messages would then be checked-out of the PIMS environment in order to permit for remote operation (e.g. modification external to the formal PIMS environment). This would allow expensive/slow communication links to be disconnected while actual modifications are made to the mail messages that are checked out. Locks would insure that certain messages could not be deleted/moved while checked-out. At the same time mail retrieval occurs, mail messages generated on PC could be sent by the remote host with DCE access. The *batch-client* presents numerous security holes and would therefore be permissible for only certain low security mail-groups and based on a user option set during a previously held secure PIMS session.

It is also permissible to have a *mail client-lite* which would be an extremely limited host capable of little or no caching and with no access to facilities such as the Cell Directory Service. In this event the *communications server*, a powerful host, would maintain a user's data cache and serve as liaison for accessing user information from the Cell Service. A myriad of techniques could be used to provide such a *mail client* with access to a *communications server*. These include communicating over a well known endpoint, reading a string binding from a shared file or regression into system dependent features such as sockets. The system power model with respect to the *mail client* is similar to the memory hierarchy found in hardware environments (cache, primary memory and disk). Local RAM storage, local storage to disk, *communications server* store and *mail server* store represent the PIMS hierarchy.

Allowing each *communications server* to act as both a pure communications channel and a client mail cache makes gauging the number of such servers required more difficult and adds undue overhead to servers that maintain no client storage. In recognition of this, a set of server decision rules are maintained in the namespace. Using the criteria established, certain classes of clients will be restricted to using certain *communications servers*. By the same token, this set of rules will be used in order to allow clients to interact with logical servers (servers on the local host or servers the same local host as a requested *mail server*). Accessing the Cell Directory Service in order to retrieve this choice profile will be a significantly more expensive operation than simply retrieving a binding handle; hence *mail clients* will not have access to such information. Clients will automatically contact the first detected *communications server*. Using the server choice profile and accessing its own load status, the contacted server will chose to either accept or reject the client. In the event of a rejection, this *communications server* assumes the responsibility of locating other such servers in order to find an accepting agent capable of handling the inquiring client. Again, maintaining a list of *communications server* binding handles is expensive with-respect to Cell Directory Service access, so for obvious reason this is an operation limited to *communications servers*. This feature will also aid in the migration of servers given a server being brought down gracefully or in the event servers are added due to the present pool becoming too heavily loaded. This configuration in general is extremely scalable and given an enforced hierarchy of servers can readily be deployed in support of thousands of hosts.

6 DCE Design and Integration Issues

Applications development within Project Pilgrim is aided by a robust suite of DCE based utilities. Conventional utilities are frequently nonreentrant in nature and hence are not suitable for use in a multi-threaded environment. Lex, Yacc and various regular expression packages are examples of this present limitation. Furthermore, DCE specific utilities expedite development as does Project Pilgrim's "build" environment which makes architecture specifications transparent to applications developers. Project Pilgrim has developed various common data structures (queues and trees), a regular expression interpreter, generalized RPC initialization, generalized security verification and a threadpool package which provides what appears to the program to be virtual infinite pool of threads.

As previously stated, the PIMS environment is asynchronous in nature; this performance feature being implemented utilizing the aforementioned utilities. Queues are used within all three components in order to transmit commands, data and status information. Each queue is allocated a thread and entries being dequeued are given a thread from the threadpool. *Mail clients* can either assign a function to be executed once a command has been processed and hence exploit the environment's asynchronous nature. Additionally, a *mail client* can wait (block) on the result of a command. This synchronous behavior facilitates PIMS integration with legacy mail readers which inherently do not exploit multi-threaded capabilities. In a similar manner PIPS uses queues so as to provide non-blocking RPC. Jobs are submitted and initially error checked before being enqueued. As mentioned previously, status is returned using PEN.

7 Conclusion

In this paper, we have outlined an architecture which provides a framework for designing systems which seek to integrate services in a distributed environment in a uniform way. We have considered two systems, PIPS and PIMS, in detail and discussed how their design fits in this framework. We believe that our architecture provides adequate flexibility and control needed in building such distributed systems.

Any operating system dependencies are localized in the Supervisor and the Client. Both of these are small lightweight processes which should be easy to implement. By isolating host specific dependencies in the outer layer, adding a new service or user interface does not change the core components. The links between the Supervisor and Client modules and the rest of the application may be non–DCE, thereby allowing the application to access non–DCE services and allowing a non–DCE client to use the application[5]. Overall, new user interfaces are easier to make available and new service providers are easy to add since only a new Supervisor has to be added. The rest of the application is not impacted[6]. Therefore, porting to a new operating system maybe done incrementally. Porting a Client and/or a Supervisor is all that would be required.

Both the Secretary and Server cache information, thus, saving on accesses to the Cell Directory Service. This is importanted because our experience at Project Pilgrim has demonstrated that accessing this DCE component could prove to be a bottleneck in large environments. Since the Secretary is designed to perform tasks such as validating the end user and maintaining static information related to the application, it relieves the Server which deals solely with the dynamic aspects of the application. Apart from such an advantage this also avoids the possibility of the Server becoming a bottleneck during the operation of the application.

The Secretary can spawn threads to handle requests from different users. Similarly, the Server can handle requests from different Secretaries. By allowing several Servers and Secretaries in the environment, we can distribute the task load of users, thus achieving a high degree of parallelism.

---

[5] Security issues, such as, is the end user a valid user will also need to be addressed, if one assumes a non–DCE communication model.

[6] If the Server and Supervisor were not separated, adding new interfaces would impact the server. Since the server would change, each new interface would mean a new version of the server, and different versions maybe running on different machines on the cell.

Management of the application is easier because of the hooks provided in the secretary and server modules. Since most of the application's critical operations are performed in these modules, a high degree of control is obtained. By formally separating the modules, and by making each module configurable, a high degree of flexibility is achieved in the organization of the application. By not restricting the instances of any of the components, the application may be reconfigured to meet the changing needs of the environment.

In conclusion, the architecture discussed in this paper provides a methodology for designing both a complicated distributed print and mail application. Both applications are operational and are being used in our environment. We believe that our architecture simplifies the process of designing distributed applications which aim at providing a consistent access to the services in a heterogeneous environment for the end users. Also, management of these services, as well as the application itself, is easier for the administrator. At Project Pilgrim, other systems are being designed based on this architecture, such as Pilgrim User Information Services (UsIS).[6].

References

[1] Open Software Foundation. *Introduction to DCE, Revision 1.0*. Open Software Foundation, 1991.

[2] Open Software Foundation. *Administration Reference*. Open Software Foundation, 1991.

[3] Open Software Foundation. *Application Development Reference*. Open Software Foundation, 1991.

[4] N. Borenstein and N Freed. *MIME (Multipurpose Internet Mail Extensious): Mechanisms for Specifying and Describing the Format of Internet Message Bodies*, June 1992. RFC 13XX.

[5] Nehru Bhandaru and Kathleen DiBella. Pilgrim event notifier (version 1.0). *Under Preparation*, 1992.

[6] Rajeev Koodli. Usis: Pilgrim user information service — design document (version 1.0.2). *Under Preparation*, 1992.

Converting Monolithic Programs for DCE Client-Server Computing Given Incomplete Cutset Information

Yi-Hsiu Wei, Shepherd S.B. Shi and David D.H. Lin

Distributed Systems Services
Personal Software Products Division
IBM Austin 11400 Burnet Road Austin,
Texas 78750, USA
{ywei, sshi, dlin}@ausvml.vnet.ibm..com

Abstract. Migrating monolithic sequential programs to distributed client-server environments enables the programs to access rich networked computing resources, distribute data to proper locations, and obtain other capabilities offered by distributed systems. However the migration task is often enormous. This paper presents a semi-automatic process for converting existing monolithic sequential programs to DCE applications. An incomplete-grouping based program partitioning algorithm is used to determine a complete partitioning strategy and to obtain a complete cutset for the program graph from a given incomplete minimal grouping information. The complete cutset determines the client-server relations among program components and defines the RPC interfaces for their interactions.

1.0 Introduction

Migrating monolithic sequential programs to the OSF's Distributed Computing Environment (DCE) [6,9] for client-server processing allows the programs to access rich network resources, distribute data to proper locations, and obtain other capabilities that distributed systems may offer (e.g. locating services dynamically, secured access).

However the migration task is often enormous. The efforts required may include:

- Reorganizing user programs to fit in client-server model.

- Partitioning user programs into subgroups of code for running on different systems.

- Defining remote procedure calls (RPC) interfaces for client-server interactions between the groups.

- Wrapping each group into a process which may behave as a client, a server or both in the network of program groups.

This work should be done automatically as much as possible to reduce the development cost and increase the reliability of the program conversion.

This paper presents a semi-automatic process for converting existing monolithic sequential programs to DCE applications. An incomplete-group based program partitioning algorithm is used to determine a complete cutset for the program graph from a given incomplete grouping information. The complete cutset defines client-server relations and forms RPC interfaces between the groups.

Given a sequential program, one needs to first analyze the program and mark a few key procedures in the program which are more significant than others: Some may carry out intensive computing task. Others may perform intensive data manipulation, or provide essential graphical user interface functions, etc. A partition algorithm will take this minimal information to derive a complete cutset for partitioning the program. According to the complete cutset, the client-server relations among the pieces of the partitioned program, and the RPC interfaces can then be generated.

In section 2, we describe the requirements of program partitioning for client-server computing and rationalize the need for key partition information from program investigator. A formal context is set up for describing the program conversion. The overall conversion process is described in section 3. The partition algorithm used in the conversion process is presented in section 4. In section 5, an example illustrates the conversion process and shows how the algorithm works.

2.0 Program Partitioning for Client-Server Computing

The general problem of program partitioning has been addressed in many previous works [7,8,11,4,2]. Most of them focused on partitioning a numerical intensive program into parallel tasks for execution on a multiprocessor system [1,3]. However, these previous researches differ from our work presented in many ways. The program partitioning algorithms on multiprocessor systems often target their goals at optimizing metrics such as job completion time, latency, load balancing, or system throughput,. A program partitioner usually have no prior information that demands certain cutpoints to use. It has to determine on its own an (sub)optimal complete cutset for the program graph using heuristic approaches to achieve the defined partition goals.

On the other hand, partitioning software for client-server computing may intend to 1) facilitate client access to software tools, 2) harness the power of networked computers, and/or 3) re-arrange resources (e.g. data or databases) to appropriate machines. This observation leads to a quite different view as to how the program conversion should be proceeded. Rather than optimizing those metrics for numerical computing and relying on a fully automated tool, a small set of high level information is used to guide a semi-automated conversion process.

The useful information may include but not limit to:

1. The procedure calls can be made remote.

2. The procedures which are better to run on high speed processors due to the computing intensive nature.

3. The procedures which are more appropriate to run on special data servers for intensive large data set manipulation.

4. The procedures which provide advanced user interfaces should run closer to users, for example on desktop systems.

We define a formal model for the program partitioning. In its context, we describe: 1) how a monolithic program is interpreted as a client-server application with a given complete cutset, 2) what information is needed to guide the program partitioning when a complete cutset is not available, and 3) how the partition algorithm derives a complete cutset from this information.

A procedural program can be modelled as a directed graph with global state. Each node of the graph is a procedure, and each arc is an ordinary local procedure call. The graph is cyclic when there are self-recursive or mutual-recursive calls. A node may have access to the global state and/or may privately hold a local state.

A complete cutset is a set of arcs in the graph for which when all arcs in the set are removed from the graph, the graph is broken up to a set of disjoint subgraphs. Each subgraph contains a group of nodes and arcs.

Given a complete cutset, a monolithic sequential program can be converted into a client-server application by having each subgroup wrapped into a single execution unit (process) which can be independently allocated resources and scheduled. For example, two processes may be running on the same or different machines.

The arc within a group represents a local procedure call. Whereas the arc at each cut point between two groups represents a remote procedure call. An arc going out of a group is a remote service requested from the group. An arc coming into a group indicates a remote service provided by the group. When a group has only outgoing arcs, the process for the group is a pure client. When a group has only incoming arcs, the process of the group is a pure server. Otherwise when a group has mixed incoming and outgoing arcs, the process is both a client and a server.

An incomplete cutset is a set of arcs for which when all the arcs are removed from the graph there are remaining connections between groups. An incomplete cutset may be given as a result of the desire to decouple particular caller/callee pairs and to make them run in different address spaces, possibly on different systems.

Since an incomplete cutset is a proper subset of a number of complete cutsets, there are many different grouping strategies available for completing the program partitioning. Thus the information defines neither the number of groups nor allocation of certain nodes to certain groups. A default option is to group each involved callee or caller node in a separate group. Otherwise more information is needed for the partitioner to come up with a more intelligent and useful grouping decision.

Therefore, a program investigator may also want to determine, in addition to which arcs to break, how nodes under consideration are grouped. For example, if a program has 10 procedures, among them the investigator is more concerned of four procedures:

1. procedure 1 has to run on different machine from procedure 2 which is the former call,

2. procedure 3 has to run closely with procedure 1, and

3. procedure 4 has to run closely with procedure 2

He should provide an incomplete grouping {{ 1, 3 }{ 2, 4 }} and have the partitioner to start from this point and find out a complete grouping and cutset.

3.0 Program Conversion Process

As shown in Figure 1, the conversion process consists of a number of steps:

1. A sequential program is observed by an investigator. The procedures of concern are marked. The marked procedures are grouped.

2. A program graph generator analyzes the program source and produces a call graph for the program. This graph is augmented with the access relations of each procedure node to the global states.

3. The graph partitioner takes the augmented call graph and the minimal grouping strategy suggested by the investigator to re-arrange the elements of graph. It completes the grouping task and derives a complete cutset from the graph.

4. Given the complete cutset, client-server relations of the program subgroups are established. The RPC Interfaces (RPC idl files) are identified and built by an interface generator.

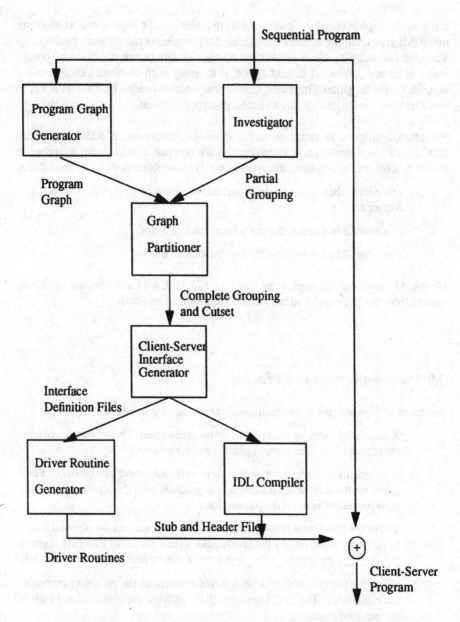

Figure 1. Converting Sequential Programs to DCE applications

5. The driver routine for each group is generated by a client-server driver generator. The driver routine is the wrapper for the program group which contains operations for setting up DCE client/server operating environment for client-server processing.

6. The RPC stubs and header files are generated by IDL compiler.

Together with the original program, the driver routines, the RPC stubs and header files form the converted DCE client-server application of the program.

4.0 Program Partitioning Algorithm

In this section, we presents the algorithm used by the program partitioner. This algorithm completes the grouping task from the given incomplete information about the intended grouping of the procedures of concern. This algorithm determines how the unmarked procedures are merged into the groups. Given a sequential program, the call graph contains a set of procedure nodes and a set of global data units.

Let
M = set of global data units
P = list of the unmarked nodes plus the global data units

Repeat
    dequeue an element from P
    if it has no connection with any group
        enqueue the element back to P
    else if it is a stateless procedure node or
    a system/language/common-environment runtime function
    copy the node to every group which has procedure call connections to it, and move
the associated connections into the group
        else if it is a global data unit
            move the unit to the group which has more access connections
            to it than other groups, and move the associated connections
            to the group
        else if it is a procedure node
                    (with local state and/or access to global states)
            if it has memory connections to global states
                move the node to the group which has more memory
                connections to this node than other groups
            else
                move the node to the group which has more procedure
                call connections to this node than other groups
    Until P is empty

Repeat
  get an element from M
  if the global data unit has cross-group access connection(s)
    construct remote access procedure(s) in the group where the
    data unit resides, connect these access procedures to the
    unit, convert the cross group access connections to remote
    procedure calls to the access procedures.
Until M is empty

We adopt a centralized shared memory strategy[5,10] by keeping one instance of each global data item in one group. Different global data items may be assigned to different groups though. These data items are centrally managed by the associated reading and writing functions in the same group. The functions can be called from other groups via RPC. The 'read' operations on the global data item, which is assigned to different group than those where the operations are, will be replaced by RPC calls to the data reading functions. The data reading functions return the desired data. Similarly, global variable assignment statements are replaced by RPCs to the data writing functions. The data reading and writing functions are generated and exported from the interface of the group.

5.0 Example

This example illustrates how the algorithm works. Given a sequential program, the graphical representation of the program is shown in Figure 2. There are 12 procedure nodes, n1 ... n12, and three global data units, m1 ... m3. The solid arrows are procedure calls. The dashed lines are global memory access connections. n5 is a stateless function which does not access to any global state. n2 holds a local state. {n1, n11, n12}, {n1, n3, n4} and {n2, n3, n4} have mutual recursive call relations.

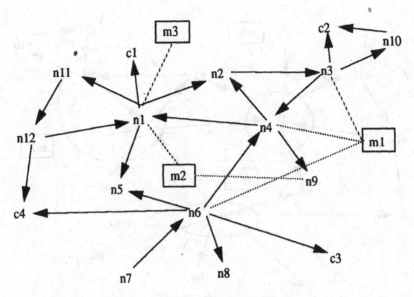

Figure 2. A Monolithic Sequential Program

An investigator examines the program. Among others, he is more concerned of four procedures. Procedure n1 processes large amount of data in m3. This work could be assigned to and run on a data server. Since both procedures n3 and n4 perform computing intensive task and closely interact to each other, the investigator decided to have them wrapped together for possibly being assigned to and run on a high-speed processor. He also recognizes that procedure n6 provides major graphical user interface functions. It has to be in a separate process to be run on a desktop or workstation with a high-function terminal. Therefore, this investigator decide to provide a simple guideline for breaking up the program: four procedure nodes must be separated in three groups: { { n1 }, { n3, n4 }, { n6 } }.

With this incomplete partition information (Figure 3), we apply the partition algorithm described earlier to break up the program into a completely defined set of groups which contains all program components. The following reveals the algorithm applied to this program:

1. Common interface calls: calls to language runtime functions or operating system services, c1 ... c4, are made locally in each group. This assumes that every system supports the common application interfaces used by the program. (e.g. printf in C)

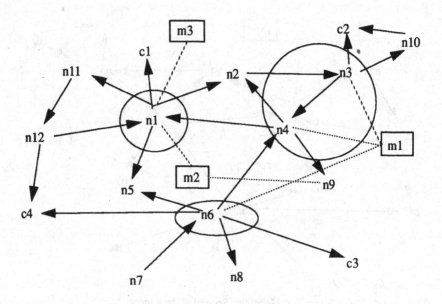

Figure 3. Procedure node marking and grouping

2.   Stateless procedures: procedure n5 does not access to global state neither hold
     a local state. The node is replicated in both G1 and G3.

3.   Procedures with state: procedure n2 has two procedure call connections with
     G2 and has one with G1. It is merged into G2. The call connection with G1
     becomes a RPC.

4.   Global memory: m1 has two access connections with G2 and one with G3. It
     is merged to G2. A remote procedure n13 is constructed to provide G3 remote
     access to m1.

5.   m2 and m3 each has one access connection with G1. Both are moved into G1.

6.   n9 has one call connection with G2 and one memory access connection with
     G1. It is moved to G1 to avoid the need for construction of a remote proce-
     dure for memory access.

7.   Procedures connecting to only one group: Since n7, n8, n10, n11, n12 have no
     access to the global states and attach to only one group, they are included in
     the group.

As a result, the program graph is completely partitioned into groups G1, G2, and G3 as
shown in Figure 4. A complete cutset is therefore found. G1, G2, and G3 are wrapped
into three separate processes. G1 and G2 processes behave both as client and server.
G3 is a pure client process. The cut points, the arcs, between G1, G2, and G3 are
remote procedure calls. The arcs within the same groups remain ordinary local proce-

dure calls. Two interfaces are identified: one for the services exported by G2 containing remote procedures n2, n3, n4, and n13, another for the services exported by process G1 containing remote procedures n1 and n9. The RPC driver programs and stubs files are then generated for G1, G2, and G3.

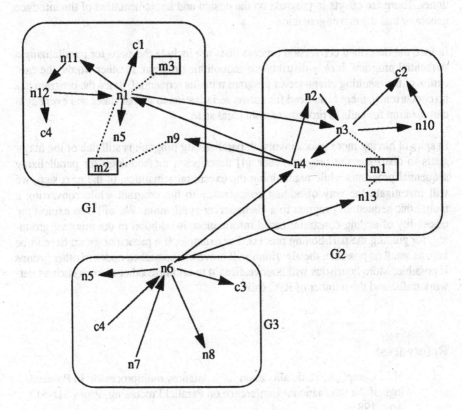

Figure 4. Complete grouping

6.0 Concluding Remarks

In this paper, we have described a program conversion process for migrating a monolithic sequential program to the DCE environment for client-server processing. We have differentiated the requirements of program partitioning for client-server computing from those for multiprocessing and rationalize the need of critical partition hints to be supplied by an program investigator. The mapping from monolithic sequential programs to client-server applications is defined via augmented program call graph. A partitioning algorithm is presented which derives a complete cutset for a graph from the hints. An example is given to illustrate the conversion processes and shows how the algorithm works.

We are beginning to prototype the system. In particular the focus is on the graph partitioner. There are efforts in progress on the design and implementation of the interface generator and the driver generator.

In fact, the described conversion process does not include the steps for parallelizing a sequential program. It only distributes a monolithic program. In other words, the execution of the resulting client-server program remains sequential. Since the program has no concurrency, there is no need for access serialization to global states and event synchronization for calls to procedures with local state.

In spite of having more issues involved, parallelizing program is still one of the major goals to distribute the program. Jade [4] describes a methodology for parallelizing sequential programs while maintaining the execution semantics. In the next step, we will investigate the way of adding concurrency to the program while converting a monolithic sequential program to a client-server application. We will also exploit the possibility of adding constraint-based information, in addition to the minimal grouping, for guiding the partitioning process. For example, if a particular group have to be kept as small as possible, the algorithm will move the unmarked nodes to other groups if possible. More heuristics will be investigated to optimize other metrics such as network traffic and the number of RPC calls.

References:

1. M.L. Campbell. Static allocation for a dataflow multiprocessor. In Proceedings of the International Conference on Parallel Processing, Pages 511-517, Aug. 1985

2. Wilson C. Hsieh. Extracting parallelism from sequential programs. Technical report, MIT, May 1988

3. P. Hudak and B. Goldberg. Serial combinators: Optimal grains of parallelism. In Proceedings of the conference on Functional Programming Languages and Computer Architecture, Pages 627-637, Jul. 1985

4. M.S. Lam and M.C. Rinard. Coarse-grain parallel programming in Jade. In Proceedings of the 3rd ACM SIGPLAN Symposium on Principles and Practice of Programming, 1991

5. B. Nitzberg and C. Lo. Distributed Shared Memory: A survey of issues and algorithms. IEEE Computer, Aug. 1991

146

6.   DCE Version 1.0 DCE Application Development Guide. Open Software
      Foundation, June 1992

7.   V. Sarkar. Automatic partitioning of a program dependence graph into paral-
      lel tasks. In IBM Journal of Research and Development, pages 779-804, Nov.
      1991

8.   V. Sarkar and J. Hennessy. Partitioning parallel programs for macro-dataflow.
      IN ACM Conference on Lisp and Functional Programming, pages 201-211,
      Aug. 1986

9.   J. Shirley. Guide to Writing DCE Applications. O'Reilly and Associates, Inc.,
      June 1992

10.   M. Stumm and S. Zhou. Algorithms implementing distributed shared mem-
      ory. IEEE COmputer, May 1990

11.   M. Weiser. Program slicing. IEEE Trans. on Software Engineering, July 1984

Managing the Transition to OSF DCE Security

Sanjay Tikku
Stephen Vinter
Siemens Nixdorf Information Systems
Burlington, MA 01803
tikku@sni-usa.com, vinter@sni-usa.com

Stephen Bertrand
Ibis Communications Inc.
Lynnfield, MA 01940
ibis@world.std.com

Abstract. OSF DCE security and UNIX system security each support independent representations of user identities. We infer from OSF's implementation of DCE security that either the two security environments are to be kept separate, or that UNIX system security is to be strictly aligned with DCE Security. Neither solution is usually practical for established UNIX system installations that are only beginning to use DCE technology. This paper describes a set of tools that enables the compatible and secure coexistence of the two security environments. These tools are provided with SNI's DCE product for our System V Release 4 based SINIX operating system and UNIX Systems Laboratories' (USL) DCE product. They are intended to be used as transition aids until migration to DCE is complete. They introduce no compromises to either security system, and they accommodate familiar and well-established UNIX system security administration practices and policies.

1 The Security Administration Problem

DCE introduces a new security administration model which involves the centralized management of users and groups that have consistent, global meanings throughout the cell [1, 2, 3]. This administration model is unlike many typical UNIX system security administration models, which involve per-host administration and, perhaps also, the host-specific identities of users and groups [5, 6].

These different administrative models follow directly from the differences between the DCE security environment, with its replicated but logically centralized database of account information (the DCE registry); and the UNIX system security environment, with its multiple and dispersed /etc/passwd, /etc/shadow and /etc/group files on the UNIX hosts (referred to as *UNIX security files* in this paper). (Note: the registry represents users and groups as UUIDs (Universal Unique Identifiers), but also maintains a mapping of UUIDs to UNIX UIDs and GIDs for UNIX compatibility.)

There are difficulties in adopting DCE security administration when DCE is introduced to sites where the UNIX security files on each host are not globally administered. In this case, users and groups may be defined inconsistently across hosts, and administrators will be concerned about the security ramifications of a global administration model.

The OSF does not define the administrative practices and policies for DCE integration with established UNIX security administration. However, the implementation of DCE security suggests two ways to handle the disparities between the two security environments:

- Maintain completely separate DCE and UNIX system security environments. The **dce_login** command establishes separate DCE privileges for each user who has already acquired UNIX system privileges via **/bin/login** (Figure 1).

- Thoroughly integrate the two security environments. The tools **passwd_import** and **passwd_export** unify and synchronize local UNIX security files on all hosts with the registry; this approach permits use of a single, integrated **login** mechanism (Figure 2).

Each of these choices, however, presents its own administrative challenges (if not problems) to the administrator, and sometimes to the user as well.

1.1 Maintaining Separate DCE and UNIX System Security Environments

The problems inherent in maintaining separate DCE and UNIX security environments affect both users and administrators. The notion of a user with multiple identities is completely contrary to the intent of DCE security, but perhaps more important, having multiple *concurrent* identities could be very confusing to the users themselves, even though they may be at ease with having different variations of their identities at different hosts. Furthermore, this scheme introduces new opportunities for unintended violations of security policy: users might inadvertently commit such violations when they are unaware of which set of local credentials, from DCE registry or from UNIX security files, is in effect at any given time.

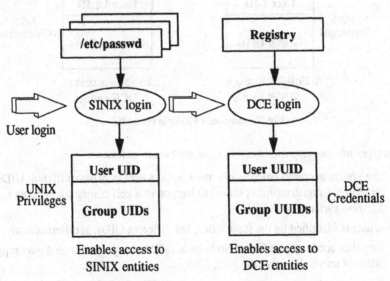

Fig. 1. Separate Logins for DCE and UNIX

The administrator's burden is also increased, since every DCE user represents an additional user to manage. Last, this approach makes DCE appear to be a poorly integrated add-on, which will delay its acceptance.

Because of the serious problems associated with this approach, we could not recommend this strategy for accommodating DCE users in a UNIX system environment.

1.2 Synchronizing DCE and UNIX System Accounts

Ideally, all UNIX system users at a DCE site would be DCE users (unified security administration under DCE is, in fact, our ultimate goal). However, this means that, as administrators import UNIX system account and group information from individual hosts to the registry (using the OSF DCE tool, **passwd_import**), they must resolve all inconsistencies related to the identities of UNIX system users and groups across all hosts.

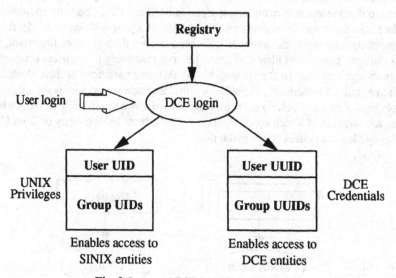

Fig. 2. Integrated DCE login from OSF

The types of inconsistencies that they must resolve are as follows:

- The system accounts (such as **bin** and **sys**) on a host may have different UIDs than those in the registry (this is bound to happen in a cell consisting of hosts running different variants of UNIX).
- A user is identified by the same name, but different UIDs, at different hosts.
- Two user accounts at different hosts have different user names (and may represent different users), but have the same UID.
- A group is identified by the same name, but different GIDs at different hosts.
- Two groups at different hosts have different names, but are associated with the same GID.

- A group is identified by the same name and GID at different hosts, but the two instances of the group define different sets of members.

Table 1 illustrates examples of these conflicts.

Table 1. Potential Conflicts

Users	Registry	/etc/passwd (host A)
name conflict	jones::10	jones::15
UID conflict	thomas::10	smith::10

Groups	Registry	/etc/group (host A)
name conflict	dev::10	dev::20
GID conflict	test::10	QA::10
membership conflict	dev::10:admin	dev::10:admin, sys

Unresolved UID or GID conflicts can cause serious security violations if not properly resolved. For example, unresolved UID conflicts can result in DCE users logging into local UNIX hosts and assuming the identities of local users. Table 1 shows an entry for the UNIX user thomas (UID 10) and another for the DCE user smith (also UID 10). When thomas logs into the cell from host A, for example, he obtains the privileges of smith on that host.

Resolving these inconsistencies involves reassigning UNIX UIDs and GIDs for those accounts that conflict, and changing the permissions of all affected files accordingly. There must also be a method for handling backed up files, as these can reintroduce identity conflicts when the files are restored.

Since all DCE users and groups must be established at a single global registry, this approach requires all conflicts to be resolved at the time the host is added to the cell. However, it is not always practical to force synchronization of the account data, partly because it may delay acceptance of DCE, and partly because of administrators' commitment to existing tools and procedures.

2 Goals for the Transition

It became apparent that achieving our ultimate goal of global security administration via DCE would take time. We realized that the problem of adopting DCE security was chiefly one of managing the transition necessary to achieve it

Our approach was to create transition aids to be used temporarily until DCE is widely accepted by our UNIX system users. We sought to avoid institutionalizing DCE and UNIX system security coexistence, because we do not believe coexistence is a correct long-term solution. We felt that this was best achieved by supporting non-DCE users (referred to as *local users* in this paper) on a DCE host. The goals we defined for our UNIX-to-DCE security transition model are as follows:

1. To disrupt as little as possible the administration and established practices of existing local users

2. To introduce no compromises to UNIX system or DCE security

3. To cause no performance degradation for local users

4. To accommodate UNIX administration tools, especially since they are often customized for site-specific needs

5. To maintain interoperability with other implementations of OSF DCE

6. To augment, rather than replace, the standard OSF DCE security tools

3   The Transition Approaches Considered

We first investigated whether our goals could be achieved within the framework of the tools supplied by OSF.

With the OSF DCE integrated login, when a host is to become a member of a cell, then all users of the host are considered DCE users. It does not offer the capability to support local users on a DCE host, so we disqualified it from further consideration.

We then investigated ways to support local users using the **passwd_override** file and the **passwd_import** and **passwd_export** tools.

3.1 passwd_override File for Local Users

We considered using the OSF DCE **passwd_override** file to list local users. This restricts a DCE user to a host-specific identity by overriding the user's network identity at the host on which **passwd_override** resides.

We first thought that the issue of local and DCE users could be solved simply by creating accounts for all users in the registry and then creating **passwd_override** file entries for local users. However, using the **passwd_override** file mechanism would create a new set of problems:

- Specifying local users in **passwd_override** file would call for mechanisms that would enable existing UNIX tools to reference the file (for example, the program **ls** reads **/etc/passwd**; in this scheme, it would have to reference **passwd_override** instead) (compromises Goal 4).

- The **passwd_override** file does not allow group overrides (compromises Goal 2)

- We would need to provide a mechanism by which system administrators could add or remove local users using their existing UNIX tools and without DCE expertise. Cloning **passwd_override** files from the **/etc/passwd** files would have accomplished this, but then local users would be listed in two places, necessitating the synchronization of these files (compromises Goal 4).

- The password for the local user is stored in the **passwd_override** file itself (following UNIX conventions). In SINIX, however, the user password is stored in the **/etc/shadow** file (which is a preferable scheme). There was no clean solution to this problem (compromises Goal 2).

- With the **passwd_override** mechanism, the local user actually logs through the registry which is a slower process than the standard SINIX login (compromises Goal 3).

For all of these reasons we abandoned the idea of using **passwd_override** files for defining local users on DCE hosts.

3.2 Resolving User and Group ID Conflicts

Another problem that we had to solve was how to import users into the registry from different hosts and resolve potential user (and group) name and ID conflicts. In existing configurations at customer sites we found that although UNIX hosts were networked, in some cases each had its own set of UNIX security files. Accounts representing a single user or group had different names and IDs at different hosts. If all of these systems were to be incorporated into a DCE cell, all the name and ID conflicts would have to be resolved. Our original plan was to require that when DCE is installed in a network then all UID conflicts be resolved at the time hosts are incorporated into the cell. Resolving all conflicts meant that at the time of importing a host into a cell:

- Any users being imported would need to be assigned new names or UIDs if they conflicted with existing names or UIDs in the registry.

- Any groups being imported would need new names or GIDs if they conflicted with existing names or GIDs in the registry.

- The ownership on all files on that host, that were owned by the user or group whose ID was changed, needed to be updated.

The requirement to resolve all conflicts at the start was not acceptable to our customers and compromised Goal 1.

We then considered allowing the mapping of DCE users to different UIDs and GIDs on different hosts. This would have enabled us to incorporate hosts in a cell that have conflicts in the UNIX security files. This idea was derived from the USL's Remote File System (RFS) approach [7].

Using this approach, the cell administrator would enter local UIDs and GIDs that conflict with registry entries into a local (per host) mapping table. Every host in the cell would optionally have a table of mapping from UUIDs to UIDs and GIDs.

Properly maintaining the mapping table would involve modifying UNIX tools that manipulate UNIX security files, compromising Goal 4. We also believed that this approach would institutionalize the mapping table, which is contrary to our intention to create transition aids.

4 The Transition Approach Adopted

We finally decided to implement a set of tools that enable administrators to manage UNIX system user account and group inconsistencies in the DCE security environment, and so allow the local and DCE security environments to coexist despite inconsistencies that cannot be immediately resolved [8, 9]. The tools we implemented for SNI's DCE product:

- Accommodate (rather than prohibit) inconsistencies between local UNIX system and registry accounts
- Increase the system administrator's ability to limit the privileges of DCE users on the UNIX system hosts for accounts that conflict
- Enable user participation in DCE to be determined by whether or not the UNIX user wishes to become a DCE user, rather than by whether or not the user's host is configured as a member of a DCE cell

We identified three development efforts that were necessary to achieve our goals:

1. Developing a mechanism to distinguish between local and DCE users, and between local groups and DCE groups.

2. Developing an integrated login that would recognize the distinctions

3. Extending the OSF DCE account import and export mechanisms (**passwd_import** and **passwd_export**).

The next three sub-sections elaborate on these mechanisms.

4.1 Local Users and Protected Groups

To distinguish local users from DCE users, entries corresponding to DCE users in the local password file are annotated as such. Unannotated entries in the password file correspond to local users. When new user entries are exported from the registry, they are automatically annotated as DCE users (refer to description of **rgy_export_accts**).

We used *DCE* as a marker string in the password field of **/etc/passwd** file. We felt this was a valid approach because the password field contains only special marker tags (in SINIX and other System V implementations the tag **x** indicates that the password is in the **/etc/shadow** file). Adding a new tag for that field does not disturb any existing UNIX system feature known to us.

We used a similar mechanism to handle groups. Entries in **/etc/group** files may be annotated as *PROTECTED* from DCE users. This means that when the registry provides a DCE user with privileges that include membership in a protected group, then the host at which the group is protected denies that privilege to the DCE user. Only if the DCE user is explicitly listed as a member of that group in the **/etc/group** file at the host is the privilege of group membership recognized at that host. The *PROTECTED* annotation appears in the password field of the **/etc/group** file.

In the case of an unprotected group in **/etc/group**, the host grants the privilege of membership in that group to DCE users even if they are not explicitly listed as members in **/etc/**

group. During export we also append all groups from the registry to the **/etc/group** file (without membership lists so as to avoid any impact on local security) so the group permissions for files created by a user in a DCE-only group are displayed properly.

4.2 The SINIX DCE Login Facility

To interpret these annotated UNIX system accounts, we implemented a special version of **login** (to replace the standard UNIX **login**) that recognizes the distinctions between local and DCE users, and between protected and unprotected groups. In doing so, it enforces the security policy that favors local users and groups when conflicts occur.

Login Behavior

When a user logs into a host, and the user's name corresponds to an unannotated (local user) entry in the UNIX password file, then that user does not obtain DCE credentials, even if an account with the same user name exists in the registry. This behavior favors local users when user name conflicts occur (preventing denial of service to local users).

When a DCE user attempts to log into an account with a UID that conflicts with the UID of a local user, the DCE login is denied on that host. This behavior guarantees that the DCE user will not obtain privileges that are associated with a local user.

Table 2 shows some these conflicts and the policies adopted to deal with them.

Table 2.   Login Policy for Resolving Conflicts

Users	Registry	/etc/passwd	Policy
name conflict	jones::10	jones::15	login for local **jones** only
UID conflict	jones::10	smith::10	DCE **jones** denied login
Groups			
name conflict	dev::10	dev::20	none necessary
GID conflict	dev::10	qa::10	protected-group policy*
membership conflict	dev::10:admin	dev::10:admin,rd	protected-group policy*

> * If the group is protected, grant the privilege of group membership to the DCE user only if the user is listed as a member of that group in **/etc/group**; if the group is unprotected, grant the privilege of membership to the DCE user if the DCE credentials specify membership in the group.

As Table 2 shows, this login also handles protected groups. Suppose the DCE user **smith** is listed as a member of the group **admin** in the registry. At host A, this group is protected and **smith** is not a member; at host B, this group is protected and **smith** is a member; at host C this group is unprotected:

- When **smith** logs in at host A, he does not obtain the **admin** privilege.

- When **smith** logs in at host B, he obtains the **admin** privilege.
- When **smith** logs in at host C, he obtains the **admin** privilege.

As we noted previously, UNIX security files are automatically synchronized with the registry. Through the use of our version of login, system administrators are guaranteed that modifications to the registry (likely to be outside of their control) will not change the privileges of local users nor the locally effective membership of protected groups.

Login Implementation

The integrated SINIX DCE login has been implemented by applying DCE changes to the UNIX system login implementation. Our integrated DCE login implementation first looks up the user name in the **/etc/passwd** file to determine whether the user is a local user or a DCE user (local users appear before DCE users in the file).

For a local user, the code path taken is the same as the standard SINIX login implementation. This preserves the SINIX login "feel" and performance characteristic.

For a DCE user, the login logic is described next (all **sec_** function calls are from the DCE security API [3, 4]):

1. Invoke **sec_login_setup_identity** to setup a DCE identity.
2. Prompt user for DCE password and validate that password by calling **sec_login_-valid_and_cert_identity**. If password validation fails then call **sec_login_purge_-context** to destroy the login context that was just created and restart the login process; else if password validation succeeds then proceed with login.
3. Call **sec_login_get_pwent** to get the password entry for the DCE user from the registry.
4. Call **getpwuid** [10] to get (from the UNIX security files) the password entry corresponding to the UID for the DCE user
5. If the UID of the DCE user conflicts with that of a local user then deny login to the DCE user; else call **setuid** to set the UID of the process. At this point, the login is committed.
6. Call **sec_login_set_context** to create network credentials for the login context.
7. If the primary group of the DCE user is protected and the DCE user is not listed as a member of that group, then set the principal group of the user to **none**. Call **setgid** to set the GID of the process.
8. Call **sec_login_get_groups** to get all groups to which the DCE user belongs.
9. For each group, test whether the group is protected (in the **/etc/group** file) and whether the user is a member. If the group is protected AND the user is not a member, remove that group from the membership set.
10. Call **setgroups** to set the locally effective supplementary group set of the process.
11. If the DCE user needs to set a new password then invoke **chpass** [10].
12. Add KRB5CCNAME environment variable to the startup environment of the user.
13. **exec** the login shell for the user.

The initial lookup of the UNIX security files and steps 4, 5, 7 and 9 distinguish the SINIX DCE login from the one supplied by OSF.

4.3 Account Import/Export Extensions

A key property of the existing OSF approach is that DCE accounts from the registry are automatically propagated to the local **/etc/passwd** files periodically, using the **passwd_export** command. DCE and UNIX system administrators need not participate in, or review the results of, this updating process.

Therefore, the critical problem to solve was how to guarantee to system administrators that the account export feature would not make changes without regard for local security policies. We did this by creating two tools, **rgy_import_accts** and **rgy_export_accts** (described in section 5), which are wrappers for **passwd_import** and **passwd_export**, respectively

5 The Transition Tools

We designed several tools that aid the transition to DCE security for our customers. Our overall goal is to make the transition easy, and to that end we have developed tools that automate, to the extent possible, the associated tasks. Because they are either local in effect or wrappers for standard DCE security tools, none of our tools affect DCE in terms of behavior or interoperability.

Our transition tools are fully compatible with the tools provided with OSF DCE and in addition provide:

- A greater level of automation
- A friendlier user interface
- Clearer output

As with any implementation of DCE, cell administrators must first decide

- Which hosts are to be members of the cell
- The configuration of DCE services in the cell

The cell administrator and the system administrator then have to decide

- Which users on these hosts are to have DCE accounts
- Which groups on these hosts are to be protected
- How to resolve various conflicts between user and group IDs

5.1 Summary of the SINIX DCE Transition Tools

This section summarizes the transition tools we developed [8].

rgy_mark_dce_user annotates entries in the **/etc/passwd** file that are to be DCE users with the string *DCE*. This tool is typically run before the host is configured as a member of a DCE cell but it can be used at any time.

rgy_unmark_dce_user removes the *DCE* annotation from the entries in the **/etc/passwd** file that are to be DCE users. This tool is used:

- When a user wants to revert to being a local user on the DCE host
- To preserve local accounts for DCE users after DCE deinstallation. Normally, all DCE users are removed from the UNIX security files when DCE is deinstalled.

rgy_mark_prot_group annotates entries in the **/etc/group** file that the system administrator wants to protect. This tool can be run at any time and all groups marked protected will be excluded from the local group set of a DCE user.

rgy_diff_accts reports on the differences between local and registry account information that, unless the differences are resolved, will result in conflicts when the host is added to the cell. This tool is typically run before user accounts from UNIX security files are imported into the registry. It gives the system and cell administrators a chance to plan how to resolve the conflicts when the accounts are actually imported.

rgy_import_accts is a wrapper for the OSF DCE tool **passwd_import**. It enables the administrator to import local account information into the registry and resolve conflicts between local and registry account information. Unlike **passwd_import**, this tool recognizes UNIX password file entries that are annotated as DCE users, and can selectively import only those users. Also, when users are being selectively imported, it imports only those groups that are needed by the users being imported into the registry. This tool retains all **passwd_import** options that are simply passed through. It is typically run, in lieu of **passwd_import**, to import user accounts into the registry. It can be run any number of times to import users in groups.

rgy_export_accts is a wrapper for the OSF DCE tool **passwd_export**. It updates the local UNIX security files with account information from the registry. It annotates the exported entries as DCE users, and appends the entries to the **/etc/passwd** file. This tool also annotates and appends group entries that were exported to the **/etc/group** file. This tool is typically run in lieu of **passwd_export** to refresh the local UNIX security files, on a regular basis and manually as needed.

rgy_init_accts is a wrapper for the OSF DCE tool **rgy_edit**. It establishes valid passwords and enables the accounts for the imported DCE users in the registry. When user accounts are imported into the cell they are set up (by default DCE security policy) with random passwords and are marked as invalid. This tool enables the cell administrator to easily turn on an account and also assign a valid starting password in a single step. The cell administrator can run this tool from any host in the cell, to turn on a DCE user account.

dce_install_login installs the integrated SINIX DCE login on the system and saves the state of the UNIX security files. This is typically run just after installing DCE onto a host but it can be run any time.

dce_deinstall_login removes the integrated SINIX DCE login program from the system and restores the original system login program. It also removes all DCE users and DCE groups from the UNIX security files. This is typically run just before removing DCE (if necessary) from a host.

6 A Sample Session

Following is a sample session that illustrates the use of the transition tools [8]. It shows the steps involved in importing *selected* user accounts from a host to the registry. It assumes that DCE installation and configuration have already been done:

1 The system administrator determines which of the local users are going to be DCE users and then runs **rgy_mark_dce_user**. For example,

```
rgy_mark_dce_user smith jones
```

annotates two users in the UNIX password files, **smith** and **jones,** as DCE users.

2 The system administrator next decides which of the groups in the UNIX security files should be protected from DCE users and runs **rgy_mark_prot_group**. For example,

```
rgy_mark_prot_group wheel
```

annotates the group **wheel** (in **/etc/group**) as protected from DCE users at the host.

3 The system administrator next informs the cell administrator that the host is ready for integration with the cell.

The cell administrator runs **rgy_diff_accts** to review the differences between account information at the host and account information in the registry that would result in conflicts. For example,

```
rgy_diff_accts -i
```

would prompt the cell administrator as follows:

```
[1] Pick up only users marked DCE
[2] Pick up only local users
[3] Pick up all users

(default: 3) [1-3,?]
```

The cell administrator is expected to pick option 1 (since he is planning to import annotated accounts only) and that would report on conflicts related to users marked as DCE users and their groups.

Using the information gained in the previous step, the system and cell administrators should now plan how the conflicts are to be resolved when the accounts are actually imported into the registry.

4 The cell administrator next runs **rgy_import_accts** to import these accounts in to the registry. The command

```
rgy_import_accts -m
```

imports all user entries that are marked (-m) as DCE users. It also imports only those groups to which these users belong. At this time the cell administrator resolves the conflicts between local and registry account data.

When this step is completed, new DCE accounts have been established in the registry for all annotated user entries.

5   The cell administrator then runs **rgy_export_accts** to propagate registry account data to the local host. For example, the command

rgy_export_accts

exports registry accounts. Now the UNIX security files have been updated with data from the registry. As they are exported, registry entries are appended to the UNIX security files and annotated as DCE entries.

6   The system administrator then runs **dce_install_login** program to install the integrated SINIX DCE login onto the host.

7   The process of installing DCE on the host is now complete and all DCE accounts are set up. However, none of the newly added DCE accounts can be used until the cell administrator explicitly turns them on.

To turn on the account for one of the imported DCE users the cell administrator runs **rgy_init_accts** to establish valid passwords for the imported user account and to mark the account and password as valid for login. For example, the command dialog

rgy_init_accts

Principal Name: **jones**

Principal's Password: *jones' password*

Cell Administrator Password: *cell admin's password*

establishes the password for the user jones and activates the account. This user can now log into the cell as a DCE user from this host.

Steps 1 through 6 are repeated on every host that is a member of the cell. Step 7 is executed for each DCE user that has been imported into the registry. It would be relatively straightforward to extend this mechanism to turn on a group of accounts using the same default password for each account or a customized password for each account.

The cell administrator would use **rgy_export_accts** regularly to keep the local user and group information synchronized with the DCE registry database. Like **passwd_export**, **rgy_export_accts** is intended to be run automatically on a regular basis (For example, as a **cron** job every night).

7 Experiences and Future Enhancements

At the time of this writing, we have released the SINIX DCE product to pilot customers. Among the suggestions these customers have made, two are notable:

- Enhance **rgy_diff_accts** utility to enable it to report on conflicts across multiple hosts; this would enable the administrator to gain a more global perspective on accounts in a cell to facilitate planning. The current implementation only lists conflicts between account entries in the registry and those being imported from one host.

- Enhance **dce_deinstall_login** so that it would restore the UNIX security files to their former state without any explicit action by the system administrator. The current tool requires the system administrator to run **rgy_unmark_dce_user** for all those accounts that need to be retained when DCE is removed from the host.

While we plan to incorporate these enhancements in our tools, we do not intend to continue upgrading and maintaining these tools beyond the time it takes for our customers to become full-fledged DCE users.

8 Conclusion

We refer to the tools we have described as transition aids because they will become unnecessary when the registry is uniformly used for UNIX security administration. Until that time, we have attempted to provide DCE cell administrators with all the advantages of the DCE without:

- Forcing administrators to make major changes to their existing system to resolve conflicts, or
- Compromising the security policies implemented on local hosts.

We believe our transition aids will speed up the acceptance of the DCE without fundamentally changing its basic approach to security administration.

9 References

1. *OSF DCE Administration Reference, Revision 1.0* (Prentice-Hall, 1993)

2. *OSF DCE Version 1.0 Administration Guide, Core Components, Update 1.0.2* (unpublished; Copyright 1993, Open Software Foundation)

3. *OSF DCE Application Development Guide, Revision 1.0* (Prentice-Hall, 1993)

4. *OSF DCE Application Development Reference, Revision 1.0* (Prentice-Hall, 1993)

5. *UNIX System V/386 Release 4 System Administrator's Reference Manual* (Prentice-Hall, 1985)

6. *UNIX System V Release 4 System Administrator's Guide* (Prentice-Hall, 1983)

7. *UNIX System V/386 Release 4 Network User's and Administrator's Guide* (Prentice-Hall, 1990)

8. *DCE (SINIX) Administration Guide - Introduction, Revision 1.0* (unpublished; Copyright 1993, Siemens Nixdorf Information Systems)

9. *SINIX DCE Compatibility and Integration Issues* (unpublished SNI Document Volume 1019, Chapter 61, Section 3; Copyright 1993, Siemens Nixdorf Information Systems)

10. *UNIX System V Release 4 Programmer's Reference Manual* (Prentice-Hall, 1990)

10 Acknowledgments

The authors thank the members of the DCE Group at Siemens Nixdorf; in particular, the expertise of Gregory Carpenter and Victor Voydock in DCE security was invaluable in designing and implementing the transition tools. We also thank the DCE engineers at Pyramid Technology and UNIX Systems Laboratories for many stimulating discussions.

11 About the Authors

Sanjay Tikku is a senior member of the DCE Group at Siemens Nixdorf, Burlington, Massachusetts. Mr. Tikku is the lead engineer of the effort to productize DCE for all Siemens Nixdorf platforms. The tools described in this paper were developed as part of that effort. He was previously the Project Leader for a multiprocessor implementation of SVR4 at Samsung Software America.

Stephen Vinter is the Project Manager of the DCE Group at Siemens Nixdorf, Burlington, Massachusetts. Dr. Vinter directs the development of the SINIX DCE Secure Core product, the OSF DCE SVR4 reference port, and the USL DCE product. Dr. Vinter previously managed the Cronus Project at Bolt, Beranek, and Newman.

Stephen Bertrand is a technical writer at Ibis Communications Inc., Lynnfield, Massachusetts. Mr. Bertrand writes user documentation for SNI's and USL's DCE Secure Core products. He was previously a Project Manager for OSF DCE 1.0 documentation, and a coauthor of *OSF DCE 1.0 Application Development Guide*.

DCE Cells under Megascope:
Pilgrim Insight into the Resource Status

Bojana Obrenić

Kathleen S. DiBella

Arthur S. Gaylord

Project Pilgrim[1]
Department of Computer Science
University of Massachusetts at Amherst
<last_name>@pilgrim.umass.edu

Abstract. Megascope is the Pilgrim utility for monitoring, reporting, managing, and presenting status information about the resources of computer systems and environment services in large, heterogeneous distributed environments.

Megascope is an autonomous distributed application, built on top of the OSF DCE.[2] It extends the basic functionality of the DCE by adding a service to it that provides the cell resource information to other applications. Most notably, Megascope provides data input necessary for successful distributed system management.

This paper discusses the functionality of Megascope and its major design characteristics.

1   Goals of Resource Monitoring in DCE Cells

The Megascope endeavor at Project Pilgrim [9] is engaged in the analysis of the specific problems associated with the resource monitoring in large, heterogeneous, DCE-based environments. This work is aimed at building a prototype of a *resource status monitoring service* that collects, reports, manages, and presents the status data about various environment resources.

By its structure and functions of an *autonomous subsystem*, Megascope follows the overall current Pilgrim strategy of building comprehensive, coherent, self-regulating environments for large-scale heterogeneous distributed computing. Central to this strategy are the DCE [7] primitives for remote procedure call, timing, naming, file system, and security. Pilgrim constructs distributed applications [10] on top of these DCE primitives, the most visible of which are user-oriented *utilities* that support various generic processing tasks, such as printing, mailing, user information, conferences. To secure the integrity, coherence, and stability of the environment, Pilgrim supports its user-oriented utilities by another group of distributed applications. These are the *system-oriented services* that are perceived by the user-oriented applications as an effective *extension of the basic DCE support*. The system-oriented facilities of Pilgrim include asynchronous event notification, generic and dynamic server instantiation, specialized editors of the cell namespace, and Megascope.

---

[1]Project Pilgrim is supported in part by Digital Equipment Corporation, Hewlett-Packard Company, and University of Massachusetts.

[2]OSF is a trademark of the Open Software Foundation.

Due to their dynamic nature, distributed environments, including DCE-based environments such as Pilgrim, require regulation. To support regulation, these environments must be able to sense their status, make decisions on the basis of their status information, and apply the necessary control actions. Megascope is designed to perform this status-sensing task. In the regulation of distributed computing environments, the essential challenge is to *achieve and verify the efficient use of environment resources*. Megascope is a part of the Pilgrim response to this challenge, since it provides the resource status information, which is a necessary input for successful resource management.

This paper reports on our approach to resource monitoring and on the design of Megascope.

Resource monitoring and cell management.   DCE environments and, in particular, the Pilgrim environment can meet the expectations of their (prospective) users only if a cell in such an environment is capable of presenting to its users a credible illusion of functioning as an integrated unit that accepts and fulfills the tasks assigned to it. In the user communities whose (current) alternative to DCE are centralized mainframe-based computing systems, the assumption of efficient and handy central management is taken for granted and built into the administrative and technical definition of such facilities. In those user communities whose highly decentralized and poorly coordinated information processing now demands higher integration, the unifying functions of the DCE are often seen as the only technically and economically feasible way to a meaningful consolidation of the available resources. Therefore, the purpose of the cell management is to enable a cell to behave as an integrated system, to maximize the efficiency of the cell operation, and to obtain the evidence of cell efficiency. Opposing this goal are several intrinsic properties of the DCE.

At the level of the basic DCE components, a DCE cell appears to be a "flat" structure consisting of a number of autonomous computing systems. The management of these individual systems is, traditionally, well understood and typically satisfactory. However, the overwhelming *number* of such systems (perhaps thousands of systems) expected to operate simultaneously in a cell precludes the human involvement on the level required for efficient management of individual facilities by the traditional procedures. The expected *heterogeneity* of DCE cells, where different systems mandate essentially different management procedures, only adds a new quality to the already prohibitive volume of the management tasks. The major goal of advanced cell management is to bridge this gap between the resource management of individual systems and the management goals of the cell as a unit. The role of resource monitoring services, in particular of Megascope, is to provide a unified view of the cell state information, which can be used as input to automated cell administration procedures (e.g., decision support, task scheduling, capacity planning.)

The role of resource monitoring services goes beyond extending the perception of human managers to cope with the number and specifics of individual providers of *classic resources,* namely computation time and memory. The adequacy of such low-level resource representations is now challenged by the *synergy of distributed environments* and *sophistication of the expected processing tasks*. The diversity of applications handled by a single cell, combined with the "maturity" and specifics of abstractions engaged by such applications, calls for a more elaborate interface between the service providers and consumers than that of traditional system management. Software and hardware compatibility, potential parallelism, communication cost and properties, geography and administrative structure, security, etc., are some of the issues arising between a cell and its users that are neither explicit in classic computing environments nor easily represented in terms of processor cycles, storage space, I/O bandwidth, or similar standard parameters based on the traditional resource models. Formulating an adequate resource description is a prerequisite for the development of successful resource monitoring services and an important goal of our Megascope project.

The sophisticated applications of the present and the future are likely to be presented to DCE cells by a *broad user community* consisting of individuals of diverse background and often non-expert abilities. Such users may have prerogatives sufficient for engaging substantial environment resources and may even command information sufficient for efficient scheduling of their tasks, while lacking the technical competence required for effecting the necessary management. The success of a cell management support, including its resource monitoring component, may turn out to depend essentially on achieving successful interaction with this class of users. The Pilgrim environment concept and, in particular, Megascope are conscious of this goal.

Understanding and defining the resource status in distributed environments. One of the goals of the Megascope project is to define and analyze a set of parameters that collectively represent the *state* of a DCE cell or the state of specific environments, including Pilgrim, that a cell supports. Thus defined, the cell status must be informative enough to serve as the input to the cell management services, while lending itself to technically feasible monitoring by Megascope. We believe that suitable cell-status descriptions will evolve together with the practice and the concepts of the DCE. Our analytical efforts aim at understanding the inherent characteristics of the DCE that must be captured by such status descriptions. Our design and implementation efforts aim at providing an operational, flexible, and extensible status monitoring service that satisfies the requirements of its distributed environment, and affords us a convenient platform for testing alternative concepts and experimenting with various types of instrumentation.

The cell resource status includes the *status of the individual systems* in the cell, so the innermost part of the status information managed by Megascope consists of the standard resource parameters of operating systems and computer hardware, e.g., processing time, memory space in various memory hierarchies, I/O capabilities, devices, etc. (cf. [15]).

The next layer of the monitored resources are the *basic DCE components* (name service, security service, file system, etc.). The exact set of monitored variables that covers the functionality of the basic DCE components is a research topic within the DCE community. The DCE SIG Instrumentation Work Group [8] considers general queuing theory metrics, applied to the cell as a system. It proposes a set of specific variables whose values should be observed in the course of the cell operation (e.g., counts of remotely executed calls, elapsed time per call, counts of requests per server, counts of directory accesses, counts of supported connections, etc.). Megascope design allows easy accommodation and modification of various data items in the status it monitors, so as to adjust easily to the imminent refinements of applicable metrics and, more importantly, to serve as a tool in the assessment of the quality of such metrics.

DCE environments may (as the Pilgrim environment does) provide their own services and utilities that act as extensions of the basic DCE functionality. The normal operation of such *dedicated applications* is in itself a resource, so the status of these applications is subject to reporting by Megascope. A detailed content of this status information also awaits further refinements. Typically, this information includes available capacity of various servers.

The Pilgrim environment offers an example of a novel level of management that accompanies the exploitation of the DCE capabilities and power. Precisely, the Pilgrim environment is able to *instantiate servers dynamically* [10], in response to run-time requests for services. In this complex situation, it is not only the capacity and behavior of cell servers, but the very *existence, number, disposition, and properties of servers* that are subject to continuous change, explicit management, and, consequently, monitoring.

Megascope, as a resource monitoring service, differs from its current alternatives in that Megascope is designed to be a *monitor of distributed environments*, while the alternatives are designed as *monitors of interconnection networks* for such environments. Internet Advisory Board has proposed [3] such a network management standard, the Simple Network Management Protocol (SNMP) [2, 16, 11], while the International Organization for Standardization (ISO) has recommended the Common Management Information Services / Common Management Information Protocol (CMIS/CMIP) [17, 4, 5, 13]. The two standards are now dominant among the non-proprietary network management protocols; both are well suited for network monitoring, and have been subsequently adapted to include monitoring of systems connected into the network. (See e.g., [1] for an illustration of such evolution.) However, the information and communication structure of these protocols remains oriented toward network entities rather than toward higher-level DCE-based abstractions of advanced distributed-computing environments. Through its own information and communication structure, Megascope attempts to report the behavior of DCE cells in more natural terms. Sophisticated monitored entities that do not map trivially onto physical systems, processing tasks that must be expressed with a high degree of independence from the physical systems, performance metrics and management actions that are defined only with respect to the cell as an integrated system, etc., have all prompted our design of Megascope. This design is presented in the following section.

2 Megascope Design

Megascope recognizes a dynamically modifiable set of *systems* that it monitors. Members of this set are computer systems as well as the utilities and services of the distributed computing environment. Monitored systems are characterized by various resources, whose status is followed by Megascope.

Megascope consists of four major components: sensors, panel, observers, and links. (See Figure 1.)

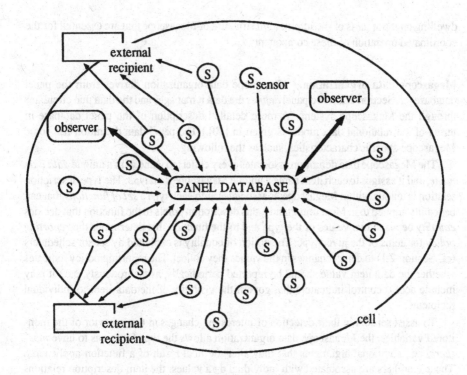

Figure 1: The Major Components of Megascope.

Sensors are components that are conceptually in one-to-one correspondence with monitored systems. Sensors continuously *run, collect* findings about the resources of their monitored systems, *recognize* those findings that qualify for reporting, and *send* the reported findings to interested recipients within Megascope and outside it.

Megascope *panel* is an on-line, in-memory database that defines and manages the instantaneous description and most recent history of the resource profile of the entire cell. The panel information content is continuously updated by sensor data and queried by Megascope users. Panels must *receive* and temporarily store sensor data, *interpret* sensor data to form system status information, *request* sensor actions in order to maintain its information content, and *respond* to remote queries that retrieve panel information.

Observers are consumers of the resource status information. Each observer corresponds to a user, i.e., a person or a program inquiring about the cell status. Observers *interface* users with Megascope panels; *form, partially evaluate, and send* user queries to panels; *receive* panel responses to the user queries; and *present* query results to users.

Links transmit data between sensors, panels, and observers, and *encapsulate* those transmission issues that depend on network protocols and on details of the RPC support.

The remainder of this section discusses individual Megascope components, after dwelling on those parts of the information structure of Megascope that are essential for the coordinated operation of these components.

Megascope data organization. Megascope data organization derives from the panel database (cf. Section 2.2.) The panel *defines* the data it manages and the data that circulates through the Megascope system. (A more detailed description of the panel database in terms of the relational data model is given in [10].) The panel data definition has some Megascope-specific characteristics, such as the following:

The Megascope data definition associates every collected value with a unique *data item name*, and it assigns to each item name a unique Megascope *data type*. The type description relation is unique within Megascope; it associates with each type a *set of functions* that can be legally applied to it. Most importantly, this description points to the function that decides *equality* between two values of the type and to the function that determines the *reporting policy* for items of the given type. The notion of equality is exploited by sensor schedulers (cf. Section 2.1) to detect changes in the values they collect. The reporting policy indicates whether the data item value should be reported periodically, asynchronously, etc.; it may include access control indicators that govern the visibility of the data item to individual recipients.

To assist sensors in their detection of interesting changes in the behavior of the monitored variables, the Megascope data organization allows the type functions to have *modifiers*, i.e., additional arguments that may alter the final result of a function application. These modifiers are associated with individual data values; the item description relations record such modifiers. The panel stores the default values of the modifiers, while sensors build a copy of their own item description relation for each recipient they serve. The purpose of this design may be illustrated by the following scenario.

Assume a data item *client_count* belongs to the data type *count*, with which Megascope associates a suitable equality function. Given two counts, say x and y, a possible choice of an equality function may be one that decides that $x = y$ if $|x - y| \leq \Delta$, where Δ is a modifier. Thus the equality of any pair of counts is always determined by the same function, specified in the count type description; the outcome of the comparison, however, depends on the value of the modifier Δ, which characterizes the instance of the comparison. Consider a sensor that detects an absolute change in the *client_count* of a server in a DCE cell, while reporting simultaneously to two applications. The first application is a security service, while the second application is a service that automatically generates and terminates servers of a certain kind, in accordance with the number of clients that contend for that service. The latter application may wish to be informed of a change in the *client_count* only if it is detected when $\Delta \geq 5$, while the security service may require $\Delta = 0$. To perform its task correctly for both recipients, the sensor applies the same equality function, defined by the panel database, to the same collected values, but allows its recipients to supply their modifiers. By the conceptual separation of the intrinsic *procedures* that govern the behavior of a data type from the *interpretation* of its values, Megascope keeps its data definition reasonable and manageable, and still sufficiently flexible.

The sensor data values passed between various Megascope components are themselves tuples whose relation schemes are defined by the panel. For each domain in such a relation scheme, the corresponding tuple contains a pair consisting of the name of the domain (item) and its value. Since the value representation is a part of the type description, these sensor data values are guaranteed to be interpreted identically throughout Megascope. The streamlined relational format of Megascope is expected to be compatible with the existing data management and presentation tools, thus enabling Megascope to exploit such tools for its conventional database functions. In particular, Megascope sensor data structure can be manipulated so that sensor data be made available in a manner compatible with the SNMP [11, 16] and CMIS/CMIP [13, 6] frameworks.

2.1 Sensors

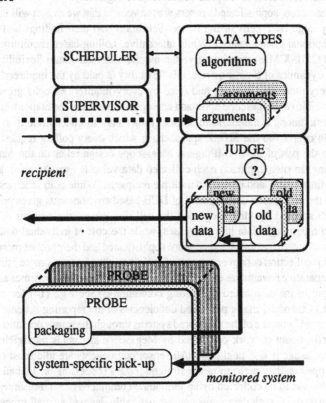

Figure 2: Megascope Sensor Structure.

Sensors are autonomous and responsible for their own configuration, startup, and correct operation. Once assigned to a system, a sensor is expected to operate whenever its monitored system operates. The functions actually performed by a sensor depend on the services requested from the sensor by its environment. Its main function is to collect data from its monitored system and to send the collected data to the *recipients* in the cell. The recipients of an individual sensor are those agents in the cell that have contacted the sensor with a request for receiving its data.

The power of sensors. Every sensor consists of one *scheduler*, one *supervisor*, and several *probes*. The scheduler, the supervisor, and the probes are each represented (conceptually) by a separate process or a thread. These processes communicate and cooperate, but are asynchronous to one another. The probes are responsible for *gathering* the resource findings and *converting* them into the internal Megascope representation. The scheduler is responsible for the sensor control and the actual data flow from the probes to the recipients, while the supervisor receives recipient requests. (See Figure 2.)[3]

The autonomous, sophisticated sensors are the vehicle that we expect will take Megascope to very large DCE cells of the future. Sensors *report* their findings and are polled only in exceptional circumstances. While alternative, polling-based monitoring schemes (SNMP and CMIS/CMIP) certainly give the inquirers the maximum flexibility as to the content and dynamics of their inquiries, this flexibility is paid by the inquirers' overhead, once for every monitored system, and once by every inquirer. As cells grow, this cost becomes prohibitive. Megascope approach attempts to distribute the responsibility for the collection task among a multitude of sensors rather than to concentrate it in individual recipients. In contrast to the SNMP approach, in which every polling request initiates a sampling on the part of the SNMP agent, Megascope design relies on the sensor-driven data gathering. In such approach each collected data value is time-stamped, kept for an appropriate time extent, and offered to multiple recipients. While both schemes have their advantages, the anticipated development of DCE-based environments gives preference to the approach adopted by Megascope. As the cell size grows, the number of recipients interested in a particular data item increases, while the cost of individual data sampling rises as the monitored systems become more sophisticated and their probes more complex. Spreading the collection cost over a group of recipients thus becomes more attractive.

The comparative advantages of polling and reporting monitoring schemes are a current research topic in the distributed-computing community. (See e.g., [14] for a survey of the problem.) One of the major perceived deficiencies of the reporting schemes is in their impact on the performance of the monitored systems through the sensor operation overhead. The expected amount of work performed by Megascope sensors is negligible, therefore their resource usage is also negligible. All sensor components are idle most of the time. When they operate, they perform rather straightforward processing on a small number of data items that are to be collected by an individual computer system. Presently, hundreds or even thousands of such data items can be justifiably deemed a small processing task, and will be even more so in the future.

Further potential disadvantage of reporting schemes is seen in the danger of overwhelming the inquirers by an uncontrolled concentration of unsolicited data. Our strategy

---

[3]Within the figures in this document, the individual boxes correspond to processing agents or large data objects, while the arcs depict data paths. The line thickness indicates the volume of flow (e.g., collected data vs. control messages) and the line continuity indicates the frequency of transmission (e.g., continuous sending vs. exceptional messages).

is to avoid this danger by investing local resources available to sensors so as to reduce the communication and processing required from recipients and other components of Megascope. The challenge is to design these components so that autonomous sensor processing matches the needs of diverse recipients. The internal sensor functions and components, designed towards this goal, are discussed in the remainder of this subsection.

Megascope probes. The repertoire of resource data monitored by Megascope ranges from events and counts associated with physical devices to possibly sophisticated descriptions of the behavior of environment utilities. To obtain these data, sensors invoke the services of the systems they monitor. These services and their invocation mechanisms vary across the set of monitored systems and the set of monitored data. The Megascope response to this diversity in the monitored data is its variety of sensor probes.

Each probe is a processing agent that obtains some subset of the monitored data. This subset contains findings that are related by their origin, so that they are best collected together. For example, a standard system call in an operating system that inquires into the status of a device usually returns exhaustive status data containing several related data items. Such a system call is typically utilized by one probe. Similarly, another probe may report several data items that together describe the transaction activity of a distributed database. Probes manage invocations of their underlying system services, select the data items of interest, and make these items available to sensor schedulers.

Every probe is special for its specific gathering goals and mechanisms. To avoid a potential pitfall of profusion of various probes, each of them being an *ad hoc* solution to a particular monitoring problem, Megascope insists on keeping the probe functions restricted to *immediate gathering of findings and their conversion to the canonical data format*. Once the data items are encoded in this universal format, their semantics becomes virtually transparent to sensor schedulers.

Probe templates. Given the size and the diversity of the environment, it is inevitable and desirable that a multitude of designers and implementors come to be concerned with the probe repertoire, while having insight into only a small subset of mutually related probes. To ensure compatibility among the probes, Megascope insists on keeping the system-dependent probe components, *probe pick-ups*, as simple and isolated and possible. Megascope strategy is to build and administrate various *probe templates*, which are incomplete probe modules that become probes by including pick-up components. Templates are responsible for probe control, interaction with the scheduler, and in general for those issues in the probe operation that are critical for maintaining the proper structure and functioning of Megascope system as a whole.

Individual probe templates correspond to specific gathering situations and anticipate them. For example, one probe template may drive various pick-ups that are all associated with a particular operating system. The structure of this template is dominated by its association with a single computer system, by the mainly periodic invocation of its pick-ups, and by its relying on the standard application interface to its monitored system. In contrast to this template type, another template is required for monitoring the level of activity in video conferences, travel reservation services, or banks. The pick-ups for all these applications may be driven by a single template type, which must enable distributed and asynchronous collection, and may require explicit cooperation of the monitored applications.

Sensor control and communication structure is identical throughout Megascope and, for a given sensor, independent of its probes. The variety of probe templates is such that can be managed by Megascope administration, while specific pick-ups are free to fill the open-ended Megascope collection repertoire, on condition that they fit properly into their templates.

Reporting changes only.   Schedulers are designed so as to keep the tasks of collection and sending separated. While the collection dynamics is maintained by probes, the sending is organized by schedulers so as to satisfy the recipient preferences. The generic strategy of Megascope is to let the *sensors send only those findings whose value is not equal* to the last value actually reported.

To implement their strategy, sensors remember the last value of every data item sent to every recipient. To test for equality, sensors compare the old and new values by invoking the Megascope-specific equality function associated with the given data type in the Megascope data definition. The modifiers to this function are supplied by each recipient, thus allowing for different interpretations of the same absolute findings by different recipients.

Schedulers may deviate from their strategy of reporting changes only and decide to report data even when no significant change has occurred. Schedulers do so when the elapsed time since the last sending is long enough to mislead a recipient to deduce that the sensor is no longer operating. Since the sensor is the active party in a regular communication, the recipient cannot distinguish a missing sensor from one that does not have any interesting findings. This problem is believed to be inherent in reporting schemes, while those based on polling may reliably detect failures of monitored systems by registering the absence of a response to their request. In reality, the anticipated size of DCE cells precludes any inquirer from exhaustive polling; it also makes it difficult for a monitored system to service polls from all interested inquirers. The Megascope approach enables sensors to confirm their existence only as often as is necessary, while the recipients may have to poll only when there is a good evidence that the sensor is not operating. The implied uncertainty in this method of failure detection depends solely on the confirmation interval, which is a part of the sensor reporting policies that can be selected and tuned in accordance with recipient preferences.

Sensor ability to avoid redundant transmission comes with a very modest cost in sensor information and control complexity. By exploiting a modest amount of those resources that are likely to be abundant in DCE cells: local memory for storing the recipient context and processing cycles for evaluating it, sensors enable their recipients to engage only in the reception of *customized, relevant information.*

Sensor command interface.   To establish connections with recipients, sensor supervisors support a simple Megascope-specific *command interface* that enables sensors to receive and service recipient requests. Sensor commands arrive asynchronously to sensor operation;

they are always initiated by sensor recipients. The first command that a recipient must issue to start receiving data from a sensor is a *connect* request to the sensor. The connect, disconnect, and modify requests are the core of the sensor command interface.

As a result of a successful connect request, the sensor scheduler builds the context information that records the specific preferences of the individual recipient as to the content and intensity of data communication. The transmission of collected data is thereafter initiated by the sensor scheduler, not by its recipient. Once the recipient has delivered its connect request to the sensor supervisor, the recipient is free to be a passive partner in the data communication, whose task is limited to the reception of the sensor data. Ideally, a sensor supports an arbitrary number of recipient connections, where each connection is unaware of the others, and serviced in a customized way.

The simplicity found in polled sensors and in their interface to inquirers is often seen as an advantage of polling schemes over the reporting schemes. Indeed, Megascope sensors are more complex than, e.g., SNMP agents (cf. [2].) However, once Megascope sensors are configured and running in the environment, their dialog with recipients is neither substantially more complex nor does it demand more communication resources than the dialog between management stations and agents of SNMP. Sensor command repertoire is small, while the commands have simple, value-setting meaning within the recipient context. Sensor commands issued by recipients having sufficient privileges are always accepted and executed unconditionally. However, the semantics of our command interface differs essentially from that of SNMP in what may be termed an extra level of indirection. While SNMP commands are issued regularly to solicit the transmission of *actual sensor data values*, Megascope sensor commands operate relatively infrequently on the *data definition* of these values. The flow of actual sensor data in Megascope has an extremely simple form: it is unconditional and asynchronous, and since it is unidirectional (from schedulers to recipients), it consumes only about one half of the bandwidth that would be required by a polling scheme operating on identical data.

Dynamically modifiable sensor policies. The recipient context kept by the sensor scheduler associates with every requested data item the modifiers required for evaluating its equality function and its actual transmission frequency, as preferred by the individual recipient. To change these preferences, or to modify the reception repertoire, the recipient issues a modify command to the scheduler. The modify command associates the specified data items with new values of their description fields, thereby establishing new reception dynamics, which remains in effect until overridden by another command. Schedulers thus support a flexible interface to multiple mutually independent parties. This interface affords a recipient an efficient *feedback path* to its sensors, through which the recipient may tune its reception to suit its instantaneous needs. In a special case of the modify command, the recipient may demand immediate transmission of its monitored repertoire, thus emulating polling.

Polling schemes are often preferred for their simplicity of sensor configuration. Such simplicity is, however, a result of the total absence of flexibility in sensor structure and operation, as all such sensors are equal and respond equally to all inquirers. Reporting schemes tend to develop many distinct specialized sensors, whose management becomes burdensome because of their diversity. While Megascope sensors all have identical control structure, each sensor may be configured for a distinct collection repertoire, and may be reconfigured to respond to specific recipient preferences. Megascope sensors thus may be all effectively distinct, while being managed identically throughout Megascope. Partially responsible for this flexibility is the panel database.

2.2 Panel

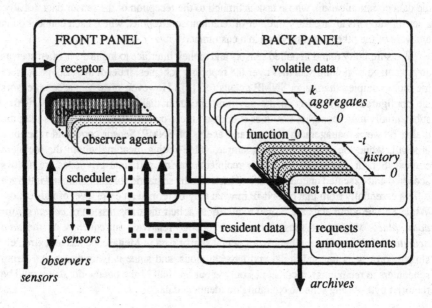

Figure 3: Megascope Panel Structure.

In the Pilgrim environment, the Megascope panel receives the data collected by all sensors. Panel stores the sensor information, maintains it for a limited period of time in its *recent history* space, and computes various aggregate functions on the sensor data. Panel responds to observer queries that retrieve the sensor information.

The Megascope panel runs continuously on its host. We assume that in very large environments it may require a dedicated computer system.

Panel database. The ultimate purpose of the panel database is to answer observer inquiries about the resource status. We term this resource information *volatile*, to emphasize its ephemeral character within the panel, and to contrast it to the *resident* information, which is persistent but dynamically modifiable. The resident information consists of two parts. The first part is the data definition of the volatile data, as found in standard database systems. The second part is a description of the relevant *static characteristics* of the monitored systems, on which the volatile information is superimposed. In terms of the relational data model one of the most important views supported by the panel database has the following relational scheme:

relational scheme *MainView* :

    <system-name> <system-resident-fields> <system-volatile-fields> <time-fields>.

Although the resident database is designed to be modifiable dynamically, these modifications need not be inexpensive. While the volatile data follows frequent fluctuations in the environment *behavior*, the resident database accomodates only the relatively infrequent changes in the environment *structure*. Dynamic modifications of the resident database grant a degree of flexibility to Megascope that is not present in the original IAB framework, where the repertoire of the monitored data is fairly static in that it cannot be easily extended by individual sensors. (See [1] for more details on the problem and a version of the solution.) Megascope design enables convenient dynamic modification of the sensor and recipient repertoire. A recompilation is required only when new data-type functions are introduced.

The power of dynamic modification of the resident database is especially important in the case of system families.

System families. A *system family* partitions the set of monitored systems in two subsets, one of which comprises the *members* of the family. The member set of each family is in turn partitioned into several subsets, where each member subset is a distinct *gender* of that family. Every system may be a member of several families, but belongs to a single gender in each family. Every family has at least one gender. One example of a conceivable system family could be a family "operating system", whose members would be only those monitored systems that are computers (rather than envirinment services), with every operating system being an individual gender.

Families and their genders are defined so as to group together those monitored systems whose equally named resources can be meaningfully compared, aggregated, and substituted for one another. Every family corresponds to such a grouping criterion; the members of the family are those systems to which the criterion applies; the family members of the same gender are equal by that criterion. Families are a means of *managing the cell heterogeneity* by making it explicit where appropriate. If type-function modifiers depend on the sensor family membership, then simple modifications of the relatively few family relations can produce far-reaching and fine-tuned impact on the behavior of many sensors and the entire Megascope system.

Families should be defined so as to represent those characteristics of monitored systems that are relevant for the interpretation of resource data in a *specific cell*. Some families may turn out to be readily accepted, like those that reflect technological, topological, or administrative properties of the monitored systems. Some families may be defined in order to improve the efficiency of Megascope administration, by associating certain properties with large groups of related systems rather than with individual systems. Obvious candidates for such management-related families are those that define access-rights and those that define arguments for normalization functions. (Normalization functions render absolute values of equal-named monitored variables in mutually compatible form, e.g., by recognizing that equal time extents on processors of different speeds amount to different processing capacities.)

Panel queries. Most of the queries *retrieve* items from the volatile data set; retrieval is the only operation that can be aplied to the volatile data. The resident database admits appropriately administered *retrieval, storage, and modification.*

The retrieval queries may be thought of as addresing the *MainView* scheme; their general form may be outlined as follows:

> **select** <*system-name*><*volatile-fields*> **from** *MainView* **where**
> <*system-resident-fields*> **satisfy** "expression" **and**
> <*system-volatile-fields*> **satisfy** "simple-expression"

To understand the content and the form of <*volatile-fields*> and the selection expressions, the query should be viewed as consisting of *two sequential stages*, where the first-stage query is issued to the resident database, while the second-stage query retrieves the volatile data. The first stage *selects* a set of interesting systems, while the second stage *retrieves* the resource data of the selected systems. We anticipate that the evaluation of the selected set may involve the unrestricted set of the standard database operations over the resident data. In contrast to the first stage, the second stage is essentially a projection with simple selections based on values of individual items, followed by applications of simple aggregate functions on the result. Two explicit stages in the query structure respond to anticipated observer interests in large homogeneous substructures within the heterogeneous environment. The first stage establishes such a substructure, while the second stage explores it.

Panel control. Most of the panel tasks are essentially parallel and mutually asynchronous. It is therefore conceptually appealing and practically advantageous to view the panel as if it were a set of largely independent agents that interact with the outside world and interfere with one another in a controlled fashion. This concept is preferable to that of a single compact panel for one more reason: facilitating distribution of panel operation over several physical hosts. On the highest level, the panel tasks are classified in two groups: the foreground tasks executed by the *front panel*, and the background tasks executed by the *back panel*.

The front panel *communicates* with sensors and observers. Its operation is completely driven by the events generated by sensors and observers. Upon receiving a *sensor message*, the front panel decodes it and stores its content into the volatile database. To avoid delays, the front panel does not attempt to analyze the received data in any way other than identifying it to the extent that is required to store it. Upon receiving an *observer query*, the front panel computes its response and sends it to the observer.

The back panel is mostly engaged in *computation* and its schedule is based on timing rather than on event occurrence. The background tasks in general consist of continuous inspection and filtering of the panel database, so that various regular and exceptional operations are performed on the data. Rich and exploitable data-level parallelism is inherent in the background processing. The background tasks include: maintaining the resident database, maintaining the recent history of the volatile data, handling exceptional values discovered in the volatile set or received by a sensor, archiving the volatile data, etc.

2.3 Observers

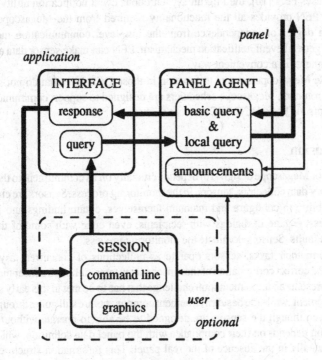

Figure 4: Megascope Observer Structure.

Observers are started on the request of users or programs that wish to retrieve the panel information. They run on the host that initiates the request.

Observer responsibilities. Observers collect *valid queries* from the user and present them to the panel, and receive *query responses* from the panel and present them to the user. As a part of this task, observers offer a convenient user interface.

In an attempt to *distribute the processing task,* Megascope observers assume partial responsibility for *computing query results*. This responsibility implies decomposing user queries into two parts whose composition is equivalent to the original query: the *basic part,* which is forwarded to the panel, and the *local part,* which is evaluated by the observer. The local part factors out those query evaluation steps that only rearrange the already retrieved data. Such steps can be performed at the user site rather than by the panel. For instance, if the user requests a normalized, sorted selection, the observer breaks this query into a basic selection plus a local normalization and sort.

2.4 Links

Megascope uses PEN [10], the Pilgrim asynchronous event notification utility, as its link component. PEN provides all the functionality required from the Megascope links and guarantees a degree of independence from the low-level communication mechanisms. Finally, as a general event notification mechanism, PEN can make sensor data available to external recipients in a convenient way.

To enable Megascope sensors to function in those DCE cells that do not support the Pilgrim environment, Megascope schedulers are designed to support communication with their recipients via basic DCE RPC services.

3 Conclusion

The success of Megascope design [10] depends crucially on its commitment to the advanced role of primary data collectors, sensors, in the monitoring process. Sensors are charged with the responsibility to configure and maintain themselves, obtain findings and judge their interestingness, engage in dialogs with recipients, even cope with some of the possible environment faults. Sensors dominate the monitoring process.

To perform their tasks, sensors operate as collections of concurrent asynchronous processes. The correct coordination of the sensor subsystems, although conceptually clear in our design, presents an implementation challenge that has to be met in this early stage of the DCE development, while the basic environment components are still going through frequent revisions. Even though the sensors are designed to be able to operate without the panel, their operation depends on their compliance with the panel data definition, which must be enforced manually in the absence of the real panel. This information structure, designed to support autonomous and ambitious sensor operation, is also challenging, because of its nonstandard meaning and nontrivial behavior.

Our proposal of sensors and the entire Megascope attempts to overcome the imminent polling bottleneck of traditional monitors by investing a moderate amount of the local computation resources and by insisting on the high-quality design and implementation. Our present work on the implementation of sensors looks for a confirmation of our concepts.

References

[1] G. Carpenter and B. Wijnen (1991): SNMP-DPI, Simple network management protocol distributed program interface. *IAB RFC* 1228.

[2] J. Case, M. Fedor, M. Schoffstall, J. Davin (1990): A simple network management protocol (SNMP). *IAB RFC* 1157.

[3] Cerf, V. (1988): IAB recommendations for the development of internet network management standards. *IAB RFC* 1052.

[4] International organization for standardization (1988): Information processing systems - Open systems interconnection, Management information service definition, Part 2: Common management information service. *ISO* 9595.

[5] International organization for standardization (1988): Information processing systems - Open systems interconnection, Management information protocol specification, Part 2: Common management information protocol. *ISO* 9596.

[6] OIM Working Group (1991): OSI internet management: Management information base. L. Labarre, ed., *IAB RFC* 1214.

[7] Open Software Foundation (1992): *Introduction to DCE*. Open Software Foundation, Cambridge, Massachusetts.

[8] OSF DCE SIG Instrumentation Work Group (1993): Requirements for performance instrumentation of DCE RPC and CDS services. R. Friedrich, ed., *OSF DCE SIG RFC* 32.0.

[9] Project Pilgrim (1992): *Pilgrim Newsletter*. May 1992, University of Massachusetts.

[10] Project Pilgrim (1992): *Project Pilgrim Document Set*. November 1992, University of Massachusetts.

[11] M. Rose and K. McCloghrie (1990): Structure and identification of management information for TCP/IP-based internets. *IAB RFC* 1155.

[12] B. Searle (1993): DCE managed objects. *OSF DCE SIG RFC* 38.0.

[13] SNMP Working Group (1991): Management information base for network management of TCP/IP-based internets: MIB-II. K. McCloghrie and M. Rose, ed., *IAB RFC* 1213.

[14] L. Steinberg (1991): Techniques for managing asynchronously generated alerts. *IAB RFC* 1224.

[15] UNIX International (1993): *Requirements and draft specifications for the Universal Measurement Architecture (UMA)*. UNIX International, Parsippany, New Jersey.

[16] S. Waldbusser (1991): Remote network monitoring management information base. *IAB RFC* 1271.

[17] U. Warrier, L. Besaw, L. LaBarre, B. Handspicker (1990): The common management information services and protocols for the internet. *IAB RFC* 1189.

Supporting Continuous Media in Open Distributed Systems Architectures

Phil Adcock, Nigel Davies, Gordon S. Blair

Distributed Multimedia Research Group,
Department of Computing,
Lancaster University,
Bailrigg,
Lancaster,
LA1 4YR,
U.K.

telephone: +44 (0)524 65201
e-mail: mpg@comp.lancs.ac.uk

Abstract. Recent developments in high-speed networks and high-performance workstations have led to the emergence of a new class of applications termed distributed multimedia applications. However, the range of distributed systems architectures currently being proposed to support open systems integration were largely conceived prior to these developments. Initial work directed towards the introduction of multimedia in environments compatible with ISO's Open Distributed Processing (ODP) standard has suggested that significant developments to the underlying architecture are required. These developments are now being reflected in new versions of the ODP standard. However, OSF's Distributed Computing Environment (DCE), currently emerging as a de-facto standard for distributed processing, does not fully address the requirements of multimedia computing. This paper reports on the impact that multimedia has had on the ODP community and examines how the community's experiences can be used as a basis for incorporating multimedia in DCE.

1 Introduction

Widespread recognition of the potential benefits of multimedia computing has prompted significant research interest in this field in recent years. A range of single workstation multimedia applications are now available combining varying sources of information such as voice, video, audio, text and graphics. Examples of these stand-alone multimedia applications include interactive video systems and computer aided learning packages.

Further benefits from multimedia computing can be achieved if support for multiple media types is provided within a *distributed* environment. Such support allows the realisation of applications including video conferencing systems, collaborative working and multimedia design environments. The emergence of high-speed networks and protocols (e.g. FDDI, ATM), high-performance workstations (executing many millions of instructions per second) and large-capacity storage devices (e.g. optical disks, disk arrays) has enabled researchers to construct such distributed multimedia systems [1].

However, in order to address the problems of operating in a hetrogeneous environment, Open Distributed Architectures must evolve to meet the requirements of this new class of applications. Researchers at a number of institutions are considering the implications of multimedia on distributed architectures (e.g. Comet [2] and the Touring Machine [3]). The results of this work are now beginning to impact on ISO's emerging standard for Open Distributed Processing (ODP) [4]. This work has not yet been mirrored in OSF's Distributed Computing Environment (DCE) which is rapidly becoming the industrial de-facto standard for distributed systems [5].

This paper describes the impact which providing support for multimedia applications has had on the ODP community and highlights aspects of DCE which will need extending if a similar level of functionality is to be provided. Section 2 of the paper presents a summary of the key requirements of any platform designed to support distributed multimedia applications. Section 3 considers the impact these requirements have had on the ODP architecture and describes a set of ODP compatible services which have been developed to support distributed multimedia applications (a brief introduction to the relevant sections of the ODP architecture is also included). Section 4 then highlights aspects of DCE which, in the authors opinion, will need to be extended in order for DCE to provide a similar level of functionality. Section 5 contains some concluding remarks.

2 Requirements of Multimedia

Experimental distributed multimedia applications are being developed in many areas such as educational systems [6], medical systems [7] and computer based conferencing [8]. In this section we consider system support requirements derived from a wide ranging study of distributed multimedia applications [9], under the following headings:-

i)   explicit support for continuous media,

ii)   quality of service (QoS) specification,

iii)   synchronisation, and,

iv)   support for group communication.

These requirements are discussed in more detail in the following sections.

2.1 Support for Continuous Media

The various forms of media in a multimedia system can be categorised as either *static* or *continuous*. Static media are those which do not have a temporal dimension. In contrast, continuous media (e.g. video and audio) have an implied temporal dimension, i.e. they are presented at a particular rate for a particular length of time

[10]. These *real-time* characteristics of continuous media demand a *continuing commitment* from the underlying system in terms of services provided. Since continuous media require sustained system support over a period of time, a means of resource reservation is required such that resources can be reserved in advance for the time they are needed. Continuous media types also require the development of new programming abstractions to model communications and storage which capture the concept of information flowing over time [11].

2.2 Quality of Service

Continuous media applications make heavy use of underlying support systems in terms of processing, storage and communications. Research effort is therefore being directed towards the development of tailorable systems which can meet the diverse requirements of such applications. A tailorable system is able to adapt itself according to application quality of service requests and resource availability.

It is important to note that, within a multimedia system, quality of service must be provided on an *end-to-end* basis. Applications need to control resource allocation completely from the information source to the information sink. Typical components in this control path include I/O devices, operating system processes and a communications network.

Quality of service configurability is also applicable to *control* information sent between system components. Control messages with bounded delay characteristics must be available to allow the system to react to real-time events in a timely manner. Again, control messages require end-to-end guarantees of service which take into account all the system components which make up the message's path. Programmers must be provided with a means of specifying their QoS requirements for both continuous media transmissions and control messages.

2.3 Synchronisation

Multimedia applications require an extensive range of *synchronisation mechanisms*. Synchronisation is required to control the event orderings and precise timings of multimedia interactions. In analysing the requirements of multimedia applications, two styles of synchronisation can be identified [12]:-

    i)   real-time events, and

    ii)   continuous synchronisation.

Real-time events occur when it is necessary to initiate an action (such as displaying a caption) in a distributed system. The timing of this action may correspond to a reference point such as a particular video frame being displayed.

Continuous synchronisation arises when data presentation devices must be tied together so that they consume data in fixed ratios. The primary example of this type of synchronisation is a 'lip-sync' relationship between a video transmission and a separately stored soundtrack.

From our experiences in handling audio and video, we believe it is likely that these styles of real-time synchronisation require a global time service providing a granularity of the order of 1 millisecond, for example to bound the latency of real-time events [13].

2.4 Support for Group Communications

The concept of process groups has been demonstrated as a useful tool for constructing distributed applications [14]. The use of this technique is likely to increase as more applications are designed to support groups of collaborating users (as is the case in many CSCW applications). The introduction of support for multimedia demands that the ability to message process groups is matched by a corresponding ability to transmit continuous media to groups of users. This requirement is particularly evident when considering the implementation of applications such as video conferencing systems where a single speaker may wish to communicate with a group of colleagues.

3 The Impact of Multimedia on ODP

The Distributed Multimedia Research Group at Lancaster has developed an application platform which addresses many of the requirements described in section 2. The platform has been designed to conform to ISO's ODP draft standards where possible and the platform and the issues it raises are described from both *computational* and *engineering* viewpoints in the following sections.

3.1 The Computational Model

The programming interface presented to the application is based on the computational model developed as part of the ANSA/ISA project [15]. The ANSA/ISA (Integrated Systems Architecture) project is funded within the C.E.C.'s Esprit program and is playing an important role in the development of standards for Open Distributed Processing.

The ANSA computational model provides a programming language model of potentially distributed objects and their modes of interaction. All interacting entities are treated uniformly as *objects*. Objects are accessed through *interfaces* which define named *operations* together with constraints on their *invocation*.

Services are made available for access by *exporting* an interface to a *trader*. The trader therefore acts as a database of services available in the system. Each entry in this 'database' describes an interface in terms of an abstract data type signature for the object and a set of attributes associated with the object. A client wishing to interact with a service interface must *import* the interface by specifying a set of requirements in terms of operations and attribute values. This is matched against the available services in the trader and a suitable candidate selected. Note that an exact match is not required: ANSA supports a subtyping policy whereby an interface providing at least the required behaviour can be substituted. Once an interface has been selected, the system can arrange a *binding* to the appropriate implementation of that object and thus allow operations to be invoked. The ANSA consortium have released a software suite called ANSAware which is a partial implementation of the ANSA model.

The authors have proposed a number of extensions to the ANSA architecture to allow the integration of continuous media types such as audio and video [12]. Support for these media types has been implemented without substantial modifications to the basic model of objects and invocation. Instead, integration has been achieved through the introduction of a number of new services. We call this set of new services the *base service platform*. It consists principally of two types of object: *devices* and *streams*. These are both seen by the higher layers as ANSA services with standard abstract data type interfaces, but they encapsulate the control, manipulation and communication of continuous media.

Devices are an abstraction of physical devices, stored continuous media, or software processes. They may be either sinks, sources or transformers of continuous media data. Most devices present two interfaces: a device dependent interface which contains operations specific to the device (e.g. a camera might have operations such as pan or tilt) and a generic control interface for controlling the device's production and consumption of continuous media. Using the control interface, clients of a device may create an *endpoint interface* on the device. This interface abstracts over all aspects of a device which are concerned with the transport of continuous media data.

Streams are the services used to connect devices together via their endpoint interfaces. They are abstractions of continuous media transmissions which map down on to underlying transport protocols. Streams may be tailored to provide a particular QoS (e.g. high-throughput, low error-rate etc.). Streams support M:N connections, i.e. they allow M sources to be connected to N sinks. This is modelled by allowing endpoint interfaces to be grouped together, and ensuring streams interconnect these groups as shown in figure 1. Note that endpoint interfaces may be dynamically added to or removed from groups.

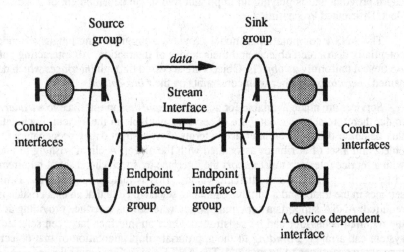

Figure 1 : Using streams to connect endpoint interface groups.

In section 2 we identified two distinct forms of synchronisation, i.e. real-time events and continuous synchronisation. Implementing both of these forms of synchronisation requires the transmission of timely control messages. At the computational level this implies that programmers may specify time bounds (i.e. earliest and latest return times) for invocations. Application synchronisation requirements may be specified using a number of techniques including complex (compound) object structures [16] and languages which include a temporal dimension [17]. Further details of the approach to multimedia synchronisation being adopted at Lancaster may be found in [17].

A prototype implementation of this model was carried out in a standard UNIX workstation environment to allow the validation of the programming interface. This has proved successful, and a number of applications including an audio/video conferencing facility have been implemented [18].

3.2 Engineering Issues

A computational model must be supported at the systems level in order to function. This is achieved by defining an engineering model which specifies the guidelines, concepts and specifications required to provide adequate support. Objects visible from the engineering viewpoint include transparency and control mechanisms, processors, memory and communications networks.

The ANSAware package provides a fairly complete implementation of the ANSA engineering model described in the ANSA Reference Manual [15]. It provides an Interface Definition Language (IDL) which allows interfaces to be defined in terms of their operations and a Distributed Processing Language (prepc) which allows a programmer to specify interactions between programs which support those interfaces. Prepc statements, which are embedded in a host language such as C, allow servers to *export* their services to a trader and allow clients to *import* any required services, establishing a binding in the computational model. Clients may then invoke operations on a server's interface.

Communications support for the invocation model is provided by a remote execution protocol (REX) which is layered on top of a message passing service (MPS). REX is a remote procedure call protocol which supports the binding necessary for invocations. MPS is a generic transport layer which provides communications support.

The functionality of the engineering model is integrated into a library which is linked with application code to form a *capsule* which may implement several computational objects. In a UNIX environment a capsule is implemented as a process. In order that objects may deal with invocations concurrently, support is also provided for multiple lightweight threads within capsules.

To meet the requirements of continuous media, the engineering model must include support for a time-constrained remote procedure call mechanism which supports the transmission of timely control messages. By specifying both a lower and an upper bound on the time at which a message should be delivered to its destination the system is able to compensate for the problem of *latency* (mainly network latency) inherent in remote procedure calls. Furthermore, the need to not only *deliver* control messages in real-time, but to have their recipients carry out the required *processing* within certain time bounds requires support from both the recipients operating system's scheduler and the capsule's thread scheduler. In particular, support is required at the threads level in the form of a pre-emptive *deadline scheduling* policy which chooses the next thread to run based on the deadline of its next waiting message. Additional support is required for streams in terms of *high performance communications protocols* which provide the QoS characteristics necessary for continuous media [19].

4 Implications for DCE

This section discusses the implications of supporting multimedia for the DCE architecture. The approach we adopt is similar to that described in section 3, namely to wherever possible augment DCE's computational and engineering models with new services without modifying existing ones. As a starting point we map the required multimedia support services on to a new set of Fundamental Distributed Services (figure 2).

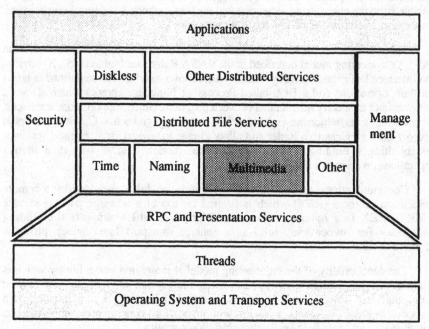

Figure 2 : Integrating multimedia services into DCE.

4.1 Computational Issues

The computational model provided by DCE is not as clearly defined as the computational model in ANSA. An interface definition language (IDL) exists in DCE which defines *attributes* for controlling features of distribution such as bindings. However, no attempt has been made to provide programmers with a uniform set of abstractions for programming distributed systems. Instead, those features of distribution defined by the integrated set of services (figure 2) are accessed by calls to subroutines (e.g. `rpc_ns_binding_import_begin` which establishes the beginning of a search for binding information in the name service database).

The integration of continuous media into the DCE computational model has repercussions for the attributes defined in the IDL such as *pipes*, *bindings*, the *name service* and for IDL itself. The following section discusses the impact of continuous media on the DCE computational model by considering how the device and stream abstractions defined in section 3 could be realised within a DCE system.

Modelling Devices

Devices are supported by two generic interfaces; a *control* interface which provides generic control operations over a continuous source or sink and an *endpoint* interface which abstracts over the transport of continuous media. Control interfaces can be provided as standard DCE interface types. However, the introduction of endpoint interfaces into DCE has implications most notably for the IDL which has no concept of media type, quality of service or continuous media. Introducing the functionality required to support endpoints can be achieved by providing the IDL with a mechanism for specifying whether an interface is discrete or continuous and by providing type/QoS annotations on the continuous interface.

The DCE *attribute configuration file* (ACF) provides additional information about an interface. Current attributes in this file control binding methods, error handling and marshalling/unmarshalling. We will introduce an attribute *continuous* into the ACF to indicate that the interface supports continuous media. If this attribute is not present in the ACF then the interface is discrete by default. Media type will be denoted by media type attributes such as *video_media* and *audio_media*.

We can specify the level of QoS in DCE by introducing a *QoS* attribute into the interface definition language (figure 3) which states the required level of QoS in terms of factors such as throughput, jitter and latency. A richer language than that illustrated in figure 3 will eventually be required to capture QoS requirements. QoS constraint languages containing declarative statements of QoS are currently under investigation [20].

```
[
uuid        (A985C864-243G-22C9-D50H-06043C1FCGA3),
version     (1.0),
QoS         ( [Throughput, 8Mbps] [Jitter, 10ms] [Latency, 20ms] )
] interface example_continuous
{
        status get_data(parameters);
        status put_data(parameters);
}
```

Figure 3 : An IDL specification including QoS information.

As discussed in section 2.4, multimedia also demands a rich model of group communications. DCE currently provides a grouping mechanism in the form of *cells* (a logical grouping of machines, resources and users). Objects within cells generally share a common purpose (for example a department or a research group) and have a greater level of trust with each other than with objects in other cells. However, cells do not provide a sufficiently general method of specifying groups to meet the requirements in section 2. Cells are intended to be reasonably static in nature while groups in continuous media systems tend to be highly dynamic (for example in a conferencing system with members joining and leaving the conference). A more flexible approach to groups is required. It is possible to denote groups by storing the relevant binding information in the name service using a *group entry* facility. This must support richer forms of group messaging than is currently possible (including multi-party continuous media connections).

DCE currently provides facilities to message single nodes and a *broadcast* attribute which is attributed to operations in the IDL. Any invocation on an operation with a broadcast attribute is automatically transmitted to all local nodes. The client which made the invocation uses the first reply received and discards the rest. This is not sufficient to implement the messaging of arbitrary groups and a multicast protocol is required.

Modelling Streams

Streams are created as the result of a binding between two continuous interfaces. A binding in the traditional distributed sense denotes a relationship between a client and a server that are involved in a remote procedure call. Binding information is stored in a data structure holding information describing the binding state such as the internet address of the machine bound to, the protocol sequence used (such as TCP or UDP) and a server process address on the host. This data structure is referenced by a pointer commonly known as a *binding handle*.

The DCE environment supports automatic, implicit and explicit bindings, each providing an application programmer with differing degrees of control over bindings. The automatic method provides the least control as bindings are managed by the client stubs. Once a remote procedure call is made, the stubs locate an appropriate server from the name service and make the call. Binding handles are invisible and the client has no choice regarding which server is used. The implicit method requires slightly more programming effort as application code must locate the required server using the name service and obtain the binding information. This allows a client to bind to a specific server. Finally, the explicit method allows a programmer to pass a binding handle explicitly as the first parameter in each remote procedure call. This allows a client to bind to a different server after each remote procedure call.

The binding models described provide no support for the binding of continuous interfaces. In particular they have no embedded notion of quality of service, continuous media types or streams. It is therefore necessary to provide a method of accommodating stream bindings (figure 1) in DCE. This can be achieved by defining a customised binding handle to store the additional binding information relating to the stream, i.e. the type and QoS of the stream. An IDL operation *continuous_bind* can be used to create a *continuous stream binding* between two continuous interfaces using the customised handle. The establishment of the binding must ensure compatibility between the required type/QoS of the stream and types/QoS capabilities of the interfaces involved in the connection. This might involve negotiation with the service requestor.

It is worth noting at this point the role of DCE pipes in the transmission of continuous media. Pipes provide a method of efficiently transmitting large amounts of typed data between a client and a server. However, they do not provide a suitable abstraction for transmitting continuous media. In particular, since pipes are invocation based there is no mechanism for expressing the continuous commitment and synchronisation requirements which can be captured using an explicit stream binding. By adding explicit stream objects to DCE the approaches to specifying synchronisation requirements in ODP (section 3) can also be used within a DCE environment.

4.2 Engineering Issues

The mechanism used to support invocation in DCE is the remote procedure call (RPC) which we use in our model as a method of communicating control information. The semantics of RPC in DCE provide a level of QoS control. However, the parameter of *latency* is not considered and must be addressed in order to provide a level of real-time control which in turn provides real-time guarantees. Our solution is to augment the current RPC model by including a timestamp as a parameter in the call to the remote procedure which specifies a deadline by which the remote procedure must be executed and the result returned. As stated earlier, such augmentation requires support from the threads scheduler. The DCE threads package supports three priority based scheduling policies, *first in first out*, *round robin* and a *timesliced* policy which is the default. However, to support time-stamped RPCs a deadline based scheduling policy is required and this will need to be added to DCE's range of scheduling policies.

In order to identify objects uniquely anywhere in a DCE network, a Universal Unique Identifier (UUID) facility is provided. There are two classes of UUID provided by DCE; Interface UUIDs and Object UUIDs. Interface UUIDs are used in remote procedure calls to give each interface type a unique signature. Object UUIDs are used to map a call to an interface to the appropriate *type managers* which execute the correct server code. No mechanism exists for the subtyping of interfaces as in ANSAware.

An example of the use of object UUIDs is the implementation of a print manager object which implements a range of generic print operations. Although there is only one interface, there may be several type managers, each of which provide different implementations for different models of printer. An object UUID is associated with each printer type and the correct type manager is referenced when an operation is called according to the UUID received with the invocation.

This is important when considering control interfaces which provide a user with a generic point of access to devices, for example when initiating and terminating a video connection. The control interface must be accessible through the name service. Since there is one generic interface which maps on to several implementations for specific multimedia devices, a relationship exists between control interfaces and interface and object UUIDs in DCE. This relationship may be used to map a call to a generic interface to instance-specific manager routines.

It is unclear whether the DCE distributed time service provides sufficient granularity to support the real-time synchronisation requirements of multimedia applications (see section 2.3) and further work must be carried out to establish whether a finer granularity is required. It is clear however that additional engineering support will be required from the underlying operating system which underpins DCE. For example, to support continuous media traffic, it must be assumed that the operating system provides a QoS constrained high performance transport service. Similarly, concepts such as split level scheduling may be required to provide the necessary real-time guarantees for DCE threads [21].

5 Concluding Remarks

Multimedia applications are likely to represent a significant percentage of all future distributed applications and distributed systems architectures must evolve to provide them with adequate support. In the first section of this paper we presented our experiences of extending one such architecture (ODP) to provide the required level of support. Based on these experiences the second section considered how a similar level of functionality could be provided within the framework of OSF's DCE.

The approach adopted is to introduce a new set of fundamental services (i.e. multimedia services) and to modify the existing services as little as possible. We can now be more specific about the contents of the fundamental multimedia services, i.e. they will include stream services and multimedia device abstractions. However, investigation has revealed that some extensions are required in at least three of the existing fundamental services: threads, RPC and the directory (name) service:-

i) Introduction of a *continuous* attribute for continuous interfaces in the IDL.

ii) IDL specification of media types with appropriate attributes.

iii) Definition of the required level of QoS in the IDL for an interface using a *required QoS* statement.

iv) New customised *binding handle* for continuous media bindings.

v) Continuous media *bind* operation for the IDL.

vi) Introduction of *time constrained RPC* with bounded delay characteristics

vii) *Deadline scheduling* policy for threads to enable engineering of time constrained RPCs.

viii) Use of the *name service* for storing continuous media binding information and group-related bindings.

ix) Potentially finer granularity for the distributed time service.

x) Additional support from the underlying operating system and transport services in terms of the communications subsystem and operating system scheduling.

As a future work item the authors hope to investigate a number of these issues further by carrying out a prototype implementation of support for continuous media devices and streams within DCE.

References

1. N.A. Davies and J.R. Nicol: A Technological Perspective on Multimedia Computing. *Computer Communications* Vol. 14 No. 5, June 1991, Pages 260-272.

2. D.P. Anderson and P. Chan: Comet - A Toolkit for Multiuser Audio/Video Applications, *Technical Report* Computer Science Division, EECS Department, University of California at Berkeley, U.S.A., October 1991.

3. P.C. Bates and M.E. Segal: Touring Machine - A Video Telecommunications Software Testbed. *Proc. International Workshop on Network and Operating System Support for Digital Audio and Video*, International Computer Science Institute, Berkeley, University of California at Berkeley, U.S.A., 8-9 November, 1990.

4. ISO. Draft Recommendation X.901: Basic Reference Model of Open Distributed Processing - Part1: Overview and Guide to Use. *Draft Report* ISO WG7 Commitee,1992.

5. Open Software Foundation: OSF DCE Application Development Guide. Rev1.0 Update 1.01, 1992.

6. R. Beckwith, D.G. Jameson and W. Tuck. Distance Learning and LiveNet. *Computer Bulletin* Vol. 2 No. 5, June 1990, Pages 2-4.

7. M. Goldberg, N.D. Georganas, J. Robertson, J. Mastronardi and S. Reed: A Prototype Multimedia Radiology Communication System. *Proc. 2nd IEEE International Workshop on Multimedia Communication*, Ottawa, Canada, April 1989.

8. S.R. Ahuja, J.R. Ensor and D.N. Horn: The Rapport Multimedia Conferencing System. *Proc. Conference on Office Information Systems*, Palo Alto, California, U.S.A., March 23-25, 1988.

9. N. Williams, G.S. Blair and R.A. Head: Multimedia Computing:Applying the Technology. *Internal Report* MPG-91-10, Computing Dept., Lancaster University, Bailrigg, Lancaster LA1 4YR, U.K., 1991.

10. D.P. Anderson, S. Tzou, R. Wahbe, R. Govindan and M. Andrews: Support for Continuous Media in the Dash System. *Proc. 10th International Conference on Distributed Computer Systems*, Paris, France, May 1990.

11. G.S. Blair, G. Coulson, N. Davies and N. Williams: Incorporating Multimedia into Distributed Open Systems. *Proc. EurOpen'91*, Tromsø, Norway, May 1991.

12. G. Coulson, G.S. Blair, N. Davies and N.Williams: Extensions to ANSA for Multimedia Computing. *Computer Networks and ISDN Systems*, Vol. 25, 1992, Pages 305-323.

13. D.B. Hehmann, M.G. Salmony, H.J. Stüttgen: Transport Services for Multimedia Applications on Broadband Networks. *Computer Communications*, Vol. 13, No. 4, 1990, Pages 197-204.

14. K.P. Birman: The Process Group Approach to Reliable Distributed Computing. *Technical Report* Dept. of Computer Science, Cornell University, U.S.A., July 1991.

15. Architecture Projects Management Ltd.: The ANSA Reference Manual Release 01.00, Architecture Projects Management Ltd., Cambridge, U.K., March 1989.

16. P. Hoepner: Synchronising the Presentation of Multimedia Objects - ODA Extensions -. *Proc. Eurographics Multimedia Workshop*, Stockholm, Sweden, April 1991.

17. G. Coulson, G.S. Blair, F. Horn, L. Hazard and J.B Stefani: Supporting the Real-Time Requirements of Continuous Media in Open Distributed Processing. *B.S.I. Document* BSI/IST21/-/1/5:94, also available as *Internal Report* MPG-92-35, Computing Dept., Lancaster University, Bailrigg, Lancaster LA1 4YR, 1992.

18. N. Davies, G. Coulson, N. Williams and G.S. Blair: Experiences of Handling Multimedia in Distributed Open Systems. *Proc. 3rd Usenix International Symposium on Experiences with Distributed and Multiprocessor Systems*, Newport

Beach, California, U.S.A., March 1992.

19. A. Campbell, G. Coulson, F. Garcia and D. Hutchinson: A Continuous Media Transport and Orchestration Service. *Proc. ACM SIGCOMM'92*, Baltimore, Maryland, U.S.A., 1992.

20. J.B. Stefani: Some Computational Aspects of QoS on ANSA, *Internal Report*, CNET, 92131 Issy-les-Moulineaux, France.

21. G.S. Blair, G. Coulson, N. Davies and N. Williams: The Role of Operating Systems in Object-Oriented Distributed Multimedia Platforms. *Proc. 2nd International Workshop on Object-Orientation in Operating Systems*, Dourdan, France, September 24-25, 1992, Pages 134-141.

Integrating RPC and Message Passing
for Distributed Programming

Yi-hsiu Wei[1] and Chuan-lin Wu[2]

[1]IBM Austin, Austin TX 78758, USA. ywei@ausvm1.vnet.ibm.com
[2]The University of Texas at Austin, Department of Electrical and Computer
Engineering, Austin TX 78712, USA. clwu@emx.utexas.edu

Abstract. Client-server and cooperative processing are two models for distributed
programming. The client-server style is simple and powerful. Remote procedure
call (RPC) is its communication mechanism. However, the cooperative processing style is more appropriate for expressing parallelism. Message passing is its
communication method. In this paper, we describe a combined programming
style and present a technique to integrate RPC and message passing in Open
Software Foundation's Distributed Computing Environment (DCE). This DCE
extension allows DCE applications to be designed and implemented in client-
server, peer cooperative processing or a combination of both.

1. Introduction

Distributed programming may adopt one of two general models: client-server computing and peer cooperative processing. These two models take different approaches to
the distribution of work to multiple systems in the network. In the client-server model,
clients are programmed to rely on access to the data, devices or computational
resources of servers to accomplish work. Remote procedure calls (RPCs) [3] are used
by clients in distributed client-server programs for clients to access remote resources.
On the other hand, peer cooperative processing is a good model for coarse granularity
concurrent processing. A peer-to-peer program contains a set of active components
running concurrently. These peer components interact with each other by exchanging
messages synchronously or asynchronously [1].

The client-server model is simple and powerful, but cooperative processing is more
suited for expressing parallelism. A combination of the two may allow a more flexible
way of designing and programming distributed applications. In the mixed style, the
components of a program may communicate with each other via RPC and message
passing at the same time, as appropriate, in different parts of the program.

The Open Software Foundation's (OSF) Distributed Computing Environment (DCE)
[11] provides a synchronous RPC facility as a uniform high-level communication
abstraction. This makes DCE a good client-server computing environment and thus
promotes client-server model of programming. DCE RPC has been used throughout
DCE core components and in all DCE applications. In this paper, we introduce an
extension to the DCE programming model to allow peer cooperative processing as

well as RPC to be used in programming distributed applications on DCE. An integrated facility provides for both synchronous RPC and synchronous/asynchronous message passing primitives in a single underlying RPC framework. As a result, DCE applications can be designed as a set of cooperative concurrent peer entities communicating with each other by exchanging messages and also accessing servers using RPCs.

Both synchronous RPC and major message passing primitives such as synchronous/asynchronous, single/multiple-point-connected, typed-data messaging and remote rendezvous calls are supported in a consistent design. Since the DCE RPC facility comes with three important capabilities: data representation conversion, typed-data marshalling/unmarshalling and support for multiple transport protocols, the integrated facility takes advantage of these capabilities to allow passing typed messages between machines in heterogeneous network environments at a low cost.

Section 2 discusses cooperative processing, client-server computing and a mixed programming style. Section 3 presents the technique for incorporating message passing capability into DCE and shows how the messaging facility is used. Section 4 describes the implementation of the integration. Section 5 is a conclusion.

2. Distributed Programming Models

In this section, we first discuss peer cooperative processing and client-server computing and then introduce a mixed style of both for programming distributed applications.

2.1. Cooperative Processing

Distributed cooperative processing extends parallel execution of programs on multiprocessors to distributed systems. In general, a parallel algorithmic solution to a problem can be represented by a directed graph, which can be considered an abstract parallel program. A node of the graph contains a number of operations. An arc represents the data flow from one node to another. Nodes cooperate with each other by exchanging data via arcs. Data may be produced during or at the end of node processing and consumed at the beginning of or during node processing. A parallel program can be executed in a distributed system by assigning its nodes to multiple machines in the network.

The abstract data flow can be implemented by either shared memory or message passing method. With shared memory, a producer node updates variables and the consumer node reads the variables. Concurrency control and synchronization between these operations are normally accomplished using semaphores, conditional variables or monitors. With message passing, the producer sends a copy of the data to the consumer. The consumer synchronizes with the producer at data 'receive' operation. These two methods are equally powerful and abstract. Either one may simulate the other [7]. Therefore, either method may be adopted exclusively as a uniform communication abstraction in a programming system. For example, NIL [8] uses message passing as the communication abstraction between its processes. While Linda [6] uses logically shared data (tuples) for program communications.

However, these two methods are also complementary to each other in the sense of execution performance. Shared memory method is efficient when two nodes are running on the same machine and have access to a common physical memory. On the other hand, message passing fits well when two nodes are located on different physical machines. Message passing across machines normally involves data copying. A local message passing between nodes in the same system may be optimized to avoid data copying at all through shared memory lazy-copying technique [10].

Since message passing is suited for communications between loosely coupled nodes running on different machines and shared memory is efficient for the communications between tightly coupled nodes running on the same machine, a refined graph model (Figure 1) allows a choice of implementation for the abstract data flow between nodes:

1. A node is a sequential thread of execution. (A node can be mapped to a thread in DCE).
2. A cluster contains a number of tightly coupled nodes which have access to a common memory in the cluster. (A cluster can be mapped to a process in DCE)
3. Inter-cluster node communication is accomplished via message passing.
4. Communications between nodes in the same cluster can be accomplished via shared memory or local message passing.

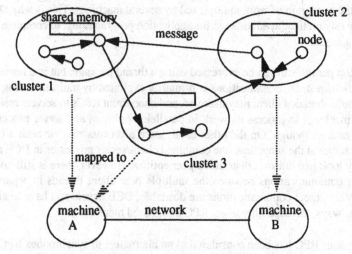

Figure 1. A refined cooperative processing model

A cluster is assigned to a physical machine as a whole. Therefore if two nodes are to be running on different machines, they have to be wrapped in different clusters. Given a number of program clusters distributed on multiple machines, the execution of all active nodes of all clusters is parallel distributed solution of the problem. This model and its variants have been adopted by a few advanced distributed programming systems [2].

The DCE process/thread model is similar to this cluster/node model except that communications between DCE clients and servers are accomplished via synchronous RPC. There is no direct communications between two peer nodes (threads). This limits the expressiveness for parallelism and the interaction among peer programs.

2.2. Client-Server Model

Other than assigning active nodes to multiple machines, work can also be distributed in a client-server style. In a client-server model, servers provide a set of services and clients request and obtain services through synchronous RPCs. Distributed processing is achieved when servers and clients are assigned to multiple machines for execution. This model is well suited to two application domains: 1) remote data services and 2) remote computation services. Example applications are distributed transaction processing and remote numerical intensive computation.

A problem with pure client-server model is that the model offers neither concurrent semantics nor a concept of communications between active program components. Therefore, programming systems such as DCE have to resort to other methods, out side of pure client-server model, for expressing parallelism. Parallelism is at least as important as work distribution. Without parallelism, a distributed processing is merely a sequential execution of work multiplexed by several machines. This is why DCE has to heavily rely on the thread package for application programming, to complete its programming model.

Application parallelism can be expressed using a thread package, but in a limited fashion. Parallelism in DCE applications is primarily exploited by multi-threading the clients. A multi-threaded client may make several concurrent RPCs to servers residing on multiple machines to process its work in parallel. The client and server processes are not peer entities though. On the other hand, since a process may be both a client as well as a server at the same time, the combined client/server processes in DCE applications may look like uniform distributed peer entities. However, there is still no facility for direct communications between the multiple peer client threads in separate processes. When direct communications are desirable, DCE developers have to simulate, in various ways, the capability using RPC and shared memory.

Asynchronous RPC has been considered as an alternative to synchronous RPC to provide some concurrent semantics [4]. An asynchronous RPC immediately returns and continues the execution of local thread after it has sent its input parameters and activated the remote procedure. The result may be left in the server environment or returned and cached in the client side for pick-up later by a subsequent synchronous

RPC from the client. Parallelism can be exploited in the sense that the client and the server can be running in parallel.

This model is restricted. Normally, a client process starts a server process by issuing an asynchronous RPC. The server process gets the input data at the beginning of its execution. It terminates when runs through the end of its routine. The two processes may not communicate freely in the middle of server routine execution. The processes are not peers, and the communication is not symmetric.

Synchronous and asynchronous RPC are therefore not sufficient for programming general peer cooperative applications. Distributed systems, such as DCE, using RPC as the only communication mechanism may not be able to directly support the programming and execution of parallel peer-to-peer applications.

2.3. The Combined Model

There are many situations in the real world where many activities are more like peer-to-peer processing than client-server computing. In the case of a project team, it is very hard (or mind-twisting) to model the activities of team members, who cooperate with each other to get a project finished, as client-server relations. It is even harder to figure out how parallelism due to the activities of individual members can be mapped to multi-threading of clients, the way DCE applications express parallelism.

Nevertheless, the client-server model is still conceptually simple for programming and powerful for reaching distributed services. Indeed, there are many real world systems which can be perfectly modeled by client-server relations. An example is that you may call a plumber to come by and fix your kitchen sink. In addition, the notion of multiple clients accessing the same server concurrently and potentially being serviced in parallel (if the server is on a multiprocessor machine) is very useful. Also, a client may contact a server any time and access it for its services dynamically. It is less straightforward to model these situations in peer-to-peer style than in client-server one.

Therefore, both models are important for describing the real world systems. They are not competitive but complementary. One is simple to program and powerful. The other has inherent parallel semantics. To allow both programming styles to co-exist in an execution environment, the environment has to provide both synchronous RPC and asynchronous/synchronous message passing facilities.

RPC involves one active program accessing remote (conceptually) passive resources. It gives the illusion of transparency. Message passing, on the other hand, involves two active programs exchanging data in various fashions: synchronous/asynchronous, blocking/nonblocking, one/two-directional, and pair/multi-party communications. Each particular message passing model is implemented by a special communication channel, which sits in between the communicating parties. We call this, a port. A port has a queue of message buffers and two operations: send and receive. With the message port, a node may send messages to another node which may in turn receive the messages.

In the combined model, a distributed program is composed of a set of clusters running on multiple machines in the network. Each cluster contains a shared global state and a set of active nodes, passive procedures and message ports. In the DCE environment, clusters are mapped to processes and nodes are mapped to POSIX threads. Threads and procedures in the same process may exchange data via shared variables. They may invoke external service operations exported by other processes. Procedures and port operations can be exported for access by other processes.

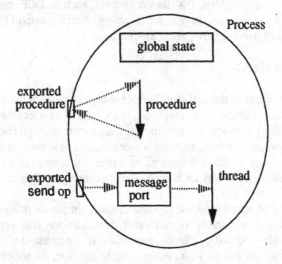

Figure 2. A process with a thread, an exported procedure, a port and a global state.

For example, the process in Figure 2 contains a global memory, a thread, an exported procedure and a port with its send operation exported. The process may contain many internal procedures not shown in the figure. Threads in other processes may send messages to the port by invoking the exported send operation of the port. The thread in this process may receive the messages by invoking the receive operation of the port.

The example distributed application shown in Figure 3 is based on the combined model. This application consists of three processes interacting with each other in a combination of client-server computing and peer cooperative processing.

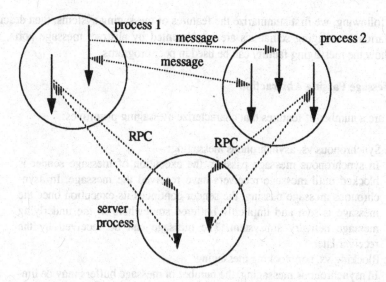

Figure 3. Combined client-server computing and peer cooperative   processing

3. Integrating RPC and Messaging Facility

To extend DCE for peer cooperative processing, a message passing abstraction has to be provided by the environment. Three important capabilities of DCE RPC are re-used to provide this abstraction:

1. Parameter marshalling/unmarshalling service to enable passing typed data between machines.
2. Data conversion capability to enable computing in heterogeneous environments.
3. Transport independent communications to protect applications from directly using low-level
   multiple transport protocols

Being built around the RPC facility, the message passing abstraction is automatically granted these high-level features. In other words, a message port can be typed and a message can contain an ordered set of typed data. A message maintains the same meaning after being transmitted from one machine to another in a heterogeneous network. And, messages can be actually transported by RPC. Thus, a powerful high-level messaging abstraction can be built at a low cost.

What needs be done to extend the system is:

1. Implement the various messaging semantics in a consistent manner
2. Provide a small but rich set (API) of messaging primitives
3. Extending IDL for defining messaging interfaces

In the following, we first summarize the features of messaging systems, then describe how various messaging semantics are implemented by abstract message ports, and show how the messaging facility can be used in peer programs.

3.1. Message Passing Abstraction

There are a number of features that characterize messaging primitives:

1. Synchronous vs. asynchronous messaging:
   In synchronous message passing, the execution of message sender is blocked until message receivers have received the message. In asynchronous message passing, the sender continues its execution once the message is sent and implicitly buffered somewhere in the underlying message delivery subsystem. The message can be received by the receiver later.
2. Blocking vs. nonblocking messaging:
   In asynchronous messaging, the number of message buffers may be limited by implementation. When a sender tries to send a message while all buffers are full, a blocking send operation will block waiting for a buffer to become available. A nonblocking send operation will return immediately with an error and drop the message.
3. One/two-directional messaging:
   Normally, send and receive operations are one directional. A two-directional messaging delivers both forward and backward messages. When a message initiator sends a message to a message responder, it blocks at the operation until a message is returned from the responder. An example of two directional messaging is Ada's entry calls to the rendezvous point in another process (Ada's Task).
4. Pair/multi-party message connection:
   There may be one/multiple senders and one/multiple receivers participate in the same messaging connection. One-sender-to-one-receiver connection is for private conversation. One-to-many connection is a broadcast. Many-to-one connection realizes a mailbox. Many-to-many connection appears in forums, newsgroups or bulletin boards.
5. Persistent Messaging:
   A message may be inspected rather than simply received so that it remains in the message buffer for others to access. This property is useful in forum type messaging.

Various combinations of these features result in versatile messaging systems. For examples, CSP and Occam use synchronous one-to-one-connected one-directional messaging. The Ada's rendezvous calls and Concurrent C's transaction calls [5] are synchronous many-to-one-connected two-directional communications. Concert RPC

[9] can be either synchronous or asynchronous, many-to-one-connected two-directional communications. Most systems have asynchronous many-to-one-connected one-directional communications. The tuple space in Linda may allow asynchronous many-to-many one-directional communications.

3.2. IDL Extension for Port Specifications

The DCE interface definition language (IDL) must be extended for specifying messaging interfaces. A messaging interface may define a number of message ports. Each port is characterized by the type of messages it delivers and the port features it has. A message port is defined by a signature (similar to a remote operation), an operation attribute port and associated features:

. A port name
. A list of message data types
. Exported port operations
. The number of message buffers
. Blocking/nonblocking send/entrycall
. Persistent/non-persistent messaging

The following is an informal syntax of port definition:

```
[port(export(send | rec | call | accept), size(n), blocking, persist)]
        portname(dtype1, dtype2, ...);
```

A message port contains a queue of message buffers and two or three operations. Each message buffer holds a message. A message is an ordered set of typed data. A port which exports send or rec is one-directional. This port thus provides operations send and receive. A send operation enqueues a message and a receive operation dequeues the message. The exported operation can be called from other processes via a normal RPC. Message queue size specifies the number of message buffers available at the port. A port is synchronous if its queue size is zero. A port is asynchronous if its queue size is non-zero. For asynchronous ports, the send operation is a blocking operation if the blocking flag is specified. Nonblocking is the default. A negative queue size means that the number of message buffers is not limited, only subject to the availability of runtime physical storage. When one-directional ports have persist flag specified, they also provide peek operation, in addition to send and receive operations. With these ports, receivers may choose to peek a message rather than receive a message. When call or accept (or both) are specified for export in the port definition, the port is a two-directional port. This port provides operations entrycall and accept for remote rendezvous calls. Port implementation ensures serialization and synchronization of multiple concurrent send and receive operations.

3.3. Using the Messaging Facility

In peer processing mode, application program components export DCE interfaces with port definitions. They use send and receive (or entrycall and accept) operations provided by the ports to exchange messages. In client-server mode, DCE applications export the interfaces with remote procedures specified as usual. In a mixed client-server and peer processing mode, the program components of an application export the interfaces with both port and procedure definitions. The program components may send and receive messages to each other and at the same time make RPCs to the services exported by others. In the following, my_message_if defines three message ports:

```
interface my_message_if
{    :
   [port(export(send), (size 0))]  port1(dtype1);
   [port(export(send), (size 10))]  port2(dtype2, dtype3);
   [port(export(call), (size 5))]  port3([in] in_dtype, [out] out_dtype);
}
```

port1 is a synchronous port, which carries a message with one data element of type dtype1. port2 is an asynchronous port which carries messages with two data elements of types dtype2 and dtype3. port3 is for remote rendezvous call which takes one input parameter of type in_dtype and returns one output parameter of type out_dtype. The send operations of port1 and port2 and the call operation of port3 are exported. Therefore, procedures port1_send and port1_rec are provided by port1. port1_send can be invoked remotely by other processes. port_rec can be invoked by any thread in the same process. Similarly, procedures port2_send and port2_rec are provided by port2. port3 has procedures port3_entrycall and port3_accept. port3_entrycall can be invoked from other processes. port3_accept can be inserted at any desirable rendezvous points in the local thread routines. The last argument of por3_accept specifies the rendezvous service function, which may be a local or remote procedure. This argument is implied and is not shown in the port signature. However, the rendezvous service function must have the same signature as that of port3.

Two peer program components my use this messaging interface:
```
process1:
{    :
   port1_send(data1);
   port2_send(data2, data3);
   port3_entrycall(in_data, out_data);
     :
}

process2:
{    :
   port1_rec(data1);
```

```
port2_rec(data2, data3);
port3_accept(in_data, out_data, entry_function);
    :
}
```

The program component in process1 sends a synchronous message and an asynchronous message. It also issues a remote rendezvous call. The messages are received by the program component in process2. The rendezvous call is also accepted and handled by the same program component. The result of the call is returned to process1 through out_data.

4. Implementation

IDL compiler is extended to generate the implementation of the specified message ports. The extended IDL implements different port types, defined in interface definition files, using a few code templates. These templates contain program structures that ensure serialization of access to a port's message queue and synchronization of send and receive (or entrycall and accept) operations for different port types.

4.1. Port Implementation

In Figure 4, myport is an asynchronous one-directional message port. The implementation of this port provides two operations: send and receive. They correspond to myport_send and myport_rec procedures. The send operation enqueues messages, which is a list of input parameters of the specialized myport_send for the port. The receive operation dequeues messages, which is a list of output parameters of the specialized myport_rec for the port. The output parameters of myport_rec correspond to the input parameters of myport_send. Only one instance of myport_send or myport_rec is running at one time. This preserves the integrity of port data. The send operation is further regulated by "buffer_full" condition to handle the situation when all buffers are full. In this situation, a send operation may either block or return immediately with an error code, depending on whether the nonblocking flag is specified in the port definition or not. Similarly, the receive operation is regulated by "buffer_empty" condition to handle the situation when no message is available. In this situation, a receive operation may either block waiting or return with a no-message error code.

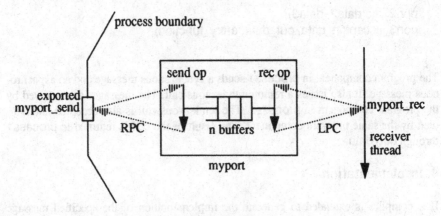

Figure 4. Port Implementation

The RPC server stub unmarshals the input parameters and passes them to myport_send, the DCE RPC manager routine. The local procedure call (LPC) returns pointers to these parameters to the receiver thread. The copy of the parameters created by the RPC server stub is used by the receiver thread.

4.2. Building and Using Message Ports

In Figure 5, foo.idl is the definition of interface foo exported by process B. This interface defines a message port portb and exports its send operation. The IDL compiler generates the implementation of portb and the client and server stub for portb_send procedure. The port implementation contains a queue of message buffers, portb_send and portb_rec procedures. If the port is persist, procedure portb_peek is also generated. portb is compiled and linked to program B and becomes part of process B. Since the send operation of the port is exported, a message sender process A can make RPCs to portb_send to enqueue messages into portb. The receiver thread of process B can dequeue the messages via LPCs to portb_rec.

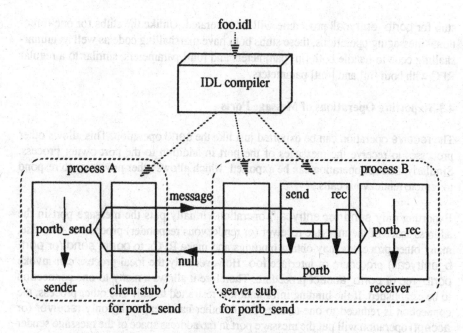

Figure 5. IDL generates a message port and RPC stubs for the interface foo

The message is in the form of RPC input parameters and the LPC output parameters. As such, the parameters of an exported send operation correspond to the [in] parameters in the stub implementation. The parameters of a receive operation, if exported, correspond to the [out] parameters in the stub implementation. In order to keep the function signature of both send and receive operations exactly the same for consistent usage of the two messaging operations, each parameter in the port definition must be a pointer to message data. The message data may be of any type.

The control flow of a message passing includes the cooperation of a message sending RPC and a message receiving LPC. The client stub of the message sender marshals RPC parameters into linear buffers and transmits them to the server stub of the message receiver. The server stub unmarshals the parameters, converts data format as necessary and invokes portb_send procedure to enqueue the message to portb. If the port is asynchronous, the enqueue operation will return quickly to the server stub which will again return immediately back to the client. Since portb_send is a simple routine which takes very little time to process, the entire event appears to be asynchronous to the sender. If the port is synchronous, the execution of portb_send will block at the port until a corresponding portb_rec is executed.

If portb is a rendezvous port, as being by exporting call or accept operation, the IDL compiler will generate a rendezvous implementation which contains portb_entrycall and portb_accept procedures. If call operation is exported, the client stub and server stub for portb_entrycall procedure will be generated. Unlike the stubs for one-directional messaging operations, these stubs both have marshalling code as well as unmarshalling code to handle both [in] parameters and [out] parameters, similar to a regular RPC with both [in] and [out] parameters.

4.3. Exporting Operations of Message Ports

The receive operation can be exported just like the send operation. This allows other processes to receive the messages of the port in addition to the port owner process. Similarly, accept operation can be exported, which allows other processes to respond to remote rendezvous calls.

Exporting only send (or entrycall) operation virtually puts the message port in the address space of the message receiver (or rendezvous responder) process. In this case, many other processes may obtain bindings and make RPCs to portb_send (or portb_entrycall) procedure of interface foo. However only the local process can invoke portb_rec or portb_accept procedure. Therefore it allows a many-to-one connection to be established. If the binding information is restricted to only one other process, the connection is reduced to one-to-one. On the other hand, exporting only receiver (or accept) operation will put the message port in the address space of the message sender (or the rendezvous caller) process. Thus it allows an one-to-many connection to be established. Similarly, if the binding to the portb_rec procedure is restricted to only one other process, the relation reduces to one-to-one connection again. If both send and receive (or both call and accept) operations are exported, the port can become a many-to-many connection port. If the port is the only program existing in the process, this process is a simple stand-alone mailbox server.

5. Conclusion

Client-server computing is a powerful and conceptually simple paradigm for distributed programming. However, peer cooperative processing can expresses parallelism of distributed applications in a more natural fashion. There are real world systems which fit very well into either one model. We have presented a technique to extend the DCE RPC facility to incorporate support for message passing. This extension allows DCE applications to be designed freely using client-server computing, peer cooperative processing or a combination of both. The technique takes advantage of DCE RPC capabilities: the data conversion, data type support, and transparent access to multiple transport protocols. As a result, a message may contain a number of high-level typed data elements and be sent across machines in heterogeneous networks.

References

1. Andrews, G.: Paradigms for Process Interaction in Distributed Programs. Comput. Survey, Vol. 23, March 1991, 49-90.
2. Bal, H., Tanenbaum, A.: Distributed Programming with Shared Data. Comput. Lang., Vol. 16, No. 2, 1991, 129-146.
3. Birrell A., Nelson, B.: Implementing Remote Procedure Calls. ACM Trans. on Comput. Syst., Feb. 1984, 39-59.
4. Chang, C.: REXDC-A Remote Execution Mechanism. Symp. of Commu. Archi. & Protocols, SIGCOMM 1989, 106-115.
5. Gehani, N., Roome, W.: The Concurrent C programming Language. Silicon Press, 1989.
6. Gelernter, D.: Generative communication in Linda. ACM Trans. Program. Lang. Syst. 7, 1, Jan. 1985, 80-112.
7. Li, K., Hudak, P.: Memory coherence in shared virtual memory systems. Proc. of the 5th Ann. ACM Symp. on Princ. of Distr. Comput. Aug. 1986, 229-239.
8. Strom, R., Yemini, S.: NIL: An Integrated Language and System for Distributed Programming. IBM T. J. Watson Research Center, Res. Report RC 9949, April 1983.
9. Yemini, S., Goldszmidt, G., Stoyenko, A., Wei, Y., Beeck, L.: Concert: A High-Level-Language Approach to Heterogeneous Distributed Systems. Proc. of IEEE Int. Conf. on Distr. Comput. Syst., 1989.
10. Acetta, M., Baron, R., Bolosky, W., Golub, D., Rashid, R., Tevanian, A., Young, A.: Mach: A New Kernel Foundation for UNIX Development. Proc. of the 1986 USENIX, Atlanta, GA, 1986, 93-112.
11. OSF DCE Version 1.0 DCE Application Development Guide. Open Software Foundation, June, 1992.

Optimized Selection of Servers for Reduced Response Time in RPC

Mittasch, Christian and Diethmann, Sven-Ingmar

Technische Universität Dresden, Fak. Informatik IBC, D-01062 Dresden Mommsenstr. 13
email: mittasch@freia.inf.tu-dresden.de

Abstract: Advanced concepts are available based on the Remote Procedure Call (RPC). They help to extend the basic functions, the techniques for error handling and to decrease the response time.

This contribution is dealing with a mechanism for reduced response time, developted and tested in the environment of DECrpc using the so called Location Broker (i.e. an agent process that provides to a client dynamically and transparently the remote server interface for the application depending on server performance and load balancing.

After a short introduction to the possiblities to reduce the response time of RPCs, the basic idea and the functionality of this tool are discussed followed by the next steps to implement and improve the tool also in the DCE/RPC environment.

1. Introduction

The response time is an essential criterion to optimize RPC-applications. Fundamental ways to decrease the response time are:

1) to feedback partial and provisional results of the server (so called bidirectional RPC, server callbacks),

2) to split the application into parallel processes, that only have to await a minimum of results of remote procedures (lightweight processes),

3) to provide RPC-server processes several times and to select dynamically the fastest one and

4) to move dynamically server procedures to other machines.

This paper is concerned with a mechanism for the load balanced selection of an RPC-server (3). That delivers primarily advantages opposite to the dynamic loading of procedures (4) - by the small amount of data to be transferred over the LAN.

Purpose of the tool is to route the remote procedure call to that service provider (server), that should bring the shortest response time at the moment of calling. The decision depends on static factors such as data rate and transmission time between client and servers, server performance and on dynamic factors such as network load and server load. Another basic criterion is to make sure that the intended mechanism may be applicable in an advanced RPC as DCE/RPC and also may be addable in other RPC expanding mechanisms as in REV [1] (shorter · response times) or in Radjoot [2] (higher level of error tolerance). Main goal is surely to be open for the supplementation of asynchronous mechanisms such as futures [1], [5] or optimized sending rules for instance without transmit-buffers (System Cronus [1]) or to buffer often called rpc's (or such with many parameters) and send them bundled (System Mercury [1]).

2. Functional principle

With the RPC implementation DECrpc by the Digital Equipment Corporation the developer is made available a tool, that manages information about remote interfaces by usable servers. It's called the Location Broker and it works very similar to the Request Broker of the RPC in the NCP (Network Control Program) by Apollo. With its help it is possible to determine the location and the port number of the server of a requested service dynamically (at the run time). That means, it realizes the principle to produce a remote procedure call transparently (from the client's view).

At the moment of providing a service, its interface is registered in the database of the Global Location Broker (GLB). It means, there exists a database containing the interfaces of all RPC services at this time. On every machine resides a so called Local Location Broker (LLB). If a client starts a RPC for the first time, it gets by means of a short data exchange between its LLB and the GLB the corresponding server interface. Repeating the same RPC simplifies the mechanism to only read the interface entry in the LLB-database. Therefore it becomes possible to the client to determine the location of the server at the runtime and so to be independent of for instance changes in the network configuration and to be able to select the server dynamically.

A possiblity to increase the performance of the client - server principle under RPC is to provide several uniform servers within a network. Up to now it is not useful to create such a redundancy. The reason is that it's only possible to register uniform servers in the GLB-database. If a client's LLB asks for an interface it gets only the first appropriate entry. The mode of operation of the location broker intends to provide to a client information about a unique service. But there is a lack, that the functionality to administrate several uniform server entries in the GLB-database and to select one of them is not possible.

A new tool shall take over these functions. It has to manipulate the database of the GLB in a manner, so that a client's LLB finds in the first entry of the uniform servers the fastest at this moment. For instance it is easily imaginable that different server machines depending on the cpu-load at different times promise to process the RPC optimally. The advantage of such a tool is to obtain dynamical mapping between the client and one of the servers. So it will be possible to take advantage of the redundancy for reducing the response time on the other side to balance the load of the service providing machines. Of course it's necessary to do this manipulation transparently to client and server processes.

The dynamic server selection causes also a disadvantage that decreases the performance of the rpc-mechanism: To make this redundancy available to the calls of the clients it is necessary to disconnect every client-server connection (using this tool) after every use so that a new RPC causes a new connection establishment calling the GLB.

3. Realization of the tool

The realization of this tool [3], called the dynamic_glb_manager, is distributed among two processes: dgm_sampler and dgm_provider.

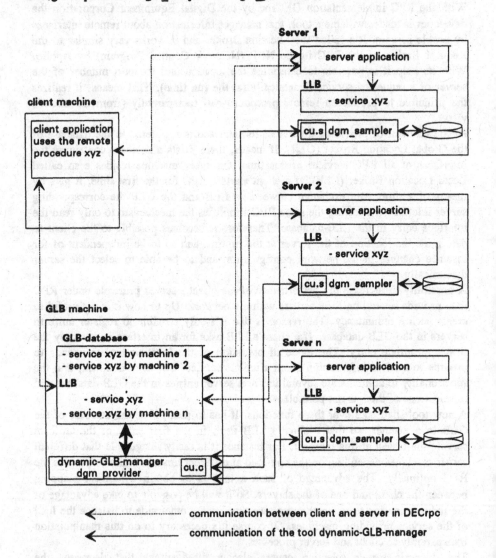

← - - - - - - - - - - - -   communication between client and server in DECrpc

← ─────────────   communication of the tool dynamic-GLB-manager

Figure 1: Functional principle of the dynamic_glb_manager .

The process dgm_sampler is located on every server machine, that exports an RPC-interface. So it has to be started automatically when the first service is registered in the GLB. This process determines cyclically an average value of the cpu-load and a value representing the performance of the concerned machine. The value cpu-load is determined with the help of the system command "cpustat". To determine the performance of the machine it measures the time used for the processing of a small load function. It would also be useful to evaluate benchmark-tests or to estimate the value depending on different priorities instead. Furthermore, the tool uses these values to determine the so called system factor that is presented for further processing.

The process dgm_provider is located exactly on the same machine as the GLB and exists only one time in the network. It processes parallel to the GLB-database an own database with the system factors of the participating servers. Its main task is to manipulate the GLB-database in such a manner, that the interface entry of the best server is set at the first position in a way that it changes its position with the previous best server. The selection of the servers is caused by the cyclic evaluation of the concerned system factors of the servers. Hence in this first realization of the tool the GLB-database is updated depending on requests of the GLB machine. Later on this principle will be replaced by a better mechanism. There are system factors only reported to the dgm_provider process if the dgm_sampler processes recognize a significant change in their system values and send a message to the dgm_provider.

If a special service is not intending to use the dynamic_glb_manager, it has no entry in the database respectively and naturally its function is not disturbed.

The communication between the processes dgm_sampler and dgm_provider is realized with an own rpc connection. It transmits the system factor (cu_s - communication unit - server) or receives and records it respectively in the database of the dgm_provider (cu_c - communication unit - client).

The principal work of the dynamic_glb_manager achieves that the general communication between rpc client and server works unchanged. An application of this tool (based on DECrpc) allows the user of distributed applications to use its advantages with only insignificant changes in its client program. Besides the starting of the parts of the dynamic_glb_manager on the concerned machines - realizable parallely by the management of the rpc, it's necessary in the client program to disconnect an rpc connection after every use (by additional order) and so to determine a GLB request before every rpc.

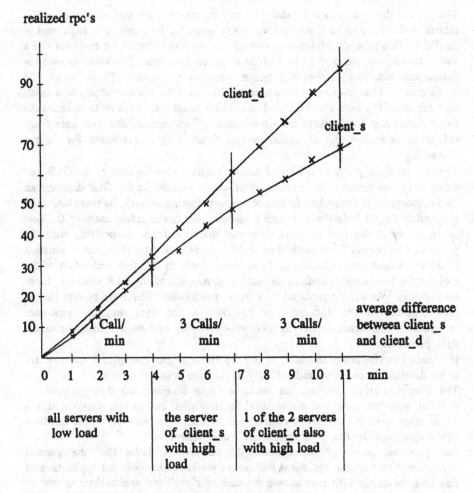

Figure 2: Difference between a static rpc (client_s) and a dynamic rpc (client_d) based on the dynamic_glb_manager measured in a subnet without other load

First tests with the dynamic_GLB-manager showed the dependence of the speed advantage of different factors: For instance it is proportional to the work load of the remote function. Furthermore it depends on the difference between the instantaneous server performance (load dependent) of the redundant servers.

4. Further analysis

An aspect for the optimization of the tool dynamic_GLB-manager is the question, how often this factor (representing the relative performance of the servers) should be refreshed. It seems, that a period of a few minutes is sufficient, if one of the servers possesses an essentially higher performance than the others. In this case switch over would only take place in the case of heavy load of this fast server. For equivalent servers for instance in a local subnet it is required to shorten the interval.

For that purpose measurements are carried out to determine an average request interval in dependance of the number of offered servers in the LAN.

Comparable with the problems of the dynamic flow control mechanisms in meshed networks for the utilization of this tool the following problems occur:

a) The servers are requested too often and increase the load (local and on the network). This problem intensifies if the transmission time between server and client increases.

b) The interval between two requests for a system factor is too long and the likelihood is high, that a rpc doesn't get the interface of the - at this time - fastest server. If this service is called in shorter intervals than the processing of such a server routine the problem intensifies - the recommended server selection increases the server load once more.

In the first realization of the tool the additional load of the participant machines is restricted to 5% of the cpu-load. Measurements showed that an interval of three minutes allows to manage six servers. With other words to request ten servers in about three minutes results in an additional load of 10% cpu-load.

That illustrates that the principle has to be improved. To reach that, two different ways are intended:

1) The load of the servers shall be reported event controlled. The events should result to essentially more efficient mechanisms to determine the system factor. In this way the server load is decreased and so it will be possible to limit it on 2% of the cpu-load and it will be possible to determine the factor in intervals of 0.1 - 0.2 seconds.

It is followed by the insertion of an additional barrier. This barrier should limit the minimum interval between two messages of the system factor to the dgm_provider process in dependence on the number of registered servers and call frequency or processing time on the server. The load of the machine running the GLB and the dgm_provider is also thus limited.

2) The system factor reported to the dgm_provider process will be extended with data about the frequency of calling the (uniform) servers. Using that allows the tool to react on a high number of (uniform) rpc's by changing the server selection principle into either a random selection or a selection dependent on the static performance of the servers (equally distributed).

The efficiency of the dgm_provider is fundamentally determined by the restricted functionality for manipulating the GLB-database. Some more comfortable read/write functions and the possibility to insert a flag into the GLB-database, that announces whether the dynamic_glb_manager is used or not, may solve the mentioned problem.

In the next stage of the problems investigation, it is planned to transfer this functional principle to DCE/RPC (under IBM's AIX). The basically analogous endpoint map [4] and its database respectively permit to do that without greater alterations. Naturally there exist more comfortable services of the CDS (Cell Directory Service) as for instance profile entries usable for the management of the dynamic_glb_manager.

References:

1. Schill, A.: Remote Procedure Call: Fortgeschrittene Konzepte und Systeme - ein Überblick, Teil2: Erweiterte RPC - Ansätze. - Informatik Spektrum 15 (1992), S. 145 - 155
2. Panzieri, F.: Shrivastata, S. K.: Radjoot: A Remote Procedure Call Facility Supporting Orphan Detection and Killing. - IEEE Trans. Softw. Eng. 14 (1988), p. 30 - 37
3. Diethmann, S.: Verteilte Verarbeitung auf der Basis von RPC. - Diplomarbeit, TU Dresden, Fakultät Informatik, 1993
4. IBM: AIX Infoexplorer - DCE Part - as online documentation of the referenced software, IBM, 1993
5. Crowcroft, J.: Lessons and Challenges of Distributed Computing. - RN/92/xx - culled from the network (anonym. ftp by cs.ucl.cc.uk), Dep. of Comp. Science, Uni. College London 1992

Extending DCE RPC by Dynamic Objects and Dynamic Typing

R. Heite and H. Eberle

IBM European Networking Center
P.O. Box 10 30 68
D-69020 Heidelberg Germany
heite@dhdibm1.bitnet

Abstract: Current DCE RPC offers an object model which is static in that objects are assumed permanent and published within a directory. Moreover, all parameters of an object's interface are typed statically. We argue that this object model should be enhanced by dynamic objects which are created as the result of a client/server interaction with parameters whose types are conveyed at creation- or call-time. Dynamic objects are a common model for context-handles and callback, as well as delegation scenarios. Dynamic typing facilitates access to generic servers through RPC. In this paper our emphasis is on motivating the need for the proposed extensions, and on showing that they can be integrated into current DCE RPC in an upward compatible manner.

Introduction

With the appearance of modern workstation technology, client/server computing has become an important programming paradigm. Besides distributed file or database servers, new applications which provide services for cooperation among users, based on shared graphical interfaces, have gained momentum. Programming environments for distributed applications should provide a systematic approach for the development of these applications[4]. They should offer higher level abstractions, either at the operating system or programming language level, that shield the developer from the details of communication and heterogeneity. Based on these, but orthogonal to them, they should additionally offer integrated services such as directories, security services, or transaction processing.

Of special importance is the support of arbitrary programming languages, which should offer a systematical approach to export services within a distributed system based on the interfaces. Exporting a service makes it available on arbitrary platforms as a local interface to clients. This approach not only accelerates the development through reuse of existing servers and transparent access, but also improves maintainability in case of service changes.

OSF-DCE [2] meets these requirements due to its wide-spread availability on many different platforms and its powerful RPC with integrated infrastructure for security and directory services. RPC is fundamental but still has functional deficiencies [10]. By their very nature, common servers are generic but cannot be integrated directly because of RPC's lack of dynamic typing. Scenarios with dynamically determined resource sharing requirements are insufficiently supported due to the static object model.

In this paper we present extensions, which offer a fuller object model, but which are nevertheless upward compatible with DCE. These extensions result in a way to offer complex servers based on their interfaces, enable new applications, and providing a scheme for shifting authorisation and access control from the application into the runtime system. By completing the object model we also get a better understanding of the current DCE object model.

We will start with a description of the object model within DCE RPC. Then we will discuss dynamic objects and dynamic typing as a completion of the existing RPC. In the fourth chapter we discuss the integration of the extensions into the DCE RPC. There we outline, how the existing IDL, stub structures and authorisation services are affected. Thereby upward compatibility will be the major concern. Finally we compare our extensions to the new emerging proposal of OMG-CORBA.

1. The Object Model within current DCE RPC

In order to motivate our extensions, we first characterise the current notion of objects within DCE RPC. We start with a rather simple model of objects within client/server computing. The active entities and units of distribution within this model are *processes*. *Objects* denote resources (data + operations) that are bound to a process. A process is called a *server* of an *object* if it offers the object to a distributed environment. A process holding a *reference* to an object is called a *client* of that object. Using this reference a client is able to call the object (i.e. client = caller). Client and server are not permanent properties of a process but a *role* a process assumes with respect to some object.

The sole informations a client has about an object are an opaque *reference* (also called a *handle*) and an *interface*. The reference uniquely identifies the object. It can be used to route a request to the object. The interface describes the operations applicable on the object and thus the visible effects from accessing it. Besides this interface, a client knows nothing about the internal object structure. This internal structure is provided by the server. It consists of a local state, a set of operations executing on that state (called together the *local object*), and the runtime environment for the object. The server is completely free in selecting an object structure, as long as that structure fulfils the *contract* defined by the interface.

DCE RPC provides a framework for realising objects accessible within an open system in languages that offer no direct support for distributed computing. A client accesses an object through a client stub that, when instantiated with a *server binding handle* imported from the directory, acts as a *proxy* object to the actual remote object. At a client side, creation of a DCE object happens at importing time.

At a server side, the local objects are called by the runtime system on an incoming request (Figure 1). The actual implementation of a local object is outside the

---

This does not mean that any client/server computation within DCE RPC follows this model, but that it is possible to realise this model within the current DCE.

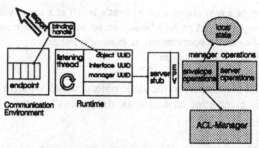

Figure 1: DCE Object at server side

scope of DCE. Local objects are encapsulated into a DCE object. The state of this DCE object consists of the entry point vector (EPV) to the manager operations, the operations are those of the server stub. A DCE object is created when it has been made accessible to clients. This means that the DCE object must have been registered to the runtime, and the binding handle of the object is exported under a name and annotated with the object's unique identifier (UUID) to the directory.

Of special importance for the discussion here is the DCE RPC facility to protect objects against unauthorised access. It is based on the fact that any acting entity, called *principal* within the context of protection, can obtain a unique identity. *Authentication* allows principals to certify their unique identity to each other. For authorisation, an object at the server side can be associated with an access control list (ACL) that defines permissions that various principals have on the object.

Whereas authentication to a large extent is a runtime matter, authorisation lies within the responsibility of the application. DCE defines an interface for remote ACL-manipulation and local ACL-management. However, any server that wants to control access to its objects, must itself provide the manager operations to these interfaces within its application. Access control is performed within the *envelope operations*. This part of the manager operations works on the *client binding handle* and additionally maps the the object UUID to the local handle of the object's state. Thus, the envelope is an application dependent stub to the server operations which, for example, might be defined within a local library.

2. Dynamic Objects

Objects denote resources (data + operations) that are *bound* to the server process. DCE RPC offers *static, global objects*. Independent of any prior client/server interaction, a server creates a DCE object at startup time, thereby publishing it within a directory under a *name*. Since the directory is replicated, publishing is an expensive operation. It can be justified only for *long-lived* objects.

This notion of a static object is not adequate to model all kinds of server-bound resources, especially when they are of a more *transient* or *dynamic* nature. Examples of such resources are

- instantiation of a new resource on a client's behalf at a server side
- granting temporary and perhaps limited access to an existing resource
- the state of a client's operation on an existing resource
- the state of a bulk data transfer

Therefore we need a counterpart to the static objects which we term *dynamic* objects. The following table gives some characteristic differences between static and dynamic objects:

Static Objects	*Dynamic Objects*
created at the server's discretion	created as a result of cooperation
exported into a (replicated) directory under a name	exported through reference passing as an anonymous reference
usually long-lived	usually short-lived
uncoupled to any client	available to specific clients
protected through static ACLs	protected through dynamic ACLs

To some extent, DCE RPC supports already something like dynamic objects with context handles and callbacks. These mechanisms are described in section 2.1. The subsequent subsections will then introduce the proposed extensions.

2.1 Context-Handle and Callback

Context-Handles: Consider a fileserver object that creates a file as the result of an open call. A more general example in object-oriented terms are the *class* operations new in the Smalltalk sense. What these operations have in common is that they return references to the created objects as result parameters (therefore we call these

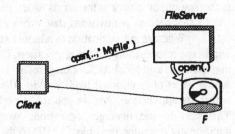

objects also *return objects*). Conceptually, the created (or *dynamic*) object is dedicated to the client. This must be enforced by the server on each subsequent access to the object. By default, the lifetime of the dynamic object is bound to that of the client. When the server detects that the client no longer runs, it deletes the dynamic object. Thus in this scenario dynamic objects realize a *creation on behalf* relationship.

Callback: Consider an object O that has to callback its client during performing some work on behalf of the client. The client creates a dynamic object P whose reference it passes as an input parameter of an operation call to O. After receiving this reference O performs the callback on P.

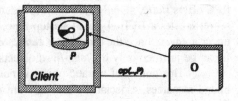

Examples of such a scenario occur, for example, in bulk data transfer as exemplified by pipes, when modeling procedure parameters or notifications. The examples exhibit different requirements of visibility of P from within O: Within the first two scenarios P is accessible to O only during executing the operation to which P was submitted as an input parameter. In the notification scenario, P is actually used to notify the client about an event that happens within O asynchronously after return of the passing request. Thus there exist two parameter passing modes for input references: *Transient* input references, where the lifetime of a dynamic object is restricted to the duration of a request (granting temporary access) and *static* input references, where the lifetime is restricted to the lifetime of the receiver.

Note the role change as a result of passing a reference to an object as an input parameter: The process that is a client of object O becomes a server of the created object P whereas the process that is the server of O becomes a client of P.

2.2 Third-Party Reference Passing

Thus far the dynamic objects of DCE are used to model reference passing as it occurs within usual client/server relationships. However it must be possible for a client of a dynamic object to grant its reference to a third process. The need for this can be demonstrated when we combine the above two scenarios, that is, a client wants to print a file F that is located on a remote file server.

In this case, the client grants the printer a reference to a remote object rather than to a local object. As within the callback scenario the printer can itself fetch the data by calling the

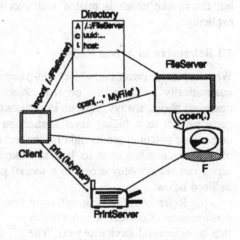

read operation on the file object. It should be opaque to the printer that it is getting the data from a different process.

Granting a reference to a third party strongly affects the access monitoring performed at the dynamic object. So far the server of a dynamic object has to ensure that only calls that originate from the client may be executed on F.

If a client wants to make its private object available to another process, it has to authorise this process at the object. Different techniques for this exist. In DCE authorisation, the client has to set the read permissions for the printer at the ACL-Manager responsible for F. The ACL-Manager for dynamic objects needs a special structure [5] which we will describe in section 4.3. The client remains the owner of the private object. As within the callback scenario, the printer is only temporarily authorised at F in order to perform some tasks on behalf of the client.

During this task, the printer itself may pass the reference of F to another object that then acts on the printer's behalf on F, but this time only within the limits of the printer's access permissions. In general the granter trusts the grantee, and this relationship is transitive. If transivity is not desired, the granter can pass the reference in *private* mode ensuring that the reference is limited to the grantee.

When the printer has finished its print task, the client revokes the corresponding read permission at F . This implies the revocation of all those permissions that were set by the printer for other processes, and so forth.

If an object should be used exclusively by only one client, the server passes its reference in *exclusive* passing mode. The client will lose access to the object as soon as it passes the reference to a third-party. Here, access rights are moved but not objects.

Passing a reference to a third-party as a result parameter must also be possible. An example of third-party reference passing with the static input references is a generalisation of the notification scenario, where the notify object P is remote to the client itself. A typical application is a customer scenario, where a client tells an object O to send the result of the request to another object P that acts as a replacement of the client. In both cases, passing a reference requires an authorise call, but the revoke either is related with receiver termination or must be performed explicitly.

2.3 References as Access Rights

When a process creates an object and passes its reference to another process, it sets automatically access rights on that object. If we assume that the authorisation described above always happens in conjunction with passing a reference to a third party we get as a higher level abstraction that a reference to a dynamic object embodies a potential access right for the receiver of a reference. Although the granter of the reference has done its best to make an object available to the receiver, the server can always deny access to a special process. Possible reasons for this will be outlined below.

Reference passing offers a new way of access right management or configuration. Consider a process A that owns several device objects. The owner can build a compound object consisting of the references of its devices and pass that to another process B , thereby authorising the receiver with only one request. Implicit revocation through transient input and client rundown, as well as the various passing modes, ensure the desired limitations on the lifetime of the passed references.

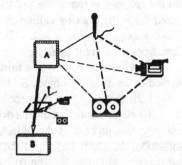

2.4 A Dynamic Object View on a Static Object

A process may import a reference of a static object from the directory and pass it as an operation parameter to another process. Such a scenario occurs, for instance, within the above file/printer scenario when the client has imported the file reference from the directory. Here the client puts a dynamic object view on a static object without the object server needing to be aware of it. The reason for doing this is to use the semantics associated with reference passing that extends the authorisation capabilities on static objects.

This scenario is often described as *delegation*. In a world of static objects with static access control, the access permissions defined within an object's ACL are usually defined in such a way that they statically cover all possible access scenarios. However, this approach is not in accordance with the *need-to-know* principle. For example, a printer should not be authorised on a static file permanently, but only while executing the print job. Delegation provides an appropriate mechanism to express the required kind of dynamic authorisation. Within the printer scenario it means that the client delegates its read-permission on the file object to the printer, in order for the printer to act on behalf of the client.

Delegation is commonly understood as [12] .. *a principal (= delegator) authorises another principal (= delegate) to perform some tasks using some of the rights of the delegator*.

Reference passing expresses a special form of delegation in that a granter delegates an access right on a well defined object. Delegation in its general form includes the granting of rights to a group of objects or to any object to which the granter has access (= *impersonation*). Note that passing a reference to a static object is more than merely calling the ACL-manipulation operations from within the client dynamically. A client may access the file but may not have the right to change its ACL. Reference passing expresses the fact that the printer is *acting on behalf* of the client and thus is given some possible set of rights that a client would have there.

3. Dynamic Typing

Stub compilation within DCE RPC is based on the fact that all IDL interface parameters are typed statically. This allows the associaton of each parameter with a compiled marshal procedure and tag-free data representations. However this scheme does not give appropriate support for *generic* servers within the IDL. A generic server can be regarded as a *container* object that offers operations, e.g., to insert and retrieve data of arbitrary type. Predominant examples are those servers that deal with persistent data, for example, structured file servers or database servers. For local clients such servers typically offer interfaces of the following form:

op_name (data-identification, format-specification-string, untyped-buffer)

Within the body of *op_name* the data in the buffer get interpreted according to the format specification. In other words, the data in the buffer are dynamically typed according to the format description.

A stub for such an interface would need to mimic the same behaviour: The format string drives an interpreter for placing the data into the stream at the sender side and exctracting plus converting the data at the receiver side. Although the number of different types, that are specified within a format description, are usually limited, IDL *unions*, even in their non-encapsulated form [7], provide no direct solution to model these interfaces within the IDL. But without IDL support, the stubs to these interfaces would have to be *hand coded*.

A reasonable concept for getting *automatically generated* stubs to generic servers is to make the standard generation of marshaling code

application interface → IDL interface specification → marshal operations

available at runtime.

In order to become application-independent we assume that the formats of dynamically typed data are described in a subset of IDL comprising basic and constructed types. The IDL is extended by a new parameter type **type**. A parameter of type **type**, called a *type variable*, contains a description of an IDL type. A parameter may reference a type variable as its parameter type, which means that its contents are dynamically typed according to the type value of the type variable. The association between a dynamically typed parameter and its type variable is analogous to the one between an open array and the parameter specifying its length.

In contrast to many other approaches (e.g., basic encoding rules in [1]) we separate the type descriptions from the data they type. We regard this approach as being superior to using a stream of tagged ("self-describing") data because the separation exists in most local interfaces to generic servers. Moreover, it is in the spirit of RPC type handling and thus does not need to modify the network data representation of the existing IDL data types. For arrays and bulk data transfer it saves bandwidth, since formats are only specified once.

Nevertheless expressing streams is possible with our concept, since type variables and dynamically typed data can be used as any other IDL data type and thus be a part of a structure. In addition type variables provide the expressive power for extending the concept of dynamically typed data to dynamically typed objects.

3.1 Dynamically Typed Objects

We will now extend a server that acts as a container object for arbitrary data types, to a server for container objects, whose type is determined dynamically but which remains fixed during their existence. A natural example is a fileserver of a structured file system that must be able to manage files whose structure is determined by a client at file creation time. Thus, what we need is object creation with dynamically determined types. Let us first clarify what *type* means within this context.

Within our object model the structure of an object's state is not visible to the DCE object unless it is reflected as a parameter type of some operation defined within the object's interface. Let Pdyn be some parameter within an object's interface whose structure is determined by the object's state (e.g., a parameter representing records of the structured file).

The server of container objects with dynamically determined structure cannot have prepared a special interface for each possible structure, since every different structure implies a different type of Pdyn . Therefore the server offers one interface I for its dynamic objects, where Pdyn is typed dynamically. For a dynamically typed object the type-description of Pdyn is determined *once* at object creation time and remains fixed during the lifetime of that object. Object creation is extended by associating a type description for Pdyn with the created (dynamic) object. At the server side, this type description belongs to the runtime-data of the object, whereas at the client side it is associated with the received reference. After object creation, the type-description is available at the server as well as at the client side. On each object request it is interpreted for marshaling Pdyn without having to be transmitted as a parameter of the request.

Let us restate the performance benefits gained from shifting the determination of type descriptions from call time to creation time: The type descriptions need to be provided, evaluated, and transmitted only once at DCE object-creation time. This makes a dynamic object view interesting for any application where the dynamic parameter type is determined once and remains fixed during a set of repeated operation calls, for example, general iteration scenarios or dynamically typed pipes. However, the interpretation of the type variable on each call remains. A scheme would be especially attractive for bulk data transfer and persistent dynamic objects, where the type variable gets dynamically compiled at object creation time, resulting in marshal operations that can be dynamically loaded at object call time.

4. Integration of the Extensions into DCE RPC

This section discusses the integration of the extensions into DCE RPC. It is assumed that the reader is familiar with the DCE IDL and DCE runtime.

One major concern of the extensions should be to maintain *upward compatibility*. Static objects as defined in current RPC should run in an extended system without restrictions. Thereby local runtime and stub structure may be extended, but existing formats and protocols should not get affected. It is obvious that the most crucial component for the extensions is the IDL. Additionaly, modifications are needed for the authorisation. For dynamic object creation and deletion we assume the API defined within [9].

4.1 DCE IDL Extensions
The following IDL support is needed for dynamic objects and dynamic typing:

- Interfaces as parameter types of object references
- Type variables and dynamically typed parameters
- Parameterized interfaces for dynamically typed objects

For a complete discussion of the extensions see [11]. Here we demonstrate the various extensions by means of the interface to the server of container objects, mentioned in section 3.1.

```
version (0), formal_is (Pdyn)]
interface container
{
        error_status_t insert([in] Pdyn rec);
        error_status_t retrieve([out] Pdyn* rec);
   [delete] error_status_t close( );
}
```

```
[version (0)]
interface container_server
{
        error_status_t create ([in] char * name, [in] type t,
                            [out, actual_is(t)] container * c );
        error_status_t open ([in] char * name, [out] type* t,
                            [out, actual_is(t)] container * c);

}
```

The container_server offers operations that return references to container objects. A container offers operations to insert or retrieve data. The structure of the data, that is inserted into or retrieved from a container, is determined when the container object is created. Afterwards, it remains fixed during the existence of the container object.

In order to describe this mechanism in the IDL, *parameterized interfaces* are introduced. Such an interface describes a template, akin to a C++ *template*, where the formal interface parameter Pdyn is referenced as a type of those operation parameters, whose structure is determined at object creation time in the container example above.

Object creation in this context happens when a reference is passed. Thus, when a parameterized interface is used as a parameter type, here in create and open, an actual interface parameter must be supplied. The actual parameter for a dynamically typed object is a type variable. Valid inputs to the type variable t are strings describing IDL data types, except pipes. Note that for the container object the type value is either specified by its client (with create) or its server (with open).

Object references are passed with the usual [in] and [out] directions. They may have additional attributes that indicate the various passing modes ([static], [exclusive] and [private], see 2.2). When an operation call results in the deletion of a dynamic object, like close, then it will be indicated through the attribute [delete].

Upward Compatibilty: Upward compatible extension of IDL means that a stub compiler understanding extended IDL is able to compile standard IDL. This is usually achieved by leaving the existing features of the IDL untouched and merely adding new parameter types. However, interfaces as parameter types supersede *context handles* and *function pointers*. In order to avoid confusion between a typed reference parameter and the untyped canonical handle parameter, we assume that the handle parameter is an implicit one. Therefore *customised handles* are superfluous. We take the convention that these constructs may only appear in interfaces offered by servers that do not require the RPC extensions.

4.2 ACF Support for the IDL Extensions

The stub compiler performs a *default mapping* from the IDL to the application language. Default mapping of an object reference parameter, for example, is based on the assumption that DCE object creation happens within the application. Therefore, a reference parameter is mapped to an opaque handle of type handle_t within the interfaces of the sender as well as the receiver side.

Through the introduction of the ACF concept, DCE RPC has already recognised the need for declarative support to specify alternative local stub structures and interfaces from the stub compiler. The rationale behind this is to shift envelope functionality into the stub, saving execution and development costs. In the following we will sketch the ACF support for object creation and for static clients to a dynamic server (for a more complete list see [11]).

Consider a manager operation for the create of the container_server interface that returns a local handle to a file from which a container object is to be built. If creation of this object should happen within the server stub, the stub compiler must know the local handle structure and the entry point vector to the manager operations. This information is supplied by extending the ACF attribute **represent_as** to be an interface attribute or even a parameter attribute for object types.

Usually a client of a dynamically typed object knows which actual type of the object is needed, for example, the structure of a file to be created. The new ACF parameter attribute **set_value** sets the value of a parameter to a constant expression. Applied to a type variable, as for instance within the create operation of the container_server interface create([set_value(my_rec)]), this means that the client needs a container object of an actual type my_rec. This actual type itself is specified in an idl file. The type variable parameter t disappears from the client stub interface of create as a result of this specification, and the client stubs of the dependent interface container become statically typed with the actual type my_rec.

4.3 Dynamic Object Authorisation

Authorisation for dynamic objects is based, as with static objects, on client PACs and on ACLs associated with the object. However, the ACL structure for dynamic objects differs from that for static objects with respect to construction, entry structure, and access checking algorithm [5].

Passing a reference of an object with interface I from a granter A to a grantee B results in the entry:

$$\langle B, \quad I\ [+restrictions], \quad A, \quad UUID\rangle \quad (*)$$

$$\quad\uparrow \qquad\qquad \uparrow \qquad\qquad \uparrow \qquad\qquad \uparrow$$

$$\text{grantee} \qquad \text{permissions} \qquad \text{granter} \qquad \text{entry UUID}$$

The permissions field lists the interface of an object, since permissions are defined in terms of operations. Optional restrictions define those operations of an interface which the grantee may not call. This field may also contain expiration dates. Based on the *granter* field, the entries belonging to a given object and user can be organised into a *tree* representing the reference passing history that originated from the user. This organisation provides efficient support for *revocation*. When the reference of this user is revoked, all the ACL entries that are part of the sub-tree rooted by that user entry are deleted.

When an object reference gets passed multiple times between a granter and a grantee, the pair (user, granter) is not sufficient to uniquely identify an ACL entry. The grantee may hold multiple references to the same object that all originate from the same granter but are associated with different restrictions. In order to distinguish the different references the entry UUID field is added.

Dynamic ACLs are manipulated through the basic operations **authorise** and **revoke**. Unlike the **sec_acl_*** interface to a static ACL, these operations manipulate only distinguished ACL-entries. The operations belong to the management operations of the object server. A handle to them can be constructed from the respective object handle. The default behaviour of an authorise-request is first to test whether the caller is a valid granter, that is either registered as the owner or a user of the object. Then it constructs the user-entry for the grantee and returns the constructed entry UUID .

The granter inserts the returned UUID as the new object UUID into the handle that subsequently is passed to the grantee. This is necessary since we do not want to extend the network representation of binding handles to dynamic objects. However, it implies a modification of the server's object dispatching. The granter has to store the returned UUID when it wants to *revoke* the passed reference subsequently.

On receiving an object call from the grantee, the server tests the dynamic ACL with the **is_authorised** operation. This operation checks the existence of an entry for the caller with the entry UUID and that the required operation belongs to the permission set of the entry. To that end the caller must present its PAC so that the server can check that it is a valid grantee with respect to the passed reference.

4.4 Handling a Dynamic Object View on a Static Object

When a reference to a static object is distributed through parameter passing, the object server might be unaware of it and thus not offer dynamic ACLs. Alternative mechanism for realising the delegation semantics inherent in reference passing are discussed in [3, 8, 12]. These mechanisms have in common that they encrypt the entry (*) into the PAC of the granter and the grantee, instead of logging it within the dynamic ACL at the object server.

The encryption method may save at most one communication step at passing time, when the entry (*) is part of the granter's PAC to the grantee [11]. However, it drastically lengthens the PAC in case of chained delegation and fails to provide efficient support for the revocation step, which is an operation frequently within reference passing.

Therefore we propose the dynamic ACL approach as described above for any reference passing. This implies that every server offers the respective interface for *authorise* and *revoke*. The authorise implementation may work together with the static ACLs as follows: If there exists no user-entry for the caller, *authorise* checks the static ACL to see whether the caller has the required permissions before it inserts the required entry. The **sec_acl_mgr_is_authorised** operation, that is called from within the server application to test the access right, must be extended to find the right ACL manager. Thus it must be determinable from a handle whether it is a reference to a dynamic or a static object.

4.5 Stub Structure for the IDL Extensions

Stub Code for Reference Parameter: Passing a reference is always accompanied by authorising the receiver to access the dynamic object. Therefore the *authorise* call can be put into the stub of the passing operation, where it is part of marshaling the reference parameter. Transient input references, that are passed, are registered internally within the stub in order to revoke them after the operation returns.

The string binding of the respective handle is the network presentation of a reference parameter (although there may be more efficient ones). The DCE RPC string binding is extended by *authentication annotations*, containing the name of the object server, the protection level and the authentication service. The object server determines the authentication annotations. Unmarshaling a received reference then consists of generating a handle from the string binding and annotating it with the received authentication information.

A server stub for a dynamic object contains by default processing of the client binding handle, comprising access control and object dispatching. For access control, the client PAC is retrieved from the binding handle and used as input to the *is_authorised* call on the dynamic ACL. For object dispatching, an *object table* is introduced into which the pair (object UUID, local object handle) is inserted at object creation time. At access time, the server stub retrieves the local handle from the table based on the object UUID within the binding handle.

Stub Code for Dynamic Typing: For the handling of dynamic typing we use a scheme similar to that described within [13].The IDL string as input to a type variable is converted into an *internal format* that is efficient for interpretation of the dependent dynamic data. The components of the internal format are indices into a table of extended marshal operations for those IDL types that are allowed to appear within a type variable. Besides the usual marshal operations, the extended operations contain the handling of the input and internal buffer.

Marshaling of dynamic data then consists of calling an interpreter operating on the two inputs, the internal format and the data to be marshaled, and producing the marshaling output. Marshaling of a reference to a dynamically typed object is extended by storing the internal format of the actual parameter into the *object table*. A similar table is needed for a client stub, since it can be called with different handles. On each subsequent access to the reference, regardless of whether used as a server- or a client-binding handle, the format is retrieved from the reference and used for marshaling typed parameters through the formal interface parameter.

As an alternative to the interpretable internal format, machine code could be generated from the contents of a type variable and then directly executed in memory. Such a scheme makes sense, where the additional costs for code generation compensate the costs for marshaling based on the interpretation scheme. The decision which scheme to use is a local matter and therefore controllable through a respective ACF attribute.

5. DCE RPC and its Extensions versus OMG CORBA

The extensions defined in this paper would enable DCE IDL to become object-based with object types that may be typed dynamically. The question now arises whether there is a need for the extensions at all, since there already exists the object-oriented IDL defined within OMG CORBA [6].

OMG IDL allows interfaces to occur as parameter types. However, since the CORBA document does not elaborate on security infrastructure, the implications of such a facility on object protection are not discussed. OMG IDL offers dynamic typing through the type **any** for "self-describing" data. Hence, it lacks the flexibility of separating type-description from dynamic data. In addition, OMG IDL does not recognise the need for *parameterised interfaces* for dynamically typed objects.

OMG IDL has been derived from C++, whereas DCE IDL has emerged from the already existing NIDL used within NCS [14]. DCE IDL reflects much more the need to have a source for stub compilation. Therefore it offers a set of special data types (e.g. non-encapsulated unions, conformant arrays, full-pointer concept and pipes), interface-,type-, parameter- and operation-attributes, richer than OMG IDL. In addition DCE already has acknowledged the need for a two-step interface specification scheme, whereas CORBA understands *language mapping* only as the default mapping the stub compiler performs.

OMG IDL is superior to our extended DCE IDL with respect to interface inheritance, more rigorous scoping rules, and attributes as abbreviations of operations. These features simplify the definition of interfaces, although they do not affect stub logic. Inheritance may define a subtyping relationship, which is almost covered by the DCE IDL concept of interface compatibility as far as binding handles are concerned.

Our concept of dynamic typing supports *generic* servers. Through the *dynamic invocation interface* CORBA supports *generic clients* who can call an object whose interfaces they do not know a priori. This is in contrast to dynamically typed objects where only parameters of an interface may be determined dynamically.

Dynamic invocation consists of a higher level interface of the RPC runtime primitives to *send* a request and *receive* a result. The parameters to these primitives are dynamically typed, but usually only at the client side. Within our context dynamic invocation combined with the concept of an interface *repository* may be useful when a process becomes a client of an object through receiving its references as part of a dynamically typed parameter. The type description of the reference within the corresponding type variable comprises only the name of the object type. Based on this name, the structure of the interfaces is retrieved from the repository. Interfaces stored there can be directly called by dynamic invocation. This means that any operation parameter is annotated by a type variable containing its type description. The type variable is already initialised by its internal format, which can be easily interpreted or even compiled at call time.

As a summary, we claim that it makes sense to extend DCE RPC even en face of CORBA because DCE provides an elaborate infrastructure consisting of stub compiler, runtime, communication, directory and security services. Moreover, the extensions defined herein are useful for CORBA since they result in stub and runtime extensions that are of general use.

6. Conclusion

The extensions proposed herein aim at completing the object model within DCE RPC and providing a facility for integrating the interfaces to complex servers. We have introduced dynamic objects as a uniform model for context-handles, callback, delegation and access right configuration. Besides offering new applications, dynamic objects simplify the development of client/server applications through integrated authorisation and access control. Extending the IDL by dynamic typing solves the data

228

heterogeneity problem of generic servers by the same IDL as introduced for RPC, which is the most economical.

Acknowledgment: Hermann Schmutz, Ulf Hollberg, both of IBM ENC, and Kurt Geihs, Univ. Frankfurt, were at the origin of many ideas discussed here. We thank F.Hofmann, Univ.Erlangen, for his support and enouragement on this work. Hermann Schmutz and Keith Hall, IBM ENC, made significant suggestions to earlier versions of this text.

References

1. International Organization for Standardization: Specification of Abstract Syntax Notation One (ASN.1). ISO 8824: 1989(E)
2. Open Software Foundation: DCE Application Development Guide and Development Reference. Documents available from OSF, Cambridge MA, Revision 1.0, Dec 31, 1991.
3. Gasser, Morrie and McDermott, Ellen: An Architecture for practical Delegation in a Distributed System. Proc. of the 1990 IEEE Computer Society Symposium on Research in Security and Privacy, (1990) pp.20-30.
4. Geihs, K: Infrastrukturen für heterogene verteilte Systeme, Informatik Spektrum,Band 16, Heft 1 (1993) pp 11-24.
5. Geihs, K., Heite, R. and Hollberg,U.: Protected Object References in Heterogeneous Distributed Systems. Accepted for publication
6. Object Management Group: The Common Object Request Broker - Architecture and Specification: OMG Document Number 91.12.1., Rev. 1.1, December 1991
7. Harrow,J: Proposed Enhancements for DCE 1.1. IDL. OSF DCE RFC 2.1, July 1992
8. Pato, J:. Extending the DCE Authorisation Model to Support Practical Delegation. OSF DCE RFC 3.0, June 1992
9. Mishkin, N.: DCE RPC API Extensions for Modular Servers. OSF DCE RFC 21.0, November 1992
10. Schmutz,H.: Autonomous Heterogeneous Computing - Some Open Problems, in Operating Systems of the 90s and Beyond, A.Karshmer J.Nehmer (Eds.), Lecture Notes in Computer Science 563, Springer-Verlag, 1991, pp. 63 - 71
11. Heite, R., Eberle, H.: DCE RPC Extensions: IDL, ACF and Runtime System Extensions. Available from the authors
12. Varadharajan,V., Allen, P. and Black, S.: An Analysis of the Proxy Problem in Distributed Systems. Proc. of the 1991 IEEE Computer Society Symposium on Research in Security and Privacy (1991) pp. 255-275
13. Wild, G., Zöller, M. Eine Lösung der Darstellungsproblematik für ein heterogenes verteiltes System, in Kommunikation in Verteilten Systemen 1987, Informatik Fachbericht 130, Springer Verlag (1987) pp 290-301
14. L. Zahn et.al., Network Computing Architecture, Prentice Hall, Englewood Cliffs, New Jersey, USA (1990)

A Simple ORB Implementation on Top of DCE

for Distributed Object Oriented Programming

Qun TENG*, Yin XIE**, Bernard MARTIN*

* BULL S.A. 7, rue Ampère 91343 MASSY; Q.Teng@frmy.bull.fr

** Télésystèmes 3-5 rue Hélène Boucher 78280 Guyancourt; yx@synergie.fr

Abstract

Recent advances on object oriented computing and distributed processing have resulted in developing new approaches for distributed application programming. The platform Object Request Broker (ORB) from the Object Management Group (OMG) proposes an elegant solution. However, the implementation of such an architecture in a heterogeneous network environment remains an open problem, due to the complexity of the communication infrastructure. In this paper, we describe a simple ORB implementation on top of OSF's DCE basic services. The benefits of using the DCE services will be demonstrated.

Key words: *DCE, Object Oriented Programming, Object Request Broker*

1. Introduction

Today, the requirements of the co-operative distributed processing become well known. However, the traditional network programming tools usually lack efficiency to construct high-performance and robust distributed applications, because there is no sufficient abstraction provided. The Object Request Broker [1] of the Object Management Group (OMG) proposes a attractive solution by combining object oriented programming and distributed computing. It offers a collection of mechanisms allowing objects to exchange messages across networks, as though they are local. The main functional components of the ORB platform will be briefly examined in the next section.

In a distributed environment, the objects are spread in the network. Thus, they do not necessarily share the same address space. They exchange messages across networks by using communications services. Therefore, a number of problems arise, for example :

- The objects should no longer be represented by their address pointer, as they may be referenced by objects in remote machines;

- Since objects can be created on whatever machine in the network and may move from one machine to another, they are not easy to be located;

- The communication services carrying invocation messages are subject to be lost or damaged, because the underlying networks are not necessarily reliable;

That is why the communication services in the ORB should be able to provide relevant mechanisms to make the distribution transparent.

DCE [2] is the perfect candidate, since it provides integrated and flexible tools and services which make the implementation of distributed applications much easier. The DCE RPC can meet the primary requirement of ORB in term of remote execution; The directory service makes the ORB applications location transparent; The DCE threads can allow ORB objects to accept several simultaneous invocations, etc.

The ORB implementation we propose in this paper is simple, because it utilises as much as possible the mechanisms provided by DCE, so as to minimise the development effort. Our implementation model will be described in the section 3. The programming language C++ will be used for the illustration purpose.

The utilisation of the DCE's remote execution mecanism requires the mapping of the ORB interface description on the DCE counterpart. In the section 4, an IDL translator is described.

The conclusion is given in the section 5.

2. ORB Architecture and Components

The Object Request Broker specifies an architecture in which an objet can transparently invoke operations on another objet within heterogeneous distributed environments. The client/server model is respected in the ORB architecture. The client is the code or the process invoking an operation on the object which is implemented in the server process. The ORB is responsible for locating the server, issueing a request to the server and returning the results to the client.

The interface between the client and the server is described in ORB IDL, an interface description language which permits powerful features such as interface inheritance. Each ORB interface specifies a type of object, which consist of a set of operations, and attributes.

The picture below shows this architecture :

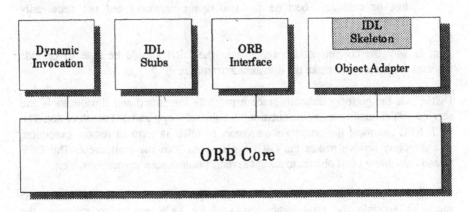

Figure 1. ORB Architecture

ORB core is the basic component of the ORB, which provides the representation of object reference and the communication support for remote operations.

ORB interface offers common ORB functions such as object reference manipulation.

Object Adapter provides the interface allowing an object implementation to access ORB functions : generation of object reference, activation/deactivation of object class implementation or individual objects, invocation of methods, etc.

IDL Skeleton implements an up-call mechanism which allows the object adapter to call the particular methods.

Dynamic Invocation Interface permits the client to construct and to issue a request at run time, rather than calling a client stub via IDL definition. Using this interface, the client can dynamically specify the object to be invoked, the operation to be performed, the set of the parameters to be passed in the operation, and so on.

IDL Stub masks to the user language the complexity of ORB remote operation mechanisms. The user request is presented by the stub in order to be forwarded to the server. The result of the invocation is then decoded and returned to the invoker.

The user application consists of a collection of objects communicating through the ORB platform. An object can play both client and server roles.

3. ORB implementation architecture

3.1. Principle

The functional specification of ORB can result in a number of implementation solutions. The system designer ought to make trade-offs such as :

- on which language (or languages) ORB interface should be mapped,

- to what extent the user language should be modified to be supported in ORB,

- how to organise the application process (single object per process or multiple),

- how to provide the distribution transparency,

- how to dynamically create objects and make them visible to other objects,

- etc.

In this section, we will present an implementation architecture of ORB on top of DCE services. To illustrate the language mapping, we will use the C++ language. Nevertheless, the mechanisms developped can also be used for other languages.

The key idea in the proposed ORB implementation is to avoid modifications in the user host programming language. i.e. The C++ programmer does not need learning new C++ extension. He or she can develop ORB based applications just like an ordinary C++ program. Besides, the development effort for ORB may be reduced, as no C++ grammar analyser is required.

To make this challenge possible, the ORB environment should give to the application an illusion of working with local objects. Thus, we introduce the concept of proxy object. The main objective of this object is to offer the same interface than that of the server object. This object acts exactly like the invoked object, except that it does not contain the real object implementation.

```
Client_Prog()
{
        ...
        Proxy_ServerObj.mtd1(p1, p2, ...);
        // Proxy_ServerObj is the local name of ServerObj;
        ...

}
```

In fact, the proxy object performs the functions of ORB stubs. It permits the client object to bind to, make the invocation on and unbind from the remote object, as shown in the code below :

```
Proxy_ServerObj::mtd1(p1, p2, ...)
{
        ...
        /*
        *       bind to the server object using the Naming Service
        */
        binding_handle = bind(ServerObjDceUuid);
        /*
        *       RPC call to the server procedure
        */
        ServerObj_RPC_mtd1(p1, p2, ...);
        /*
        *       unbind from the server object
        */
        unbind(binding_handle);
        ...
}
```

There is always one proxy object for each remote object[1] on which clients of that server object may issue invocations. The reason for this is to keep the server object's behavior uniform for all the client objects in the same process and to avoid redundancy.

At the server side, the RPC procedure performs the functions of ORB object adapter and skeleton. It invokes the method implementation and returns results. The code below shows the RPC function making the up-call to the server object :

```
ServerObj_RPC_mtd1(p1, p2, ...)
{
        ...
        ServerObj.mtd1(p1, p2);
        ...
}
```

3.2. Architecture

The principle is quite simple. But, to achieve this in the DCE environment, we should be able to answer the following questions :

- how to locate objects?
- how to create proxy object for a object dynamically bound?
- how to organise object implementations?

The implementation architecture we propose is fully bsed on the DCE distributed services. An ORB application involves several processes distributed in the network. A ORB process can support both client and server functions which are implemented in the DCE client and server stub procedures. The ORB core functions are provided by the DCE RPC service.

---

[1]To ensure the uniformity, the local invocations are treated as remote.

The following picture shows the proposed implementation architecture :

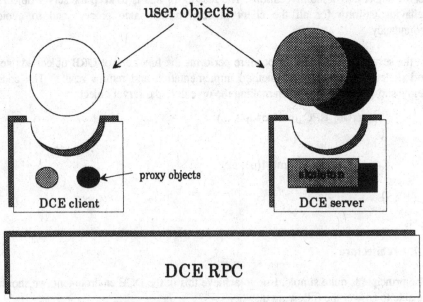

Figure 2. ORB implementation architecture

The user application is made of one or more objects which can be created statically or at run time. The object implementations[2] are distributed in the network according to the configuration policy defined by the application designer(i.e. processing power, storage capacity, security measure, etc.). The instances of an object type can only be created on the hosts which support that particular implementation. One object can invoke another by issuing an ORB request containing the reference of the invoked object. The invocation is performed without knowledge about the location of the object. However, an invocation is possible only if the invoker succeeds to import the service interface exported by the server objet.

Since DCE provides location transparency for RPC procedures, ORB implementation can directly make use of this mechanism. Therefore, An ORB object invocation is mapped on a DCE RPC call. This mapping will be straightforward if the semantic of the invocation is preserved. Thus, the ORB IDL interfaces must be translated into DCE IDL interfaces. For this effect, we have developed a IDL translation tool which will be presented later in this section. Furthermore, there must be an one-to-one relation between an ORB object and its DCE interface. Fortunately, DCE provides object oriented programming capacity. One server can support more than one type of DCE object and manage several object UUID of the same type. The objects of the

---

[2]The term "object implementation" here refers to the notion of the class of the object oriented languages.

same type share the same set of stubs. This feature allows to dynamically create objects without changing the stub procedures.

When an ORB object is created, it will be allocated an ORB reference. The reference will contain the uuid of the corresponding DCE object, which allows the ORB to take advantage of the location transparency provided by the DCE.

The ORB maintains a reference table in which an object is represented as a 3-tuple <localReference, ORBReference, DCEuuid>. If the object implementation is local, the localReference is the C++ reference of the object. If the object is remote, it contains the C++ reference of the proxy object. ORBReference contains the ORB reference of the object. DCEuuid contains the *uuid* of the corresponding DCE RPC object. Each time that a new object is created, one entry with the object's C++ reference is added to the local table. However, when a new object is referenced by the client for the first time, a new entry with its proxy reference is added to the table. Within the same ORB entity, there is only one proxy object for a referenced remote object.

The host language such as C++ usually provides the class definition which describes the behaviour of the objects of the same implementation. This class definition can be completely or partially mapped on the ORB interface. Thus, each ORB object may perform the same or a subset of behaviour of its corresponding C++ object. The ORB interface is then translated to the DCE interface to generate stub procedures. This translation is performed by using the IDL translator.

3.3. Example

The example given here attempts to show the mechanisms described above.

The object objectX invokes the method mtdA1() of the object ObjectA with a argument containing the reference of ObjectC. In the mtdA1(), ObjectA will create ObjectB and invoke mtdC1() of ObjectC.

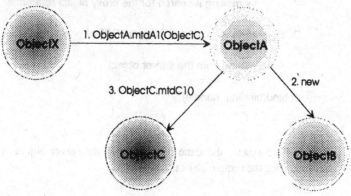

Figure 3. Example

The object ObjectX is the client of ObjectA. we suppose that ObjectX utilises the service of ObjectA in the method *prog()* :

- The client procedure in ObjectX is as follows :

```
ClassX::prog()
{
    ...
    /*
    *           invokes ObjectA
    */
    Proxy_ObjectA.mtdA1(ClassC &proxy_refC);
    ...
}
```

The invocation is not performed directly on ObjectA, but on its proxy in the local ORB process.

- The mtdA() of the proxy object for ObjectA :

```
Proxy_ClassA::mtdA1(ClassC &proxy_refC)
{
    ...
    /*
    *           bind to the ObjectA using the Naming Service
    */
    binding_handle = bind(ObjectADceUuid);
    /*
    *           The proxy object makes a RPC call to the server
    *           procedure, passing the ORB reference of ObjectC
    *           in the argument.
    *           This ORB reference can be found in the reference table
    *           by making a search for the proxy object reference.
    */
    DCE_InterfaceA_mtdA1(ORB_getORBRef(proxy_refC));
    /*
    *           unbind from the server object
    */
    unbind(binding_handle);
    ...
}
```

The proxy object offers exactly the same interface than the server object. It makes a DCE RPC call to invoke the remote object.

ObjectA is the server of ObjectX and the client of ObjectC. In addition, it dynamicly creates the ObjectB. Its ORB interface is translated into DCE interface. Its DCE server procedure is shown below :

```
DCE_InterfaceA_mtdA1(ORBRefType ocRef)
{
        ClassC  &proxyC1;
        /*
        *       call DCE primitive to obtain the object uuid from
        *       the binding handle
        */
        rpc_binding_inq_object(binding_handle, &uuid, status);
        /*
        *       search for local object reference in reference
        *       table using its DCE uuid
        */
        objRef = ORB_getObjRefFromDCEuuid(uuid);
        /*
        *       search for entry corresponding to OC from ORB
        *       reference table
        */
        proxyC1 = ORB_getObjRefFromORBRef(ocRef);
        /*
        *       If this object reference ocRef is found in the reference
        *       table, e.g. the ObjectC has been referenced,
        *       The ORB run time can take the its proxy object and
        *       pass it as parameter in the method call.
        *       If not, the ORB run time should invoke the operator New
        *       to bind to the object and create its proxy object.
        */
        if (proxyC1 != nullRef)
        {
                /*
                *       object C1 has been already referenced
                */
                ((ClassA &)objRef)->mtdA1(proxyC1);
        }
        else
        {
                /*
                *       the object reference is missing from the
                *       reference table.
                */
                proxyC1 = new (ocRef) ClassC();
```

```
                  ((ClassA &)objRef)->mtdA1(proxyC1);
         }
    }
```

In order to make invocation on the ORB server object (ObjectA), the DCE procedure needs the ORB object's local reference which can be obtained by its DCE uuid. This invocation requires the reference of ObjectC. However, the local ORB process may never refer to this object before. If so, the proxy object for ObjectC ought to be created to perform this dynamic binding.

The ORB object implementation for ObjectA is shown below :

```
ClassA::mtdA1(ClassC &refC1)
{
    ...
    /*
     *         create dynamically an instance of ClassB
     *         Only the proxy object is created
     *         The server object will be generated by
     *         the proxy object in the implementation site
     */
    ClassB proxyB1 = new ClassB();
    ...
    /*
     *         Invoke a method on the proxy object.
     */
    refC1.mtdC1();
    ...
}
```

When an object creation is required, only its proxy is created in the user code. The real object is created during the construction of this proxy object.

Only this part of code is writen by the user. It does not require any language extension.

4. ORB/DCE interface translator

To meet the ORB to DCE interface mapping requirements, we have developed a tool which performs the translation from ORB IDL interfaces to DCE IDL interfaces.

The syntax of the DCE IDL is quite similar to that of the ORB IDL. The translation might be straightforward, if the ORB interface definition did not provide special features.

Unfortunately, the ORB IDL allows a number of features which are not directly supported in the DCE IDL such as : attribute definition, interface inheritance, etc. Therefore, the ORB/DCE interface translator aims to provide relevant mechanisms to facilitate this mapping.

The translator performs normal syntax conversion from the ORB interface definition to the its symmetry in the DCE IDL.

If the ORB interface definition uses the direct attribute manipulation feature, we define a pair of operations : "get" and "set" in the DCE interface to perform the counterpart in the DCE IDL. The "get" operation reads the attribute value; The "set" operation changes this attribute to a specified value. If the ORB IDL attribute is read only. Only the "get" operation is specified.

i.e.

IDL interface definition :

```
interface A {
        attribute long          x;
        readonly attribute short    y;
};
```

Corresponding DCE interface definition :

```
interface A
{
        long    _get_x( );
        void    _set_x( [in] long x);
        short   _get_y( );
}
```

The interface inheritance mapping is more complicated. Suppose that we have the following ORB interface definition :

```
interface A: B, C{
        void mA1();
};
```

The ORB interface *A* is derived from *B* and *C* which are defined as follows :

```
interface B{
        void mB1();
};
interface C{
        void mC1();
};
```

When the interface *A* is directly translated to its DCE interface, it will only contain the operation *mA1*. Thus, the translator should be able to recognise the inheritance, to include *mB1* and *mC1* and to create the corresponding stubs. One solution is to copy all the operations and attributes of the base interfaces in the derived interface according to inheritance rules (ex. overloading, conflict resolution) and to generate the stub procedures. A naming problem may arise when overloaded operations are defined. Therefore, the name of the DCE procedures should take into account the number of arguments and their types *(i.e. DCE_IntfA_mtdA_int_char_float() for mtdA(int x, char y, float z))*.

5. Conclusion

This paper has proposed a simple ORB platform implementation using DCE services. It is demonstrated that the development effort can be reduced, since DCE provides effective communication mechanisms. The key idea of this implementation is the utilisation of the proxy object concept. A proxy object offers to the client the same interface as that of the server objet. It encapsulates the ORB client stub procedures.

This implementation architecture is under prototype development in the aim of providing a simple object oriented programming environment over the DCE. The performance aspects are not yet taken into account in this phase.

6. Reference

[1]   "The Common Object Request Broker : Architecture and Specification", OMG Document, Draft 1991.

[2]   "Introduction to BULL DCM/DCE", BULL, 1992.

[3]   "Application Development Guide DCM/DCE", BULL, 1992.

DCE++: Distributing C++-Objects using OSF DCE

Markus U. Mock

University of Karlsruhe, Institute of Telematics
76128 Karlsruhe, Germany; e-mail: mock@ira.uka.de

Abstract

This paper describes the design and implementation of an extended distributed object-oriented environment, DCE++, on top of DCE. The design goal was to overcome some observed shortcomings of DCE namely that is only well-suited for client-server applications. Opposed to DCE DCE++ supports a uniform object model, location independent invocation of fine-grained objects, remote reference parameter passing, dynamic migration of objects between nodes, and C++ language integration. Moreover, the implementation is fully integrated with DCE, using DCE UUIDs for object identification, DCE threads for interobject concurrency, DCE RPC for remote object invocation, and the DCE Cell Directory Service (CDS) for optional retrieval of objects by name. An additional stub compiler enables automatic generation of C++-based object communication interfaces. Low-level parameter encoding is done by DCE RPC's stub generation facility using the C-based DCE interface definition language (IDL). The system has been fully implemented and tested by implementing an office application. Experiences with the existing system and performance results are also reported in the paper.

1 Introduction

The OSF Distributed Computing Environment (DCE) [6,7,8,9] is becoming an industry standard for open distributed computing. It offers a rich set of services such as RPC, threads, naming, to enumerate just a few. For these reasons, DCE has been the choice for our research and development projects, too. However, like other authors [5], we have also observed several deficiencies of the traditional client/server-model supported by DCE:

- Granularity: Clients and servers are heavyweight instances. Therefore, it is costly to install them dynamically and it is virtually impossible to relocate them at run-time.

- *Communication:* The communication paradigm in asymmetric: Invocations are usually client-to-server round-trip. Server-to-client invocations require cumbersome implementation techniques but are desirable within many applications.

- *Parameter semantics:* RPC reference parameters are dereferenced and their contents are copied by value into the peer's address space. This can lead to anomalies in case of concurrent access to client and server copies. Moreover, parameter passing by remote reference would also be more efficient in some cases.

- *Remote data access:* Data structures managed by a server can only be accessed indirectly, i.e. by invoking data management operations of the server. Many applications could be facilitated by enabling direct remote access to data objects.

- *Entity identity:* Data objects do not have a globally unique identity. Therefore, they cannot be arbitrarily addressed from remote locations, one of the reasons for the lack of direct remote data access. Client and server entities only have a global identity by application-specific composition of low-level address and identifier information.

We designed and implemented a distributed object-oriented extension of DCE to address these problems. It supports the following features:

- *Fine-grained distributed objects:* The programming model is based on fine-grained, dynamically created C++ objects located at several distributed network nodes. An initial remote location can optionally be specified at object creation time. C++ objects therefore are the basic units of distribution. However, objects can also contain nested C++ data structures, leading to objects of arbitrary granularity.

- *Systemwide identity:* All distributable objects are internally referenced via system-wide unique identifiers based on DCE's *universal unique identifiers (UUIDs)*.

- *Location independent invocation:* Objects communicate by method invocations, no matter whether the peer object is local or remote. The task of locating peer objects is performed by our system. Remote invocations are internally mapped onto DCE RPC. This is achieved by an own stub generation facility working together with DCE's IDL-based stub compiler.

- *Dynamic object migration:* Upon request by the application, objects can dynamically move between nodes, e.g. to co-locate communicating objects or to distribute parallel computations onto different nodes. An important property of our approach is that migrated objects can still be accessed in a uniform way, and that concurrent migration and invocation requests are synchronized.

- *Concurrency support:* Object invocations at a given node can be performed concurrently based on multithreaded RPC servers. Moreover, applications can explicitly create concurrent computations by using a thread-related class library; this class library of our system is internally mapped onto DCE threads.

- *Decentralization and dynamics:* The implementation is based on a decentralized architecture. In particular, the algorithm to locate objects is fully decentralized. Moreover, object creation and deletion is fully dynamic, and the node structure can also be reconfigured dynamically. Based on these properties, there are no system-inherent scalability limitations.

- *Full integration with DCE:* One of the most important and distinguishing properties of our system is its full integration with DCE mechanisms. It solely uses DCE

RPC for implementing interobject communication, and DCE threads for concurrency. Moreover, UUIDs serve as object identifiers, nodes are addressed by DCE binding handles, and the DCE Cell Directory Service is used for optionally registering objects by logical names. Based on DCE, the implementation is highly portable and enables heterogeneous systems interoperability.

The approach is based on concepts introduced by earlier approaches such as *Emerald* [1], *Amber* [2], *Arjuna* [12], and *Amadeus* [4]. However, as opposed to these systems, it is integrated with DCE mechanisms, an issue that guided many detailed design choices. Moreover, the approach does not introduce any C++ language modifications - therefore, it is a system service on top of DCE and C++ and not a new language.

We first discuss our system architecture and design choices. Thereafter, we describe details of our implementation and discuss experiences and performance results. We also illustrate the functionality by an example application.

1.1 DCE++ Architecture and Basic Concepts

DCE++ uses fundamental DCE services, namely threads, RPC, and CDS. The time service is also operating in our environment but is only exploited internally, especially by CDS timestamps for name entries. The other services can be integrated with our approach in the future. Fig. 1 shows the extended architecture of DCE++ based on a simple example configuration.

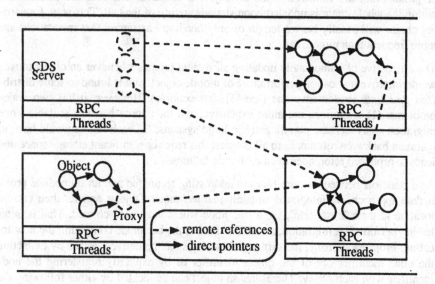

Fig. 1: DCE++ Architecture

On each node, a DCE RPC demon is installed and serves RPC invocations. Moreover, threads are used for handling concurrent invocation requests and can be exploited by the application with object-oriented class capsules. Distributed objects are allocated at various nodes and have local and remote interobject references. A remote reference is implemented by a proxy indirection; a proxy contains a location hint for the referenced object and transparently forwards invocations based on DCE RPC. Each node maintains a hash table for mapping the global object identifiers within incoming invocations onto actual storage addresses of C++ objects.

One or more DCE CDS servers are also part of the environment. Objects can be named upon creation which has the side effect that their names are registered with the name server along with the binding handle for the creating node. This mechanism is used to obtain initial references to objects and solve the problem of binding. However, it is not necessary to name an object. In fact, most objects will be nameless and references to them will only be obtained as references in remote method calls. While this gives the application developer some control over the accessibility of objects its main purpose is performance. Accessing the name service is an expensive operation taking several hundreds of milliseconds while passing object references in a method call requires only in the order of ten milliseconds making it one order of magnitude faster.

1.2 Proxy Management and Object Access

A proxy is installed whenever a node learns about the existence of a remote object. This is the case when a reference to a remote object is passed as a parameter of an invocation. In addition, when an object moves and has references to remote objects, proxies must be installed at the destination node for each reference. Moreover, a migrating object leaves a proxy at its former location. This results in forwarding chains of proxies that are followed when an object is invoked. The location information within the whole chain is updated upon stepwise return of the call. This way, forwarding chains will usually have a length of only one hop - assuming that invocations are more frequent than migrations.

The alternative of immediately updating all remote proxies whenever an object moves would improve invocation performance of mobile objects and is found in some distributed *Smalltalk* implementations (see [3], for example). However, it has two major problems: (1) migrations are more expensive, and the approach is not scalable since migration costs increase significantly in large systems; (2) each object would have to maintain backward references to all proxies; this requires significant storage space and leads to orphaned references in case of node failures.

As a trade-off between a pure forward addressing technique and an immediate proxy update approach, we integrated an additional technique: Objects register their current location at their "birthnode", i.e. at the node where they were created. That is, after having performed a migration, an RPC is sent to the birthnode containing the new location. From each proxy, the birthnode's address can be derived, either by extracting the node identifier out of the object identifier or by explicitly registering the node identifier with each proxy. Therefore, an object can be located by either following the forwarding chain or by querying the birthnode. The first option is used in the fault-free case. However, if a forwarding chain is broken by a failed intermediate node, the birthnode is queried for an object's location. In the normal case, forward addressing is more efficient - it requires one RPC if the location information is up-to-date, while the birthnode option would require at least two RPCs for locating the object at a third-party node.

1.3 Object Mobility

Object migrations are requested by the application by calling an automatically generated method of an object. Basically, a migration consists of the following internal operations (see fig. 2 for an example of moving an object *O1* from *node 1* to *node 2*): (1) First, the object to be moved is locked by a semaphore. This is required for synchronization with ongoing invocation requests. (2) Then the object is replaced by a proxy at the source node and unlocked; however, the object data is still kept for failure recovery. (3) Next, an RPC installation operation is invoked remotely at the destination node, passing the object's data as an RPC parameter. All object data structures are defined in IDL so that marshalling and unmarshalling can be done completely by DCE RPC. (4) The destination node installs the object and inserts its identifier into the local hash table. If there has been a proxy before, it is replaced by the object. (5) Upon receiving the reply of the remote installation RPC, (6) the source node of the migration informs the birthnode about the new location. (7) Finally, the original object data is deleted at the source node.

This approach has some interesting characteristics: Although migrations and invocations are synchronized by semaphores, locks are not held at the source node until the migration has fully completed. This is not necessary as the source node can immediately forward invocations when the proxy has been installed. The birthnode is informed only when a migration is completed so that it does not receive incorrect information if a migration fails. If an object should be located via the birthnode in the meantime, the operation would still work: The birthnode would direct the invocation to the former location of the object which then already has a proxy pointing to the new destination. Migration requests can also go to remote objects. In this case, the request is forwarded like a usual method invocation until it reaches the destination node. Then the migration is performed as discussed above.

Instead of specifying an absolute destination, a relative migration method is also supported. It takes a peer object as a relative destination specification, locates the given object as discussed above, and then performs the regular migration to the found location.

Since IDL requires the interface definition to be available before compiling and linking the application the current system does not allow new object types (i.e. classes) to be added dynamically to a running application. Also, all the code implementing the methods must be available at all nodes, such that an object of each defined class can possibly migrate to every node in the system.

1.4 Class Structure

The described functionality is offered by a set of classes shown in fig. 3 together with the most important relationships with application and system components. The class *Object_Reference* implements all required data and basic functionality for remote object access and object migration.

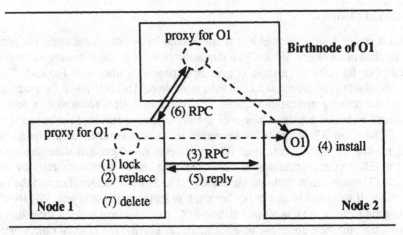

Fig. 2: Object Migration

For each application class with distributed instances, two implementations are required. The first one, denoted _<Application_Class> in the figure, is derived from *Object_Reference* and represents an auxiliary class. It mainly implements the proxies with code to distinguish between local and remote invocations. However, an instance of an auxiliary class is also present for each local object as an external capsule for each class. The class offers the required code to migrate objects with application-specific data structures, too. In case of remote invocations and migrations, it makes direct use of DCE RPC as indicated in the figure. Most importantly, this class can be generated automatically based on an interface description as described below.

The "real" implementation of each application class, denoted *<Application_Class>* in the figure, is identical with a regular class implementation as found in a corresponding non-distributed application. Each object of an auxiliary class has a local reference to the associated "real" object of the application class.

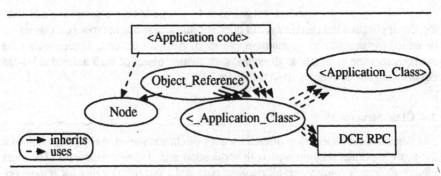

Fig. 3: Class/Module Structure

Network nodes are also represented by objects, for example to specify destination locations of migrations. The derived class *Node* offers the corresponding functionality. In particular, each object of class node contains the required address information as a DCE RPC binding handle. An application only uses objects of class *Node* and of auxiliary application classes directly. Several other auxiliary classes are part of the system, namely classes for threads, semaphores, hash tables, and directory service name entries.

The concrete structure, use, and automatic generation of these classes are described below.

2 Implementation

The implementation was done on a network of DECStations 5000 and 5240 under Ultrix 4.2, using AT&T C++ 2.1 and DEC's C++ compiler, named cxx. Our DCE prototype has been provided by DEC (version 1.0). Basic transport-level communication is performed by TCP/IP, UDP/IP or DECnet via an Ethernet. The actual communication protocol can be selected at RPC initialization time. For implementing the stub generation, the Unix tools *awk* and *sed* have been used.

The following subsections describe our implementation. We first discuss the system classes provided by our approach and then show some uxiliary application classes.

2.1 System Classes

Object_Reference: Much of the functionality of our approach is given by class *Object_Reference*. It has the following (simplified) structure:

```
class Object_Reference {
  private:
            uuid_t        object_id;              // object UUID
            char          *object_name;           // object name
            Node          *suspected_loc;         // suspected (NOT necessar-
ily current) location
            Node          *creating_node;         // creating node of object
            pthread_mutex_t mutex;                // semaphore
  public:   Object_Reference (char*);             // used for application ob-
jects and nodes
            Object_Reference (RPC_Obj_Ref*);      // used for migrated objects
and location hint evaluation
            ~Object_Reference ();                 // destructor
            void          lock();                 // lock semaphore
            void          unlock();               // unlock semaphore
            uuid_t        get_oid ();             // return id
            char*         get_name ();            // return name
            Node*         get_cre_loc ();         // return birthnode
            Node*         get_sus_loc ();         // return location hint
            void          update (Location *loc); // update location hint
            int           migrate (Object_Reference*);// relative migration
            virtual int   migrate (Node*);        // absolute migration
```

```
        virtual Location* locate ();                    // locate objects
};
```

Objects of this class contain a DCE UUID to identify them (*object_id*). It is generated by the constructor using a DCE system function. They also have an optional name (*object_name*) that is registered with CDS. The location hint of proxies and the birth-node of the corresponding object are stored in separate instance variables, *suspected_loc* and *creating_node*, respectively. In principle, it would be possible to derive the birthnode from the object UUID (the node address would be part of the UUID to make it globally unique); however, this did not work with the given DCE implementation. The semaphore for synchronizing invocations and migrations is also part of *Object_Reference*.

Most of the methods are pretty straightforward. It may be worthwhile to note that the second contructor is used to install proxies when a new object reference is passed to a given node. The required address information is provided via a parameter of type *RPC_Obj_Ref* that contains the internal RPC address information for an object's location. The *update* method is called when a proxy chain is updated upon return of a remote invocation. The relative migration method is application-independent as it only calls the absolute migration method after having located the object. However, the absolute migration method that performs the physical migration must be provided by the application-specific subclass and is therefore virtual. The method to locate an object is implemented differently by application objects and nodes and is therefore also virtual.

Node: An object of class *Node* is created locally for each node that is known by a given peer node, including itself. It provides the required information to invoke an RPC at a suspected object location. This includes a unique identifier for the node, and a corresponding RPC binding handle.

```
class Node : public Object_Reference {
    private:
                    uuid_t          loc_id;                     // id from binding handle
                    rpc_binding_handle_t binding_handle;        // DCE binding handle
        public:     Node (char*);                               // nodes defined by applica-
tion
                    ~Node ();                                   // destructor
                    Location*       locate ();                  // return suspected_loc from
base
                    void            Shutdown ();                // stop RPC listener
                    uuid_t          get_id ();                  // get node id
                    rpc_binding_handle_t get_bh ();             // get binding handle
};
```

The constructor of this class creates a representative for foreign nodes if a node name is given. In this case, a CDS inquiry is performed for importing the required binding handle and identifier information (using the CDS interface operations *rpc_ns_binding_import_begin, ..._next, ..._done*). Otherwise, the representative for the local node is generated. In this case, the constructor exports the local binding information to CDS (using *rpc_ns_binding_export*) so that other nodes can import it. The *locate* method just returns the suspected location of the superclass component as nodes never move. In addition to basic access operations for instance variables for internal use, a method to shut down the RPC server of a node is provided. It is useful for remote housekeeping within an application. It is implemented by calling a remote DCE RPC management function at the actual location. Note that all other methods can be implemented locally - except the interaction with CDS within the constructors.

The implementation of the other application classes, namely of the threads and hash tables are relatively straightforward and are therefore not described in closer detail.

2.2 Application Classes

Class structure: The actual implementation of the "real" application classes is similar to ordinary C++. However, the auxiliary application classes, i.e. the capsule classes around the real classes, are generated automatically. They basically have the following class structure (_<A>) for an application class <A>:

```
class _<A> : public Object_Reference
  private:
              _<A> (char*);                          // internal constructor for
proxies
  public:     <A> *obj_ptr;                          // pointer to application ob-
ject
              _<A> (<A>_data*, RPC_Obj_Ref*);        // used within manager after
migration
              _<A> (RPC_Obj_Ref*);                   // used within location hint
evaluation
              ~_<A> ();                              // destructor
              int migrate (Node*);                   // absolute migration
              static _<A>* get_ref_by_name (char*);  // get reference to existing
object
              // for all application-specific constructors:
              _<A> :: _<A> ( ... , Object_Reference *or = here, char* name = "");
                                                     // regular application-
specific constructor
              // for all application-specific methods:
              result_type _<A> :: method_name ( ... , Object_Reference *or = NULL,
RPC_call_data *cd = NULL);
```

Each object has an internal pointer to the actual object data of class <A> (*obj_ptr*). This pointer is dereferenced for all local invocations, passing them to the real object. Two internal constructors are used for installing objects after a migration and for generating proxies, respectively. <A>_*data** is a pointer to the data structure of the application class, however given in C instead of C++ for conformance with DCE's IDL. The implementation of the *migrate* method also accesses this data structure definition in order to perform the remote object installation by an RPC call. Details are expounded in [11].

3 Example Application

To test our system we implemented a small application, modeling an office scenario, see figure 4.

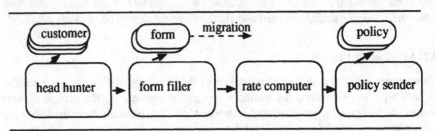

Fig. 4: Example Application

A "head hunter" creates a number of customers and for each customer a form is created that has to be filled out. After initializing and filling in some basic data such as the customer name the head hunter is done. The form filler periodically checks the forms' state and as soon as they are available for further processing it requests them being migrated to its own node and fills in more data. Likewise the "rate computer" periodically checks whether the form filler is done, as soon as the form is in state "form_filled_in" it requests a migration to its own node. Then it computes the rates for the customers (we model insurance policies being filled out). Finally the filled-in policies are migrated to the "policy sender" upon request by the policy sender. As can be inferred from the description of the scenario various migrations are involved. Moreover, the form filler, rate computer and policy sender access the forms remotely to find out in which state they are. Therefore the application also makes use of remote method invocations.

To develop an application one has to go through the following steps:

- write the application classes
- write a corresponding IDL-description
- write a corresponding DCE++ description

Once one has gone through those steps one generates the migration code by running the DCE++ stub generator, then the IDL-compiler, and finally the C++ compiler and linker to create the application code. More details on the development process and the way the code really looks like can be found in [11].

4 Performance and Experiences

In this section we will look at the performance of the system. Moreover, we will discuss the general experiences gained by designing and implementing DCE++.

Performance:

To gather performance data of our DCE++ system we chose to time migration within our sample application. For that purpose we used different amounts of data within the form that is filled in and migrated in the application. First, we timed the migration of the form containing only system relevant data that is inherited by each appliation class such as the object's ID. Then we increased the additional user data from 100 bytes to 1000 bytes and finally 10000 bytes. All reported times are in milli-seconds and shortest, longest and median time to complete the migration are shown. The measurements were made on lightly loaded DEC 5000 stations connected by an Ethernet. The communication protocol chosen to be used for RPC was UDP.

The figures show that the overhead incurred by DCE++ is negligable. In previous measurements in the same environment we had measured about 6 ms for a raw empty RPC call. Moreover, the figures show that the migration time is not very sensitive to the amount of data being transfered. This, however, must be attributed to the tested data sizes - which all fit into a UDP packet - and the type of data used (arrays) which allows the IDL-compiler an efficient and fast encoding and decoding. A median time of 35 ms for the migration of an object containing about 1000 bytes makes DCE++ suited for use in real applications.

time [ms]	Empty	100 bytes	1000 bytes	10000 bytes
Minimum	16	16	16	59
Maximum	176	254	176	543
Median	31	31	35	82

Fig 5: Performance

Experiences:

Based on our implementation and on the example application, we gathered a number of important experiences:

- *Object model:* The object model seems to be more suited for distributed programming than the traditional client/server approach. Within our application (and within former projects), we observed that a uniform object model simplifies application design. Location independent invocation based on globally unique object identifiers makes distribution transparent to a large degree - except the problem of failure handling, of course. Remote object reference passing contributes to this fact as it is a natural passing mechanism in local applications, too.

- *Object mobility:* Mobility is an essential feature of distributed object-oriented approaches. It allows for modeling physical data transfer (such as document shipping) at a very high level of abstraction. Moreover, it provides explicit control of distribution when an application requires it (e.g. to co-locate communicating objects).

- *Use of RPC:* In spite of our criticism of RPC, this mechanism has proven as a workable base for implementing such a distributed object management facility. Based on the one-to-one mapping of method invocations onto application-specific RPCs, most of the parameter marshalling problems were just passed down to the RPC level; this simplified our implementation significantly. Moreover, the recursive implementation of the algorithm to locate objects based on RPC has proven quite elegant and easy to test and maintain. It would be more efficient to send results back to the caller via a direct message from the callee, but this slight disadvantage is outweighed by the chance of updating all intermediate location information.

- *Use of standards:* The use of DCE as an industry standard also had many advantages. As opposed to ad-hoc mechanisms, the environment was rather stable. Moreover, we did not have to deal with heterogeneity problems; they are hidden by the RPC protocol. Finally, the high portability of applications based on a standardized platform is an important advantage in open systems.

- *Use of system services:* The use of system services as offered by DCE made a rapid implementation possible. In particular, we exploited CDS for node and object management and threads for concurrency support - in addition to RPC, of course.

- *Interface definition:* Our interface definition and stub generation approach is only an intermediate solution. Its capabilities regarding the language syntax are limited. Moreover, a partially redundant specification must be given. Therefore, a major goal of our future work is a full C++-based interface definition and stub generation facility.

5 Limitations

Although we think that our current system is already usable for application development, it still has its shortcomings.

Most notably there are currently two description files the user has to write: the IDL-description to be used by the IDL-compiler and the DCE++ description file that is used to generate support code for migration and remote access. However, this is not a design limitation, since it is possible to generate the DCE++ description file from an augmented IDL-description. Work is in progress to enhance the IDL-description to allow the description of C++ class interfaces. From such a description the DCE++ description file could be generated automatically, maybe even by the IDL-compiler itself. This would render the need for writing a second (redundant) description unnecessary, which - apart from being a nuisance - also introduces the possibility of errors.

Another limitation of the system related to the IDL-description restricts the range of data types that can be used in migratable objects. Since the IDL-description must conform with the corresponding C++ classes it it currently impossible to support class hierarchies with virtual member functions.

Finally, although IDL allows complex data types such as linked lists it is currently impossible to migrate them. The reason is that the RPC runtime system allocates some parameters of a RPC on the server's stack and deallocates them once the call has completed. This is desired behavior for RPC and for a remote method invocation as well, however, when sending object data to another node to install the object there, i.e. when a migration is being performed, the data on the (RPC) server's side must persist. For simple flat data types DCE++ can simply do the allocation itself, when more complex (user-defined) data structures are involved, though, it would be necessary to have access to the IDL-description to take appropriate action. A possible solution would be to allow an attribute for an RPC call specifying that parameter data has to persist after the call completes thus enabling migration. How to do this exactly is another topic being investigated.

6 Conclusion

This paper described the design and implementation of a distributed object-oriented extension of the OSF Distributed Computing Environment. The major features of the approach, location independent object invocation and object mobility, have proven very useful for application development. Moreover, the use of DCE as a standard has provided significant implementation benefits.

Acknowledgements: I would like to thank Markus Person who implemented the described concepts within his diploma thesis [10].

References

1. Black, A., Hutchinson, N., Jul, E., Levy, H., Carter, L.: Distribution and Abstract Types in Emerald; *IEEE Trans. on Softw. Eng., Vol. 13, No. 1, Jan. 1987, pp. 65-75*

2. Chase, J.S., Amador, F.G., Lazowska, E.D., Levy, H.M., Littlefield, R.J.: The Amber System: Parallel Programming on a Network of Multiprocessors; *12th ACM Symp. on Operating Systems Principles, Litchfield Park, Arizona, 1989, pp. 147-158*

3. Decouchant, D.: Design of a Distributed Object Manager for the Smalltalk-80 System; *ACM OOPSLA Conf., Portland, Oregon 1986, pp. 444-452*

4. Horn, C., Cahill, V.: Supporting Distributed Applications in the Amadeus Environment; *Computer Communications, Vol. 14, No. 6, Juli/Aug. 1991, pp. 358-365*

5. Levy, H.M., Tempero, E.D.: Modules, Objects and Distributed Programming: Issues in RPC and Remote Object Invocation; *Software - Practice and Experience, Vol. 21, No. 1, Jan. 1991, pp. 77-90*

6. Open Software Foundation: Introduction to OSF DCE; *Open Software Foundation, Cambridge, USA, 1992*

7. Open Software Foundation: DCE Users Guide and Reference; *Open Software Foundation, Cambridge, USA, 1992*

8. Open Software Foundation: DCE Application Development Guide; *Open Software Foundation, Cambridge, USA, 1992*

9. Open Software Foundation: DCE Application Development Reference; *Open Software Foundation, Cambridge, USA, 1992*

10. Person, M.: Verteilte Objektverwaltung auf der Basis von DCE; *Diplomarbeit an der Fakultät für Informatik der Universität Karlsruhe, 1993 (in German)*

11. Schill A., Mock M.: DCE++ - Distributed Object-Oriented Support on Top of OSF DCE, Submitted for Publication

12. Shrivastava, S.K., Dixon, G.N., Parrington, G.D.: An Overview of the Arjuna Distributed Programming System; *IEEE Software, Jan. 1991, pp. 66-73*

Object-Oriented Distributed Computing With C++ and OSF DCE

John Dilley <jad@nsa.hp.com>

Distributed Systems Architecture Team
Hewlett-Packard Company
19410 Homestead Road, MS 43UA
Cupertino, California 95014-9810 **USA**

HP Document Number NSA-93-014

Abstract. This paper suggests a method for developing object-oriented distributed applications using the C++ and DCE technologies. It presents the benefits provided by the use of object-oriented design and development techniques when writing distributed applications. It describes a model to map DCE onto C++, a structure for distributed C++ applications and it presents a set of challenges we encountered while integrating C++ with DCE, along with the solutions we chose for them. Through this approach we saw a significant decrease in application code size as well as an increase in developer productivity.

1   Overview

This paper reports on the results of a project aimed at simplifying the development of distributed applications based upon the OSF Distributed Computing Environment.

This project defines a class library that hides complexity from DCE developers and a compiler that converts DCE interface definition files into customized C++ client and server classes. Server developers implement the server class methods to implement server behavior. Client developers use the client class methods to access corresponding servers across the network. Using this approach, client writers use the same model they use for making local method calls, but an RPC is being made transparently for them.

Standard DCE functions such as security and namespace registration can be packaged in C++ classes and reused automatically by applications. This reduces application complexity and can increase the consistency of distributed applications.

By integrating the DCE exception model with C++ exceptions we were able to make consistent use of language support for remote and local exceptions.

1.1   Why DCE in C++

We chose to use C++ to encapsulate and abstract DCE functionality for a number of reasons.

- Object orientation provides many benefits for abstracting interfaces and hiding data, allowing developers to work at a higher level. C++ also facilitates interface and code reuse.

- C++ is becoming a very prevalent language for object-based systems development. Increasing numbers of C++ class libraries and development tools are becoming available.

- C++ has a clean and natural interface to C, and therefore to the existing DCE implementation.

- The C++ object model is also similar to the object model used in DCE.

These last two factors make the resulting system more intuitive and therefore easier to learn.

1.2 Benefits

The benefits of building systems using object-oriented techniques have been well studied in the literature. Korson and McGregor [1] provide a thorough examination of the concepts and benefits of object-oriented development. Nicol, et al [2] present some benefits of object orientation for building distributed systems and discuss some current distributed object-based systems including the existing DCE object model and OMG's CORBA [3] distributed object system.

In our work the primary benefits that relate to the construction of DCE-based distributed applications were the abstraction of complex DCE interfaces and integration of the DCE object and exception models with the C++ language. Other benefits were seen in the use of encapsulation, error handling, initialization, and cleanup.

A higher-level interface to the DCE allows greater productivity because less code needs to be written to deal with the DCE in each new application. Access to DCE functionality is provided through common access to base class member functions. Encapsulation of DCE data types within C++ types allows convenient access to DCE data through C++-supported type conversions. And integrating the DCE object model into C++ provides access to that model in a more natural, language supported way.

We believe that using the DCE class libraries will produce more readable and reliable code, and make it easier for new DCE users to learn how to create their first DCE-based distributed applications. This is mainly due to the complexity of the environment which is hidden by the class libraries.

2 The DCE Object Model

DCE *interfaces* (IDL specifications) define a set of related data types and remote operations that can be performed using those data types. A client performs a remote operation by making a Remote Procedure Call to a compatible server (a server which implements the interface the client wishes to use).

A DCE *object* is a logical entity supported by a DCE server. Each object has an *implementation type* which is effectively the class of the object. Each implementation type is supported by a set of *manager routines* that perform remote operations defined in an interface definition file. A server can support multiple interfaces; each interface can have multiple implementation types associated with it. Implementation types are typically associated with different categories of entities the server is manipulating. For example, a server could support database access by its clients. The server may support multiple database implementations transparently, while providing clients the same logical view (interface). The server in Figure 1 supports multiple interfaces; within its database interface it has implementation types A and B, with associated manager routines.

Each implementation type can have a set of objects associated with it. These objects are often logical representations of the entities the server manages, such as individual databases or perhaps tables in a database.

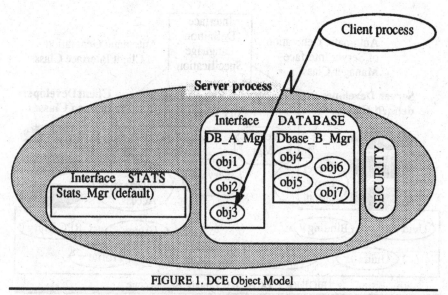

FIGURE 1. DCE Object Model

A server registers the interfaces and objects it supports with the DCE environment and awaits incoming RPCs. Each RPC is dispatched by the runtime to the specific manager function that supports the interface and object requested by the client.

DCE clients establish a binding to an object by specifying an interface and object identifier. The client and the DCE runtime use this information to select an appropriate server and initiate the RPC. By selecting an object, the client can select which logical entity it wishes to access; in Figure 1 the client has bound to the object obj3.

3   Description of Approach

We considered two approaches to constructing a set of class libraries for use as an interface to a particular technology (in this case DCE). One was to write *wrapper classes* for each of the basic data types and *wrapper functions* for each of the interfaces defined by the technology. These classes and functions are patterned directly after the data types and functions defined in the technology specification and tend to look and operate just like the underlying types and functions.

The other approach was to create a set of classes that build an abstract model of the data and functions needed by an application. These classes are not patterned after the data types themselves but rather based upon a set of *tasks* or *responsibilities*. The implementations use the underlying data types but do so within an infrastructure that may be independent of those data types.

With the wrapper classes, each underlying interface is typically mapped into a method call, providing little simplification over the current API. With wrapper classes you are tied to a particular implementation of the underlying technology. To work with a different implementation or underlying technology you will need to write and use another set of wrapper classes. Wrapper classes are still essential in many instances to encapsulate basic data types even when using a task-based model. One example is to encapsulate native data types into cleaner objects making use of polymorphism or C++ operators.

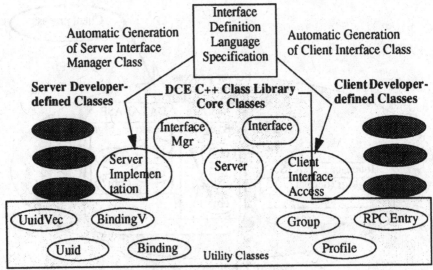

FIGURE 2. DCE Class Library Architecture

The task-based approach requires more up-front design work by the package developer, but in the end can yield a system that is cleaner and more consistent for the application developer. Task-based systems may also be able to survive changes in underlying technologies, provided the model presented by the technology remains similar.

We chose to create a set of task-based classes to support the DCE object model, along with a set of wrapper classes to encapsulate basic DCE data types.

4 The DCE C++ Object Model

The DCE C++ object model attempts to preserve the DCE object model while providing convenient, natural C++ access to DCE objects. In the DCE C++ object model an interface defines a set of abstract client and server classes. Member functions of these abstract classes correspond to the remote operations defined in the IDL file. Additional abstract classes are provided that encapsulate and simplify the interaction with DCE and a set of wrapper classes are provided to encapsulate the basic DCE data types into a C++ representation consistent with the DCE object model. On the server side DCE objects provide the desired behavior; on the client side they provide transparent access to the object via the DCE RPC mechanism.

4.1 Class Library Components

The components of the class library include the core abstract base classes providing the framework for the object model and a set of utility (wrapper) classes that encapsulate the basic DCE data types.

DCE Core Abstract Base Classes

The DCE core classes are responsible for providing the DCE interface abstraction. They define the view of the distributed object system with which you interact. Client and server implementation classes, generated by the IDL to C++ compiler, inherit their interface and default behavior from these core classes, which provide members common to all interfaces. The core classes are:

- Server—this class implements the portion of the server that interacts with the DCE environment. A single instance of the server class registers the objects, interfaces and bindings supported by the server process with the DCE runtime. The server class also takes an optional location in the name space under which the server should register itself. The server class has a listen method that performs all the necessary registration with the environment and begins listening for incoming RPC requests.

- InterfaceMgr—this is the server-side abstract base class. Each interface manager is associated with a DCE interface handle and optional type and object identifiers (UUIDs). The interface manager class defines a set of conversions and access routines to get the stored data. Derived classes of InterfaceMgr, generated by the IDL to C++ compiler, provide the member functions that must be implemented by the server developer corresponding to the interface-defined remote operations. These classes are referred to as implementation classes.

- Interface—this is the client abstract base class. It holds the common client functions for specifying a remote object with which to communicate. The constructor requires as parameters interface and server binding information. The Interface class provides the ability to control binding policies, and to convert an Interface object to a string binding representation. Derived classes of Interface, generated by the IDL to C++ compiler provide the client member functions to access the interface-defined remote operations. These classes are referred to as client access classes.

Utility Classes

The utility classes encapsulate the behavior of basic DCE data types to make their use more convenient within C++. The purpose of these wrappers is to allow convenient construction and use of these data types. Many of them provide conversions to the corresponding DCE representation (such as to string or `uuid_t`), allowing them to be passed directly to DCE calls without need for separate translation. The primary utility classes are:

- Binding—encapsulates `rpc_binding_handle_t`. Can be constructed from string or from binding handle components. Provides conversion back to `rpc_binding_handle_t` or to `char*`.

- Uuid—encapsulates `uuid_t`. Can be constructed from string form or `uuid_t`. Equality tests against `uuid_t` and `char*` are provided for convenience. Conversion operators are provided for `uuid_t` and `char*`, as well as to hash value.

- BindingVec—implements a vector of binding handle objects. Can be converted into the DCE vector type. There is also a UuidVec class.

Generated Classes

The generated classes are created from the interface definition by the IDL to C++ compiler. Their structure is described in detail in the following sections.

Developer-Defined Classes

The solid ovals represent classes the developer defines (derives) to provide the implementation and access to the distributed functionality.

4.2 IDL to C++ Compiler

The idl++ "compiler" is actually a `perl` script that translates an interface definition into the interface-specific client and server access classes. The compiler first runs the standard DCE IDL compiler to create the client and server C stubs and the interface header file containing the operation and data type declarations. The compiler parses the header file to create a set of C++ classes for each interface defined in the IDL file. The client access classes contain member functions that allow C++ method calls to invoke the RPCs defined in the IDL file. On the server side the compiler generates two classes: an abstract implementation class corresponding to the interface defined in the IDL file and a default instantiable implementation class derived from this abstract class (see Figure 3).

In addition to the server-side implementation classes the compiler generates a C++ entry point vector (EPV) data structure, and an object mapper, which maps an interface and object ID pair to a C++ object instance. The C++ EPV is called by the DCE runtime when an RPC is received for a given interface. The C++ EPV calls the object mapper to get the specific C++ object instance to which the call is being made. The C++ EPV calls the desired member function on the object returned by the object mapper and handles the mapping of DCE exceptions; see §7.2 for a discussion of exceptions.

The data types specified in the header file are left untouched by idl++: no mapping of user data types for C++ is done. Data types defined in the IDL file are simply used by the application developer as basic C++ data types. IDL data types are a subset of C++ types (see the IDL specification [4]). This prototype does not permit the passing of C++ objects as arguments to remote procedure calls.

4.3 Client Access Class

The client-side access class inherits from the abstract base class Interface. The access class includes the methods corresponding to the operations (remote procedures) defined in the IDL interface. The client access methods manage binding to a server and then call the corresponding C stub generated by the DCE IDL compiler. The client methods also map DCE exceptions returned by the RPC into C++ exceptions.

4.4 Server Implementation Class

For the server the compiler generates an abstract implementation class derived from InterfaceMgr. The implementation abstract class provides specifications for the member functions corresponding to the remote operations declared in the interface definition file. Instantiable classes derived from the abstract implementation class must implement the member functions defined in the abstract implementation class to provide the operational characteristics of the server. Each of these instantiable classes is of a distinct imple-

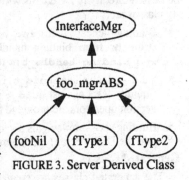

FIGURE 3. Server Derived Class

mentation type (i.e., has an associated manager type UUID). The compiler generates one such class by default with a nil manager type UUID (the nil manager class). If multiple implementation types (and therefore multiple managers) are to be used, you must derive additional classes from the abstract manager class.

Each object (instance) of an implementation class must have its own object UUID and must be registered with the server class so the C++ runtime (object mapper) can locate it when a call comes in for that object UUID.

The implementation classes implement the manager methods in C++ in the same way the manager functions are implemented in a C-based DCE server. The manager methods use the data passed in as arguments, perform their task, and possibly return data to the caller.

If manager methods throw C++ exceptions they will be caught in the C++ EPV and transmitted back to the C++ client (as a DCE-compatible data type) where they are raised again as C++ exceptions for the client to handle.

5 Applications Ported

We ported a set of sample applications from the HP DCE Toolkit to experiment with the class libraries, with the InterViews C++-based GUI [5][6], and with object database technologies. The applications ported are described in the following sections. More detail about these applications can be found in [7].

Our application development environment was HP-UX 8.0 and 9.0, with the HP DCE Developer's Environment release, based upon OSF DCE 1.0.1.

5.1 sleeper

The sleeper sample application is a very simple application whose interface takes an integer number of seconds to sleep. The manager sleeps for that many seconds and then returns. We used this application for basic experimentation and testing of the libraries.

5.2 rmt_load

The remote load application is used to monitor the load average of a group of server systems. The application client concurrently requests the load average of each of a set of servers by doing RPCs in separate threads. Each server returns its one-minute load average (as emitted by the standard uptime program) which is then reported by the client.

In our prototype, the remote load client was given an InterViews-based GUI to display the load averages. Only the client was ported; it contacted existing C-based servers to demonstrate interoperability between C and C++ DCE applications.

5.3 phone_db

The phone database application is used to look up personal phone and email information. The UI allows specification of name or regular expression search criteria. With that information the client makes an RPC to the database server and displays the results. The phone_db server maintains a database of names and related information. It is implemented in C++ and uses the HP OpenODB object database to hold the data.

The interface for this application defines data types for a database entry, a simple structure of strings, and a linked list of database entries. Operations defined include a search by name (the name is set up as the key field in the database), an arbitrary search for an intersection of fields, and operations to add and remove entries from the database. The server exports its bindings to the namespace and the client uses the name service interface to locate a compatible server.

The server manager functions were leveraged from the C version. They maintained the same interface but were reimplemented to use OpenODB underneath. The client was almost entirely rewritten due to the new InterViews graphical user interface.

6 Results

Porting the existing C applications to C++ took very little time—the main time-consuming tasks were the removal of the code to interface with the DCE and the addition of the InterViews GUI. Since the interface definitions remained the same, the code dealing with the data types and remote procedures was highly leveraged. In some of the applications the manager code remained in C, as it was perfectly adequate. This saved development time, and illustrates the integration of the C and C++ environments.

All the GUI work was done in C++. Since we were using a new technology that the sample applications had not been using previously, this was all new code. We found that interfacing the GUI code with the C++ client access class was quite natural.

6.1 Benefits

The primary benefits we experienced after use of this technology were:

- Providing powerful abstractions on top of DCE allowed us to concentrate on the application, not the environment.

- Application development and debugging time were shortened because the basic DCE calls are encapsulated in an already-tested library. Also, having sensible defaults for many DCE values prevented the need for much redundant code by allowing code reuse.

- The C++ DCE application code size is significantly smaller than the C code. We noted a five-to-one decrease in the actual lines of code that dealt with the DCE environment in the sleeper application. The new C++ code was also easier to develop than it had been to develop the original equivalent code in C.

- The C++ DCE application object size is predictably larger than the C version. The object size grew by 30-40%, mainly due to the addition of the C++ exception mechanism and the DCE C++ exception model we added. Use of shared libraries should minimize this increase.

- The C++ exception model is more powerful and useful than the DCE exception model. A greater variety of exceptions can be transmitted more easily across the RPC and handled in the client in a natural way supported by the language.

- Having standard policies defined for namespace registration and security should assist in making future applications using this code more consistent with each other. This will reduce the management effort required to maintain a set of client/server applications.

- The higher-level abstractions seem to be easier to learn than when using DCE directly. It is hard for us to judge this fairly as we were all proficient with DCE before porting the sample applications.

7 Issues with technology

The main issues encountered in integrating the DCE with C++ were in the areas of threads and exceptions.

7.1 Handling DCE Threads

The DCE threads package provides significant benefits but places the requirement of being threadsafe on all components linked into an application. Be sure to verify whether your C++ compiler emits thread-safe code (most do), and whether its libraries are thread-safe (most aren't). Also, if using X11 or other libraries, be sure to determine whether they can be called from multiple threads concurrently. If not you will have to wrap calls to those subsystems to prevent reentrance problems.

7.2 Mapping DCE Exceptions into C++

The area of exceptions required quite a bit of work in the design of the class library. The C++ language-based exception model is by far more powerful and better integrated than the DCE exception package. It was used as the basis for all exception handling in our prototype since DCE exceptions are incompatible with C++ destructors.

The first challenge was that the C++ and C-based DCE exception mechanisms cannot interoperate—an exception thrown or raised by one mechanism cannot be caught and interpreted by the other. Furthermore, an exception raised in one language context cannot be allowed to pass through blocks from the other language. If this is allowed to happen, cleanup code might not be properly executed. The DCE exception facility uses the **setjmp** and **longjmp** calls. The **longjmp** call allows control to pass from one stack frame to another frame, possibly much earlier in the call stack. The trouble is the C++ compiler can emit code at the end of blocks to call destructors for automatic variables and to handle C++ exceptions. Allowing a DCE exception to skip over this code can cause consistency problems and memory leaks in the C++ application.

Exception Model

To model exceptions in C++ an abstract base class OSFException was defined to specify the common behavior for all exceptions. Two more base classes, DCEexception and CMAexception, were derived from OSFException to model the distinct types of exceptions that can be raised by the DCE and CMA (threads) subsystems. The DCEexception class was further subdivided into RPC, security, and directory service exceptions. Each exception that can be raised either by the DCE or CMA subsystem was created as a subclass derived from one of these base classes. Each of the specific exception classes has a method that will print out an informative description of the exception, and can be converted into a string through an **operator char***.

The choice to model exceptions as individual classes, instead of as a generic class with an exception value, allows individual exceptions to be caught by class—in the C++ exception model any specified data type can be caught. With the generic exception with value model, fewer classes would be needed but if you want to catch a particular exception you must catch the generic exception and test its value.

Server Stubs

C++ exceptions cannot be passed across the network back to the DCE client. Any exceptions raised by the C++ manager methods must be caught and translated into a data type that can be raised again as a C++ exception in the client. To facilitate this, the idl++ compiler adds a hidden status parameter to the interface definition. That status parameter is used to hold the unique integer value of the exception that was raised. On the client-side that integer is thrown again as a C++ exception. Since an integer type is used, only the DCE **error_status_t** and **unsigned32** data types can currently be transmitted back to the client. Any other exception type is mapped to a generic exception code.

Client Stubs

The C++ access method calls the DCE C stub, which can raise a variety of DCE exceptions, including communication status, fault status, and user defined DCE exceptions. To prevent problems caused by the inconsistent DCE and C++ exception models, the DCE C stub call is wrapped by a CMA **TRY/CATCH** clause. If an exception is caught in the C++ stub, it is rethrown in C++ as the corresponding exception subclass.

8 Recommendations

We have demonstrated it is possible and useful to develop object-oriented distributed applications with C++ and DCE, but there are still technical issues with doing so. We have come up with a set of recommendations intended to smooth the road for others developing distributed object-oriented applications using DCE and C++. Our recommendations fall into two classes: vendor and user recommendations.

8.1 Vendor Recommendations

The sooner thread-safe libraries are available, the easier it will be to develop applications using DCE threads. In particular, the C++ runtime library, X11 and GUI technologies built upon it, and commercial products such as databases must be made thread-safe.

The availability of thread-aware distributed debuggers will also greatly aid in the creation of DCE applications.

8.2 User Recommendations

The most important issues to be aware of are those that would impede integration of the object-oriented and distributed computing technologies.

- Determine which system components are thread-safe. Develop a plan for working around the non-thread-safe components, either by writing wrappers, serializing, or ensuring that only a single manager thread will run.

- Make sure the DCE exception mechanism is properly dealt with: do not allow DCE or CMA exceptions to escape past C++ blocks.

9 Related Work

There are many distributed object systems documented in the literature with a variety of goals. The Arjuna system [8][9] focuses on fault tolerance and persistence using a custom RPC mechanism built atop an existing kernel. The Clouds project [10] built a distributed, object-based operating system using a custom microkernel and remote object invocation implementation. Like Clouds, Emerald [11] uses an object-thread approach to provide distributed object communication. These are primarily research projects exploring the operation of distributed object systems using custom platforms. Schill [12] presents a model for building an object-oriented distributed system within the framework of Open Distributed Processing (ODP) on top of an existing OSI-based infrastructure.

By contrast, our work focuses on integrating C++ within the existing DCE system infrastructure, and to simplify the use of the DCE object model.

OMG CORBA[3] will address creating distributed object systems in C++; some implementations will run on top of DCE. CORBA IDL provides for interface inheritance, which DCE IDL is lacking, and provides a more C++-like syntax for interface specification. The CORBA object model is different from the DCE model, but not significantly—both are distributed object models with the concepts of interfaces, remote operations, and data hiding.

We suggest that our work may assist in the migration from DCE to CORBA by providing an intermediate C++-based distributed object system until CORBA implementations are widely available. Migrating from DCE/C++ to CORBA should be much easier than migrating directly from C or from C++ using direct DCE calls.

10 Conclusions

Our conclusion from this work is that using object-oriented design and development techniques can provide significant benefits in distributed systems. In particular, the class libraries and compiler we developed significantly reduced the burden of creating DCE-based object systems.

There are several enhancements that we have considered for this work. The obvious candidates are other DCE-based systems, such as threads, naming, security, and transaction processing with Encina. Migration of this approach to the CORBA environment should also be studied.

11 Acknowledgments

The idea and initial design and implementation of this project were done by Jeff Morgan. We wish to thank Bob Fraley for his expert advice and contribution to this effort.

12 References

1. T. Korson, J. McGregor: *Understanding Object-Oriented: A Unifying Paradigm.* CACM Vol. 33, No. 9, September, 1990, p 40-60.

2. J. Nicol, C. Wilkes, F. Manola: *Object Orientation in Heterogeneous Distributed Computing Systems.* IEEE Computer, Vol. 26 No. 6, June 1993, p 57-67.

3. *Common Object Request Broker Architecture and Specification.* Object Management Group Document Number 91.12.1, Revision 1.1.

4. Open Software Foundation: *OSF DCE Application Development Guide.*

5. M. Linton, J. Vlissides, P. Calder: *Composing User Interfaces With InterViews.* IEEE Computer, Vol 22, No 2, February 1989.

6. *InterViews Plus Programmer's Guide.* Hewlett-Packard, 1992.

7. *HP DCE Sample Applications Overview,* Hewlett-Packard Document NSA-92-024, 1992.

8. S. Shrivastava, G. Dixon, G. Parrington: *An Overview of the Arjuna Distributed Programming System.* IEEE Software, Vol. 8, No. 1, January, 1991.

9. G. Parrington: *Reliable Distributed Programming in C++: the Arjuna Approach.* USENIX C++ 1990.

10. P. Dasgupta, R. LeBlanc Jr., M. Ahamad, U. Ramachandran: *The Clouds Distributed Operating System.* IEEE Computer (*to appear*).

11. R. Raj, E. Tempero, H. Levy, A. Black, N. Hutchinson, E. Jul: *Emerald: A General-Purpose Programming Language.* Software Practical Experiences, Vol. 21 No. 1, January, 1991.

12. A. Schill: *OSI, ODP and Distributed Applications: Towards and Integrated Approach.* IEEE Global Telecommunications Conference and Exhibition, 1991. p 638-642.

OSF is a trademark of the Open Software Foundation.

Graphical Design Support for DCE Applications

Hans-W. Gellersen

Telecooperations Group, Institute of Telematics, University of Karlsruhe,
76128 Karlsruhe, Germany; e-mail: hwg@tk.telematik.informatik.uni-karlsruhe.de

Abstract. DCE and especially object-oriented extensions on top of it provide rich functionality for implementation of distributed applications. Yet, we observe a lack of support for the design of distributed applications. Available object-oriented design methods do not cater for distribution. In this paper, the Visual Distributed Application Builder (VDAB), a new graphical model for design of distributed applications is presented. VDAB extends common object-oriented design support towards distribution and introduces new visual programming concepts to address the inherent complexity of large distributed applications. VDAB is integrated with DCE and its object-oriented extension DCE++. VDAB application designs are eventually mapped automically to DCE++.

1 Introduction

The development of distributed applications is considerably more difficult than the development of centralized software due to their well-known characteristics, such as low-level communication, locality, heterogeneity, risk of node failure. The complexity of developing distributed applications requires dedicated lifecycle spanning software engineering support.

The OSF Distributed Computing Environment eases the task of developing distributed software by providing RPC as communication mechanism, threads for concurrency support, distributed name management, distributed file management and security services [15]. Moreover, DCE supports interoperability in heterogeneous environments. However, it has been pointed out, that the support is limited to client/server-style applications. A number of deficiencies inherent with client/server computing are listed in [16], namely the coarse distribution grain, the asymmetric communication, the parameter semantics and the lack of systemwide data object identity.

DCE++ has been implemented as an extended distributed object-oriented system on top of DCE. It tightly integrates distributed o-o concepts introduced by approaches such as Emerald [2], Amber [5], and DOWL [1], with DCE mechanisms. DCE++ makes DCE available for the o-o programming community; it even stays within the language boundaries of C++. Further, it achieves a high extent of distribution transparency. Moreover, it overcomes the listed shortcomings of client/server computing.
DCE and DCE++ on top of it simplify the task of distributed programming considerably. Yet, they focus on implementation and do not address upper CASE issues.

Object-oriented design methods like OOD [3], OOA [6], and HOOD [10] do support early lifecycle stages, yet they do not support much more semantics than common o-o programming languages. In fact, they do not treat distribution aspects at all. An exception is the DOCASE system around the distributed o-o design and implementation language DODL [7, 13]. VDAB is based on the DOCASE experience, but is rather a tool than a language approach. Instead of providing the application developer with yet another language (and it would be a complex one due to distribution), VDAB provides tool support on top of widely accepted environments. DCE was chosen as it promises to become an industry standard. C and later C++ were chosen because of their widespread acceptance. A first prototype was based on C and DCE, a second one is now fully integrated with the recently developed DCE++.

In the following section the VDAB design model for distributed applications will be introduced. Section 3 describes the graphical design concepts and tools implemented in VDAB. The integration of VDAB and DCE is discussed in section 4. VDAB's functionality from early graphical design to code generation is illustrated along a sample application development in section 5. Finally, a conclusion summarizes the ideas introduced and points out future work.

2 The VDAB Model for Design of Distributed Applications

In this section we first describe the distributed object-oriented approach and its extension to object categories. These concepts form the foundation of the VDAB model, which is described in terms of design elements, design steps and design rules.

2.1 Objects and Categories

Distribution and Objects: In order to simplify the task of developing distributed applications it is desirable to achieve a large extent of distribution transparency. The distributed object-oriented approach has been proven to be adequate for hiding unpleasant distribution characteristics from the developer. In this approach, objects are not only units of modularization, but function also as units of distribution (moreover, they can also be used as units of concurrency).

A basic feature of this approach is location independent method invocation. That is, the invocation syntax and semantics is the same for both local and remote invocations, thus implementing abstraction from low-level communication and from locality. Another important feature of the distributed o-o approach is object mobility, i. e. the facility to dynamically migrate objects between system nodes. The ability to migrate objects dynamically has an often underestimated and disregarded impact on availability, reliability, and performance of a distributed application. Of course, the distributed o-o approach also inherits the well-known o-o characteristics encapsulation, data abstraction and inheritance. These features have been proven to ease the development of complex applications and to increase software reusability.

The Category Approach for Structuring Objects: The distributed o-o approach fits best into our requirements. Yet, it is not sufficient as it lacks expressive design elements. In the o-o model *everything is an object*, but not more. When it comes to modeling large real-world applications, a larger set of distinguished design elements is required.

The category approach addresses this concern by structuring objects into distinct categories with predefined semantics. This approach has already been implemented in the DOCASE project [13]. To the user (the application developer) the object categories appear as a complete set of orthogonal building blocks. The user defines each application object class as a descendent of a category, thus combining user defined semantics with the system defined category-specific semantics. This violation of the *small is beautiful* rule introduces additional system complexity which requires countermeasures to increase ease-of-use. First of all, the design methodology has to assist the application developer in categorizing his class definitions. Further, the category-specific semantics have to be made visible for all tools and to be supported throughout the software lifecycle.

While the categories appear as a canonical set on the user-level, they form a single rooted hierarchy on system-level. Obviously, a root category has to define all semantics that are common for all categories (e.g., objects of all categories have a location). Subcategories are defined in a single inheritance tree. Category inheritance has to be clearly distinguished from application inheritance. Category inheritance specifies the inheritance of category semantics to be provided by subcategories, and is invisible for the user. Application inheritance is specified by the user and defines the inheritance of behavior along the class hierarchy [8].

The current VDAB prototype implements five object categories, which are described subsequently. We think of the category system as extensible to cater for future requirements (e.g. support of multimedia, CSCW, etc.). Introduction of additional categories will require extension of the graphical language and of the VDAB tools.

2.2 VDAB Design Framework

The VDAB Design Elements: Object Categories and Relations

Currently, five object categories are defined and supported by VDAB. They serve as design elements for the application developer:

- **Active Objects** have a highly independent activity (own thread of control). Active Objects are the *substantial* components of an application. They are thought of as instances, i.e. in known or predictable quantities, and they are rather long-lived.

- **Passive Objects** are controlled by Active Objects. They are thought of in a type-oriented way. Instances would be created dynamically, be mobile (probably exchanged between Active Objects) and have a rather short lifetime.

- **Logical Nodes** are required to express locality of distributed objects while abstracting from physical network nodes. They allow for definition of initial object placement and other object configuration issues. At first glance, the strong support of locality may seem to contradict the stated goal of hiding distribution aspects from the user. Nevertheless, we found Logical Nodes an essential design element required for modeling locality aspects which are inherent in real-world applications.

- **UI Agents** are for the encapsulation of user interface functionality to increase portability and interoperability. UI Agent objects communicate with other objects thru a distinct interaction protocol.

- **Environment Agents** support the integration of legacy software.

Further, VDAB defines a number of built-in relations between VDAB objects for modeling structural (*is part of*, *knows*, ...), behavioral (*creates*, *deletes*, *uses*, *activates*, ...) and distribution aspects (*moves to*, *visits*, ...).

Design Elements, Design Steps and Design Rules

Gerteis describes a set-theoretic model for design methods, and the generic Design Method Assistant (DMA), a tool-building-tool for guided interactive design [9]. A design method is defined as a system consisting of a set of design elements, a set of design steps, a set of design rules and a design procedure.

The DMA is currently customized into the VDAB Design Method Assistant. In the VDAB model we have object categories and inter-object relations as design elements. Design steps are the operations that can be performed on design elements (creation, modification, deletion), e.g., the assertion of a relation between VDAB objects. Design rules are predefined constraints between design elements. In VDAB, they specify how VDAB objects can be interrelated, e.g., Passive Objects can not create or use Active Objects. Finally, the design procedure specifies the process of design reasoning and decision making. Design decisions result in distinct design steps.

3 The VDAB Graphical Design Tool Set

Analogous to the design method we can describe a graphical design method as consisting of a set of graphical elements, a set of graphical rules, a set of graphical steps and a graphical design method. In order to build a graphical tool for a given design method graphical equivalents for the design elements have to be defined, thereby introducing the graphical notation. Further, design steps and design rules have to be mapped into the tool. This is considerably more difficult as human interaction aspects introduce graphical rules which are not related to application semantics.

3.1 Customization of a Tool-Building-Tool for Graphical Editors

The development of graphical tools for the VDAB design model was based on the following goals:

1. Customization of a tool-building-tool for rapid prototyping of graphical editing facilities

2. Strict separation of design and graphical representation

3. Extensive support of the design method in the tools (by achieving a good mapping of design steps and rules to graphical steps and rules)

For building the VDAB graphical editing tools we chose to costumize ODE, an extensible tool-building-tool [12]. ODE provides powerful visualization techniques and is highly customizable and extensible based on a simple yet expressive functional language. ODE proved to meet the desired rapid prototyping requirements. Further, ODE also supported the second goal, as it enforces strict distinction of models (e.g. design artifacts) and views (e.g. graphical design techniques), similar to the model-viewcontroler paradigm in Smalltalk [14]. ODE's constraint evaluation mechanism supported the third goal. It allowed implementation of consistency constraints among different views of the same model, and other graphical rules like context-sensitive disabling/enabling of command buttons. Constraint maintenance among graphical representations further requires automatic graph layout, which is also provided by ODE.

3.2 VDAB Graphical Views

Subsequently, we will refer to the various graphical editors of VDAB simply as views. Recently, a number of graphical notations for visualization of object-oriented software structures have been introduced: e.g. OOD allows for graphical specification of class structure, object structure, modules and processes [3]. For description of dynamics, a state transition diagram and a timing diagram are provided. OOA [6], OOSD [18] and OOSE [11] suggest similar notations. All these notations focus mainly on visualizing structural aspects. Description of behavior is poor. Distribution is not considered. We further criticize the poor support for identification of required objects and methods.

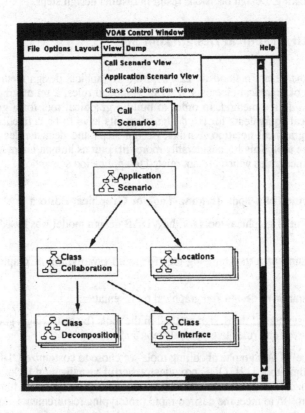

Figure 1: VDAB Control View

The VDAB tool set introduces new graphical design concepts to address the listed concerns. First of all, instance-oriented scenario views are introduced to support intuitive problem solving strategies. These views aim at very intuitive identification of system requirements. Further, VDAB introduces an intuitive notation for system behavior. To cater for distribution, object configuration views are defined. Finally, VDAB introduces a visualization of the graphical design process itself to guide the developer thru application design.

Subsequently, we first describe the *Control View*. Next, the instance-oriented *Application* and *Call Scenario Views* are described. Then, a brief overview over type-oriented VDAB views is given. Finally, we reflect how distribution aspects are addressed in the VDAB tool environment.

Development Guidance: As stated above, the complexity of distributed application development requires measures to ease the application developer's task. The VDAB approach to this end is to provide different views for different application aspects and application contexts, thus allowing the developer to concentrate on certain aspects while the system keeps track of side effects. Yet, the developer needs guidance lest he gets lost in a jungle of views. Therefore, VDAB visualizes the design procedure in its *Control View* (fig. 1). Further, it implements a dynamic hyperstructure among views for navigation thru the design process.

Note: the depicted graph in figure 1 suggests a sequential development process to give the developer a general idea of how to proceed. VDAB allows for much more flexibility, e.g. additional call scenarios can be specified at any time, of course.

Application Scenario View: The application scenario view has been designed in analogy to what a developer might put down on a notepad or whiteboard as first sketch of an application. The view is instance-oriented as we believe a first draft of a problem would rather be in terms of instances or examples than in more abstract type-oriented terms. To underline instance-orientation, *cloning* is among the design steps supported by the application scenario view. The graphical design elements are the object categories and abstract relations such as *uses, is collocated with, is UI of*. As in most VDAB views, the design elements are provided on a palette. Selected objects can be placed anywhere in the graph area, selected relations can be drawn from one object to another (unless a graphical design rule prohibits it!). Objects and relations can both be manipulated directly thru popup menus.

At any time, certain aspects of the scenario, e.g. user interaction or locality, can be folded away, allowing to concentrate on other aspects, or simply to reduce the number of visible items. As the application scenario is supposed to be developed rather intuitively, graphical design decisions are of course reversible (that holds for all VDAB views). An application scenario provides an easy to grasp overview of an application. As it is supposed to be a first draft it does not claim completeness. Rather, it is supposed to assist the developer with identifying application requirements, e.g. classes that need to be defined.

User guidance for design of the application scenario will be based on a dictionary of keywords generated from the list of requirements. These keywords may directly hint to the object categories, e.g. they might denote a location. Throughout application design the dictionary can serve for appropriate naming of design elements and relations.

Call Scenario Views: While the application scenario view aims at capturing an application overview, call scenario views display *arbitrarily chosen* behavioral aspects.

They describe call chains, thus defining *timethreads* taking place on certain events. The graphical notation was inspired by work of Buhr [4] and implemented in VDAB with extensions for description of synchronization aspects. Call scenarios support explorative specification of operational interfaces. They further help gathering requirements for method implementation. Moreover, call scenarios can be envisioned as test scenarios for validation of application functionality.

Type-oriented VDAB Views:

- **Class Collaboration View:** the type-oriented equivalent to the application scenario; it displays application classes and *knows* relations. The *knows* relations can be qualified as persistent (permanent reference from one class to another) or temporary (temporary reference in the form of a parameter or local variable).

- **Inheritance View:** displays the subclass relations.

- **Decomposition View:** specification of the *knows* and *has part* relations of objects, thereby defining their data structure.

- **Interface View:** specification of the operational interfaces.

- **Method Implementation View:** editor for method bodies; this view is not fully integrated with the others; changes in it are not reflected by other views.

The Distribution Aspect in VDAB Views: VDAB provides the developer with very simple means to describe the distribution inherent in his application: he can specify the initial object configuration and he can select routines to run at startup time on the application's logical nodes. Object configuration can be specified explicitly by binding objects to logical nodes or implicitly by binding objects to each other (collocation).

Runtime object configuration aspects remain hidden to the developer. Yet, he is provided with means to specify object migrations explicitly or implicitly (by specifying collocations). Further, he can specify distribution attributes for parameter objects: they can either stay where they are, move to the called object or visit the called object for the time of method execution.

4 From Design to Implementation: Integration of VDAB and DCE

Fig. 2 depicts the integration of VDAB and DCE. A number of graphical tools allow for manipulation of the VDAB model of an application; the model itself is a graph of interconnected design elements. Based on the internal design model, VDAB generates input files for the DCE++ system. Based on these files, DCE++ generates additional code to implement low-level communication for the distributed application. This additional code, which remains hidden in the VDAB environment, customizes the DCE RPC, threads, and naming services. The VDAB code generation facility abstracts from DCE. Only the threads service is used directly (to implement Active Objects), other services are only indirectly used thru DCE++.

In this section, we first sketch out how distributed applications are implemented with DCE++. Then, we will describe the VDAB code generation facility. Finally, we will discuss the need for tight integration of design and implementation in general, and compare a desired integrated framework with the VDAB reality.

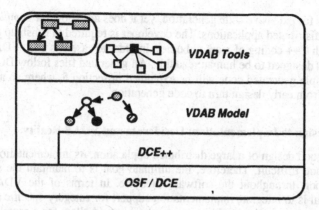

Figure 2: VDAB integration with DCE and DCE++

4.1 Programming with DCE++

DCE++ programming is only roughly sketched out here, for details cf. [16]. The description refers to an early DCE++ implementation; future versions are expected to hide even more of the underlying communication, e.g. by means of a stub compiler.

In order to enable C++ objects in the DCE++ system to be invoked location-independently and to migrate across node boundaries, additional classes have to be provided for each application class. This tedious task is, fortunately!, hidden from the developer by the DCE++ system. Yet, DCE++ requires the developer to provide a specification *common.dce++* of all remote classes and their methods. Further, DCE++ requires the user to write an IDL file *common.idl* describing all remote methods. Finally, the developer has to fill in a template for each logical node in his DCE++ applications, thereby defining the initial object configuration. The implementation of the actual application objects does not differ from ordinary C++ coding. Yet, the developer has to take care for consistency of application object implementation and the *common.dce++* and *common.idl* descriptions.

4.2 VDAB Code Generation

VDAB does not only support design of distributed applications but is also capable of writing most of the code an application developer otherwise would have to provide. In a first prototype, VDAB designs were mapped to C and DCE code. A major part of the code generation was for implementation of the low-level communication based on DCE services. The use of DCE++ as intermediate layer allows VDAB to abstract from low-level communication. The VDAB code generation now only specifies *what* communication is required; *how* the communication is realized is responsibility of DCE++.

The graphical specification of classes and their operational interface is sufficient for automatic generation of the *common.dce++*, *common.idl* and application object header files. The graphical specification of logical nodes allows for automatic generation of DCE++ logical node files. Finally, even rudimentary implementations of method bodies can be generated based on call scenario specifications.

VDAB allows for extensive code generation, yet it does not allow for *complete* implementation of distributed applications. The developer is required to finish up the implementation with C++ coding of method bodies. In order to ease this task, VDAB generated code was designed to be human readable. All generated files follow DCE++ conventions. Sample generated code will be explained in section 5, where an application is developed from early design thru to code generation.

4.3 From Design to Implementation: Desiderata and VDAB Reality

Even with a good design of a large distributed application, its implementation will still be complex and difficult. Therefore, the ultimate goal is to maintain the same high level of support throughout the software lifecycle. In terms of the VDAB design model the goal is to integrate implementation support for category-specific semantics. Design-level support in the implementation phase would allow for a seamless transition from design to implementation. Yet, current implementation languages are not sufficient to achieve this goal. With current languages, important application aspects are often handled by calling out to libraries and toolkits, which only allows for syntactic but not for semantic checking.

The VDAB reality is far from an integrated design and implementation modeling framework. Yet, VDAB goes well beyond other graphical design methods by generating effective and human readable code. That means, based on the design VDAB already provides a good deal of the implementation. Moreover, the generated code is in a form which makes it relatively easy for the application developer to provide the rest of the implementation. Still, once the developer moves from graphical design to textual implementation he loses VDAB support irreversibly. As VDAB does not (yet) understand DCE++ files (C++, IDL and DCE++ class descriptions), VDAB semantics can not be checked and iterations over design and implementation remain unsupported. In order to overcome this shortage to some degree, we are now working on interpretation of DCE++ files for VDAB. This will be restricted to a subset of C++ and IDL.

In comparison with DODL, the design and implementation language of the DOCASE system [7], the integration of design and implementation is less tight in VDAB. Yet, VDAB as opposed to DODL is of immediate use for application developers, as it does not require the developer to learn a new language. While VDAB does not provide sufficient means for implementation, it eases the implementation task considerably by generating highly comprehensible code.

5 A Sample Application: Automatic Call Distribution

In this section, a sample application is developed with VDAB. *Automatic Call Distribution* (ACD), a telecommunications application, was chosen to highlight the applicability of VDAB to real-world task. ACD distributes telephone calls in switch systems automically. Incoming telephone calls are directed by ACD (instead of an intermediate operator) to certain operators who then process the telephone calls (using a central client database). This system is inherently distributed: a central node (probably a workstation) processes incoming calls; operators work on operator nodes (e.g. PCs); client and statistics databases are located on database server nodes.

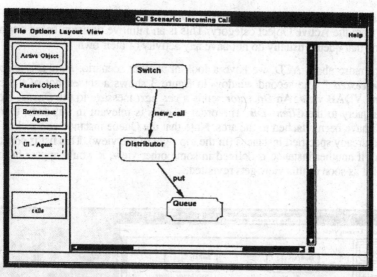

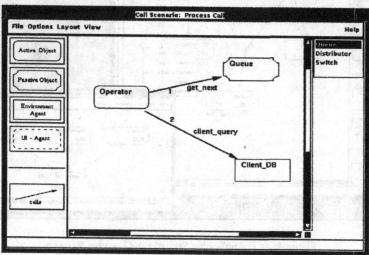

Figure 3: ACD Call Scenarios *Incoming Call* and *Process Call*

5.1 ACD Call Scenarios

How ACD works is best described along typical scenarios: e.g. *What does happen, when a telephone call comes in ?* VDAB supports this approach and allows us to sketch an "Incoming Call" scenario as given in figure 3, upper window. The scenario specifies that in the event "Incoming Call" the *Switch* sends a *new_call* message to the *Distributor*. The *Distributor* then sends a *put* message to the *Queue* instance. Note that the *Queue* was designed to be a Passive Object whereas the other instances were picked from the Active Object category. This is an intuitive decision based on the assumption that queues usually do not have any activity of their own.

To learn more about ACD, we have a look at another scenario: *How are telephone calls processed ?* The second window in figure 3 shows a screenshot of the corresponding VDAB view. An *Operator* sends a *get_next* message to the *Queue*. He also sends a query to the *Client_DB*. The order of calls is relevant in this case, therefore ordinals have been attached to the arcs. Note that the Queue instance was picked from a list of already specified instances (in the top right of the view). This list is constantly updated: if another instance is defined in some other view, it would appear in the instance list as soon as this view gets revisited.

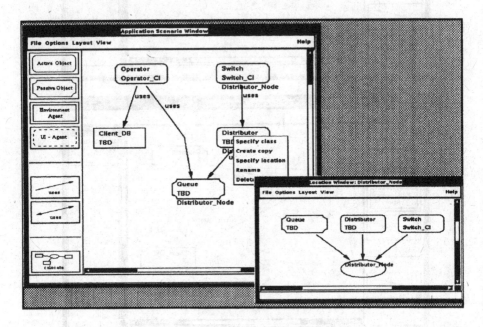

Figure 4: ACD Application Scenario and Location View

5.2 ACD Application Scenario

With the quick specification of call scenarios we have already introduced major components of the ACD system and gathered some information about how they interact. Yet, so far the information is distributed over a number of views. What we would like to have now is some sort of overview displaying all yet specified components and their interrelations. VDAB provides the application scenario view to this end. It generates automatically an application overview based on call scenario specifications. The larger window in figure 4 shows the resulting view.

As the application scenario gives an overview over system components it is a good place to say something about their distribution. We can either explicitly introduce logical node instances and place application instances on them (graphically), or we can define collocations among application objects. In our sample design we decided to collocate *Switch*, *Distributor* and *Queue* on a logical node *Distributor_Node*. A location view displays the result and allows for specification of further configuration details (fig. 4, small window). The application scenario further allows for identification of classes and thus to proceed from instance-orientation to type-orientation. Yet, the developer is not forced to explicitly classify his instances. In that case, the system takes care for implicit generation of class definitions while the developer keeps his instance-oriented view, which is often more intuitive.

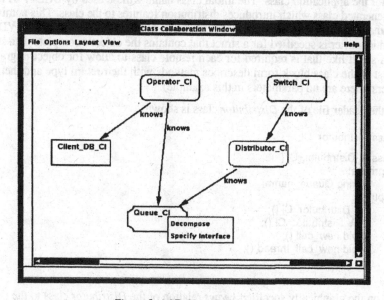

Figure 5: ACD Class Collaboration

5.3 Type-oriented Views of ACD

Based on the instance-oriented specifications in call and application scenarios VDAB can generate a *Class Collaboration View* (fig. 5). It shows which classes have to be known by others. Classes in this view can be further specified by bringing up *Decomposition Views* for description of their data structure, or *Interface Views* for description of their operational interfaces. It is important to note, that the developer can return from a type-oriented view to an instance-oriented view at any time: e.g. it will in general be more intuitive to specify method parameter lists in the context of call scenarios than in an abstract type-oriented view.

5.4 Automatically Generated ACD Code

Subsequently, the code generation will be illustrated for the *Distributor* class of the ACD system. First, the class description for *common.dce++* is shown:

```
###########################################################
# class block form class Distributor_CI
```

```
##########################################################
A_Distributor_Cl  : Distributor_Cl        : A_Distributor_Cl_data
#
                  : Distributor           :
void              : new_call              :
void              : new_call_thread       :
...
```

In a class block form the DCE++ system is provided with the information it needs to make classes remote. The description specifies A_Distributor_Cl as DCE++ internal name for the application class. The initial class name will be used by DCE++ as name for a generated class which introduces distribution features to the class. This naming is somewhat confusing for the DCE++ programmer, but is made transparent by VDAB. A third identifier is specified for a struct that contains the object's complete data structure. A struct like that is required for each remote class to allow for object migration. The rest of the class block form describes methods with their return type and their parameters (there are no parameters in this example).

Next, the header file of the *Distributor* class is shown.

```
class Distributor_Cl;

class A_Distributor_Cl {
    private:
        string Queue_name;
    public:
        A_Distributor_Cl ();
        ~A_Distributor_Cl ();
        void new_call ();
        void new_call_thread ();
};
```

Based on the graphically specified *knows* relation of the *Distributor* class to the *Queue* class, Queue_name is specified for *reference by name*. The method new_call () is derived from our call scenario specification.. As for all methods of active objects, VDAB generates an additional method, in this case new_call_thread (). These additional methods implement asynchronous method execution using the DCE Threads service; this remains transparent for the developer.

Finally, let us have a look at the *common.idl* file which VDAB generates for DCE++, and which the DCE++ system uses for stub compilation:

```
...
/* ############ Class Distributor_Cl ################## */
typedef struct {
    string        Queue_name;
} A_Distributor_Cl_data;

void A_Distributor_Cl_Migrate (
    [in]          handle_t             bh,
    [in]          uuid_t               oid,
    [out, ref]    error_status_t       *status,
    [in, string]  char                 *loc   );
```

```
void A_Distributor_Cl_install_object (
    [in]            handle_t                bh,
    [in]            RPC_Obj_Ref             r,
    [in]            A_Distributor_Cl_data *p     );

void A_Distributor_Cl_new_call (
    [in]            handle_t                bh,
    [in,out]        RPC_call_data          *data );

void A_Distributor_Cl_new_call_thread (
    [in]            handle_t                bh,
    [in,out]        RPC_call_data          *data );
...
```

For each class a struct containing its data structure has to be defined for the idl compiler. Further, *Migrate* and *install_object* methods have to described for each class. The actual methods are generated by DCE++. Finally, all user defined methods have to be specified here, too.

6 Conclusion

This paper described VDAB, a new approach for extensive design support for large distributed applications. Whereas existing support for distributed applications and in particular for DCE applications focuses on implementation issues, VDAB aims at life-cycle spanning support. The strong emphasis on instance-oriented intuitive views supports early design. Iteration over a number of graphical design tools allows for increasing detail. Finally, the code generation facility produces most of the application code in a human readable form, thus catering for further manual coding and maintenance. The applicability of VDAB has been demonstrated along a sample application development.

VDAB has been designed to be immediately applicable for development of DCE applications, but also to be extensible towards further application aspects. Future design model extensions (implemented as additional object categories), will support teamwork, multimedia and workflows to meet the huge demand for support of physically remote teams, long-lived business procedures, and human-human interaction. Further, advanced support for human interaction development will be incorporated in VDAB. DCE supports portability and interoperability, yet platform-bound user interfaces remain the portability bottlenecks of DCE applications. As opposed to currently developed GUI portability kits which only support the least common denominator of a number of GUI toolkits [17], we will investigate in paradigm-independent human interaction.

References

1. B. Achauer: The DOWL distributed object-oriented language. Communications of the ACM, Vol. 36, No. 9, Sep. 1993.

2. A. Black, N. Hutchinson, E. Jul, H. Levy, L. Charter: Distribution and abstract types in Emerald. IEEE Trans. on Software Engineering, Vol. 13, No. 1, Jan. 1987, pp. 65-75

3. G. Booch: Object Oriented Design with Applications, The Benjamin/Cummings Publishing Company, 1991.

4. R. Buhr, R. Casselman. Architectures With Pictures. In Proc. of OOPSLA '92, Vancouver, BC, Oct. 1992, pp. 466-483

5. J. Chase, F. Amador, E. Lazowska. H. Levy, R. J. Littlefield: The Amber system: Parallel programming on a network of multiprocessors. 12th ACM Symposium on Operating Systems principles, Litchfield Park, Ar, 1989, pp. 147-158

6. P. Coad, E. Yourdon: Object-Oriented Analysis. Prentice-Hall, 1990.

7. W. Gerteis, Ch. Zeidler, L. Heuser, M. Mühlhäuser: DOCASE: A Development Environment and a Design Language for Distributed Object-Oriented Applications. In Proc. of TOOLS Pacific '90 (Technology on Object-Oriented Languages and Systems), Sydney, Australia. Nov. 1990, pp. 298-312.

8. W. Gerteis, L. Heuser, M. Mühlhäuser: The ABCD-Architecture of Hybrid Design/Implementation Languages for Large Distributed Applications. OOPSLA '91 Workshop OLDA-1, Phoenix, Ar, Oct. 1991.

9. W. Gerteis: An Approach Towards Guided Interactive Design. Proc. 2nd Great Lakes Computer Science Conf., Kalamazoo, Mi, Oct. 1991.

10. M. Heitz: HOOD Reference Manual. CISI Ingenierie, Midi Pyrénées, Sep. 1989.

11. I. Jacobsen: Object-Oriented Software Engineering. Addison Wesley, 1992.

12. T. Leidig, M. Mühlhäuser. Graphische Unterstützung der Entwicklung verteilter Anwendungen (in german). In Proc. of GI/NTG-Fachtagung Kommunikation in verteilten Systemen, pp. 494-508, GI, Springer Verlag, 1991.

13. M. Mühlhäuser, W. Gerteis: DOCASE: A Methodic Approach to Distributed Object-Oriented Programming. Communications of the ACM, Vol. 36, No. 9, Sep. 1993.

14. MVC Architecture. ObjectWork / Smalltalk, User's Guide, Part Three.

15. Open Software Foundation: Introduction to OSF DCE. Cambridge, Ma, 1992.

16. A. Schill, M. Mock: DCE++: Distributed Object-Oriented System Support on top of OSF DCE. Submitted for publication.

17. G. Singh: Requirements for User Interface Programming Languages. In B. Myers, editor, Languages for Developing User Interfaces. Jones and Bartlett Publishers, 1992.

18. A. Wasserman, P. Pircher, R. Müller: The object-oriented structured design notation for software design representation. IEEE Computer, March 1990, pp. 50-62.

Taming Heterogeneity in Networked Environments

Liba Svobodova

IBM Research Division
Zurich Research Laboratory
Saumerstrasse 4
8803 Rüschlikon
Switzerland
e-mail: svo@zurich.ibm.com

- Invited Talk -

Distributed computing has been a very active research area for at least fifteen years. Many research projects focused on the development of a native distributed operating system that would support distributed processing in a natural and efficient way. New kernels, distribution and communication paradigms and protocols, languages, abstractions and algorithms were developed to enable and facilitate distributed computing, and many interesting experimental systems incorporating the new ideas and concepts were built. Distributed environments based on local-area networks that not only interconnect personal computers and workstations but also provide low-cost resource sharing became attractive for many business and industry applications; a variety of commercial solutions emerged. There is now a steadily growing need to interconnect the various LAN-based systems and to enable distributed applications across an entire enterprise and even across networked environments encompassing several companies. The multifaceted heterogeneity of such environments has been hindering the development and deployment of distributed applications; the developers have to deal with different operating systems, file systems, naming conventions, user interfaces, communication subsystems, management procedures. It is clearly not feasible to replace the installed systems with a common homogeneous base; instead, it is necessary to agree on common standards at some level of abstraction that can be supported by most existing systems.

The OSF DCE constitutes a major step towards interoperability at the distributed system level. Still, many open issues remain, and new ones are emerging. The overview paper [1] presents quite a comprehensive list of topics to be addressed. There are two additional fundamental issues that are beyond the scope of the DCE, yet crucial to conquering the heterogeneity and complexity of the networked environments: interoperability of the communication subsystems, and distributed system/network management. As DCE does not prescribe the communication protocols below its RPC, it is necessary to provide a separate solution to the heterogeneity at this level, such as the multi-protocol transport networking (MPTN) architecture [2,3]; the X/Open consortium is evaluating MPTN for potential standardization. The overall management of distributed systems presents a great technical challenge. It must be linked to network management, yet hide low-level network management problems. It must be user-friendly and highly automated. It must be capable of scaling up to tens and hundreds of thousands of nodes, and of accommodating the growing population of mobile users. Although several projects under the EC programs RACE and ESPRIT are working on relevant issues, a comprehensive integrated solution is not yet in sight. This is clearly an area that requires a major effort in research, experimental work, and standardization.

References

1. Bever et al.: Distributed Systems, OSF DCE, and Beyond; *these proceedings*.

2. Multiprotocol Transport Networking (MPTN) Architecture: Technical Overview; *GC31-7073, IBM Corp., April 1993.*

3. Britton et al.: Multiprotocol Transport Networking: A General Internetworking Solution; *Proc. IEEE Intl. Conf. on Network Protocols, San Francisco, October 19-22, 1993.*

Author Index

Lecture Notes in Computer Science

For information about Vols. 1–655
please contact your bookseller or Springer-Verlag

Vol. 693: P. E. Lauer (Ed.), Functional Programming, Concurrency, Simulation and Automated Reasoning. Proceedings, 1991/1992. XI, 398 pages. 1993.

Vol. 694: A. Bode, M. Reeve, G. Wolf (Eds.), PARLE '93. Parallel Architectures and Languages Europe. Proceedings, 1993. XVII, 770 pages. 1993.

Vol. 695: E. P. Klement, W. Slany (Eds.), Fuzzy Logic in Artificial Intelligence. Proceedings, 1993. VIII, 192 pages. 1993. (Subseries LNAI).

Vol. 696: M. Worboys, A. F. Grundy (Eds.), Advances in Databases. Proceedings, 1993. X, 276 pages. 1993.

Vol. 697: C. Courcoubetis (Ed.), Computer Aided Verification. Proceedings, 1993. IX, 504 pages. 1993.

Vol. 698: A. Voronkov (Ed.), Logic Programming and Automated Reasoning. Proceedings, 1993. XIII, 386 pages. 1993. (Subseries LNAI).

Vol. 699: G. W. Mineau, B. Moulin, J. F. Sowa (Eds.), Conceptual Graphs for Knowledge Representation. Proceedings, 1993. IX, 451 pages. 1993. (Subseries LNAI).

Vol. 700: A. Lingas, R. Karlsson, S. Carlsson (Eds.), Automata, Languages and Programming. Proceedings, 1993. XII, 697 pages. 1993.

Vol. 701: P. Atzeni (Ed.), LOGIDATA+: Deductive Databases with Complex Objects. VIII, 273 pages. 1993.

Vol. 702: E. Börger, G. Jäger, H. Kleine Büning, S. Martini, M. M. Richter (Eds.), Computer Science Logic. Proceedings, 1992. VIII, 439 pages. 1993.

Vol. 703: M. de Berg, Ray Shooting, Depth Orders and Hidden Surface Removal. X, 201 pages. 1993.

Vol. 704: F. N. Paulisch, The Design of an Extendible Graph Editor. XV, 184 pages. 1993.

Vol. 705: H. Grünbacher, R. W. Hartenstein (Eds.), Field-Programmable Gate Arrays. Proceedings, 1992. VIII, 218 pages. 1993.

Vol. 706: H. D. Rombach, V. R. Basili, R. W. Selby (Eds.), Experimental Software Engineering Issues. Proceedings, 1992. XVIII, 261 pages. 1993.

Vol. 707: O. M. Nierstrasz (Ed.), ECOOP '93 – Object-Oriented Programming. Proceedings, 1993. XI, 531 pages. 1993.

Vol. 708: C. Laugier (Ed.), Geometric Reasoning for Perception and Action. Proceedings, 1991. VIII, 281 pages. 1993.

Vol. 709: F. Dehne, J.-R. Sack, N. Santoro, S. Whitesides (Eds.), Algorithms and Data Structures. Proceedings, 1993. XII, 634 pages. 1993.

Vol. 710: Z. Ésik (Ed.), Fundamentals of Computation Theory. Proceedings, 1993. IX, 471 pages. 1993.

Vol. 711: A. M. Borzyszkowski, S. Sokołowski (Eds.), Mathematical Foundations of Computer Science 1993. Proceedings, 1993. XIII, 782 pages. 1993.

Vol. 712: P. V. Rangan (Ed.), Network and Operating System Support for Digital Audio and Video. Proceedings, 1992. X, 416 pages. 1993.

Vol. 713: G. Gottlob, A. Leitsch, D. Mundici (Eds.), Computational Logic and Proof Theory. Proceedings, 1993. XI, 348 pages. 1993.

Vol. 714: M. Bruynooghe, J. Penjam (Eds.), Programming Language Implementation and Logic Programming. Proceedings, 1993. XI, 421 pages. 1993.

Vol. 715: E. Best (Ed.), CONCUR'93. Proceedings, 1993. IX, 541 pages. 1993.

Vol. 716: A. U. Frank, I. Campari (Eds.), Spatial Information Theory. Proceedings, 1993. XI, 478 pages. 1993.

Vol. 717: I. Sommerville, M. Paul (Eds.), Software Engineering – ESEC '93. Proceedings, 1993. XII, 516 pages. 1993.

Vol. 718: J. Seberry, Y. Zheng (Eds.), Advances in Cryptology – AUSCRYPT '92. Proceedings, 1992. XIII, 543 pages. 1993.

Vol. 719: D. Chetverikov, W.G. Kropatsch (Eds.), Computer Analysis of Images and Patterns. Proceedings, 1993. XVI, 857 pages. 1993.

Vol. 720: V.Mařík, J. Lažanský, R.R. Wagner (Eds.), Database and Expert Systems Applications. Proceedings, 1993. XV, 768 pages. 1993.

Vol. 721: J. Fitch (Ed.), Design and Implementation of Symbolic Computation Systems. Proceedings, 1992. VIII, 215 pages. 1993.

Vol. 722: A. Miola (Ed.), Design and Implementation of Symbolic Computation Systems. Proceedings, 1993. XII, 384 pages. 1993.

Vol. 723: N. Aussenac, G. Boy, B. Gaines, M. Linster, J.-G. Ganascia, Y. Kodratoff (Eds.), Knowledge Acquisition for Knowledge-Based Systems. Proceedings, 1993. XIII, 446 pages. 1993. (Subseries LNAI).

Vol. 724: P. Cousot, M. Falaschi, G. Filè, A. Rauzy (Eds.), Static Analysis. Proceedings, 1993. IX, 283 pages. 1993.

Vol. 725: A. Schiper (Ed.), Distributed Algorithms. Proceedings, 1993. VIII, 325 pages. 1993.

Vol. 726: T. Lengauer (Ed.), Algorithms – ESA '93. Proceedings, 1993. IX, 419 pages. 1993

Vol. 727: M. Filgueiras, L. Damas (Eds.), Progress in Artificial Intelligence. Proceedings, 1993. X, 362 pages. 1993. (Subseries LNAI).

Vol. 728: P. Torasso (Ed.), Advances in Artificial Intelligence. Proceedings, 1993. XI, 336 pages. 1993. (Subseries LNAI).

Vol. 729: L. Donatiello, R. Nelson (Eds.), Performance Evaluation of Computer and Communication Systems. Proceedings, 1993. VIII, 675 pages. 1993.

Vol. 730: D. B. Lomet (Ed.), Foundations of Data Organization and Algorithms. Proceedings, 1993. XII, 412 pages. 1993.

Vol. 731: A. Schill (Ed.), DCE – The OSF Distributed Computing Environment. Proceedings, 1993. VIII, 285 pages. 1993.

Vol. 732: A. Bode, M. Dal Cin (Eds.), Parallel Computer Architectures. IX, 311 pages. 1993.